MW00941513

The Souls Conflict

Richard Sibbes

BIBLIOLIFE

Copyright © BiblioLife, LLC

This book represents a historical reproduction of a work originally published before 1923 that is part of a unique project which provides opportunities for readers, educators and researchers by bringing hard-to-find original publications back into print at reasonable prices. Because this and other works are culturally important, we have made them available as part of our commitment to protecting, preserving and promoting the world's literature. These books are in the "public domain" and were digitized and made available in cooperation with libraries, archives, and open source initiatives around the world dedicated to this important mission.

We believe that when we undertake the difficult task of re-creating these works as attractive, readable and affordable books, we further the goal of sharing these works with a global audience, and preserving a vanishing wealth of human knowledge.

Many historical books were originally published in small fonts, which can make them very difficult to read. Accordingly, in order to improve the reading experience of these books, we have created "enlarged print" versions of our books. Because of font size variation in the original books, some of these may not technically qualify as "large print" books, as that term is generally defined; however, we believe these versions provide an overall improved reading experience for many.

THE

SOUL'S CONFLICT

AND

VICTORY OVER ITSELF BY FAITH.

BY THE

Rev. RICHARD SIBBES, D.D.

Psalm cxvi.—Return unto thy rest, O my soul; for the Lord hath dealt bountifully with thee.

PHILADELPHIA:

PRESBYTERIAN BOARD OF PUBLICATION.

PAUL T. JONES, PUBLISHING AGENT.

1842.

Printed by
WILLIAM S. MARTIEN.

CONTENTS.

4 CONTENTS.

TO THE CHRISTIAN READER.

THERE be two sorts of people always in the visible Church; one that Satan keeps under with false peace, whose life is nothing but a diversion to present contentments, and a running away from God and their own hearts, which they know can speak no good unto them, these speak peace to themselves, but God speaks none. Such have nothing to do with this Scripture; the way for these men to enjoy comfort, is to be soundly troubled. True peace arises from knowing the worst first, and then our freedom from it. It is a miserable peace that ariseth from ignorance of evil. The angel *troubled the waters,* John v., and then cured those that stepped in. It is Christ's manner to trouble our souls first, and then to come with healing in his wings.

But there is another sort of people, who being drawn out of Satan's kingdom and within the covenant of grace, whom Satan labours to unsettle and disquiet: being the *god of the world,* he is vexed to see men in the world, walk above the world. Since he cannot hinder their estate, he will trouble their peace, and damp their spirits, and cut asunder the sinews of all their endeavours. These should take themselves to task as David doth here, and labour to maintain their portion, and the glory of a Christian profession. For whatsoever is in God, or comes from God, is for their comfort. Himself is the God of comfort; his Spirit most known by that office. Our blessed Saviour was so careful that his disciples should not be too much dejected, that he forgot his own bitter passion to comfort them, whom yet he knew would all forsake him: *let not your hearts be troubled,* saith he. And his own soul was troubled to death, that we should not be troubled: *whatsoever is written is written for this end;* every article of faith hath a special influence in comforting a believing soul. They are not only food, but cordials; yea, he put himself to his oath, that we might not only have consolation but strong consolation. The sacraments seal unto us all the comforts we have by the death of Christ; the exercise of religion, as *Prayer, Hearing, Reading,* &c., is that *our joy may be full:* the *communion of saints* is chiefly ordained to *comfort the feeble minded* and to *strengthen the weak.* God's government of his Church tends to this. Why doth he sweeten our pilgrimage, and let us see so many comfortable days in the world, but that we should serve him with cheerful and good hearts? As for crosses, he doth but cast us down, to raise us up, and empty us that he may fill us, and melt us that we may be *vessels of glory,* loving us as well in the furnace, as when we are out, and standing by us all the while. *We are troubled, but not distressed; perplexed, but not in despair; persecuted but not forsaken.* 2 Cor. iv. 8. If we consider from what *fatherly love* afflictions come, how they are not only moderated, but sweetened and sanctified in the issue to us, how can it but minister matter of comfort in the greatest seeming discomforts? How then can we let the reins of our affections loose to sorrow without being injurious to God and his providence? as if we would teach him how to govern his Church.

What unthankfulness is it to forget our consolation, and to look only upon matter of grievance? to think so much upon two or three crosses, as to forget a hundred blessings? To suck poison out of that, from which we should suck honey? What folly is it to straiten, and darken our own spirits? and indispose ourselves from doing or taking good? A limb out of joint can do nothing without deformity and pain; dejection takes off the wheels of the soul.

Of all other, Satan hath most advantage of discontented persons, as most agreeable to his disposition; being the most discontented creature under heaven, he hammers all his dark plots in their brains. The discontentment of the *Israelites in the wilderness* provoked God to *swear* that *they should never enter into his rest.* Psalm xcv. ult. There is *another spirit in my servant Caleb*, saith God; the spirit of God's people is an encouraging spirit. Wisdom teaches them, if they feel any grievances, to conceal them from others that are weaker, lest they be disheartened. God threatens it as a *curse* to give a *trembling heart*, and *sorrow of mind*, Deut. xxviii. 65; whereas on the contrary, joy is as oil to the soul, it makes duties come off cheerfully and sweetly from ourselves, graciously to others, and acceptably to God. A prince cannot endure it in his subjects, nor a father in his children, to be lowering at their presence. Such usually have stolen waters to delight themselves in.

How many are there that upon the disgrace that follows religion, are frighted from it? But what are discouragements to the encouragements religion brings

with it? which are such as the very angels themselves admire at. Religion indeed brings crosses
with it, but then it brings comforts above those crosses. What a dishonour is it to religion to conceive
that God will not maintain and honour his followers?
as if his service were not the best service; what a
shame is it for an heir of heaven to be cast down for
every petty loss and cross? to be afraid of a man whose
breath is in his nostrils, in not standing to a good cause,
when we are sure God will stand by us, assisting and
comforting us, whose presence is able to make the
greatest torments sweet?

My discourse tends not to take men off from all
grief and mourning; *Light for the righteous is sown
in sorrow.* Our state of absence from the Lord, and
living here in a vale of tears, our daily infirmities, and
our sympathy with others, requires it; and where
most grace is, there is most sensibleness, as in Christ.
But we must distinguish between grief and that sul-
lenness and dejection of spirit, which is with a repining
and taking off from duty; when Joshua was overmuch
cast down at Israel's turning their backs before their
enemies, God reproves him, *Get thee up, Joshua,
why liest thou upon thy face?* Joshua vii. 10.

Some would have men after the committing of gross
sins to be presently comfortable, and believe without
humbling themselves at all; indeed when we are once
in Christ, we ought not to question our state in him;
and if we do, it comes not from the Spirit; but yet a
guilty conscience will be clamorous and full of objections, and God will not speak peace unto it till it be
humbled. God will let his best children know what
it is to be too bold with sin, as we see in David and
Peter, who felt no peace till they had renewed their

repentance: the way to rejoice *with joy unspeakable and glorious*, 2 Pet. x., is to stir up sighs *that cannot be uttered*. And it is so far, that the knowledge of our state in grace should not humble us, that very ingenuity considering God's love to us, out of the nature of the thing itself works sorrow and shame in us, to offend his Majesty.

One main stop that hinders Christians from rejoicing is, that they give themselves too much liberty to question their grounds of comfort and interest in the promises. This is wonderfully comfortable say they, but what is it to me? the promise belongs not to me. This ariseth from want of giving all *diligence to make their calling sure* to themselves. In watchfulness and diligence we sooner meet with comfort than in idle complaining. Our care therefore should be to get sound evidence of a good estate, and then likewise to keep our *evidence clear;* wherein we are not to hearken to our own fears and doubts, or the suggestion of our enemy, who studies to falsify our evidence: but to the word, and our own consciences enlightened by the Spirit; and then it is pride and pettishness to stand out against comfort to themselves. Christians should study to corroborate their title; we are never more in heaven, before we come thither, than when we can read our evidences: it makes us converse much with God, it sweetens all conditions, and makes us willing to do and suffer any thing. It makes us have comfortable and honourable thoughts of ourselves, as too good for the service of any base lust, and brings confidence in God both in life and death.

But what if our condition be so dark, that we cannot read our evidence at all?

Here look up to God's infinite mercy in Christ as

we did at the first when we found no goodness in ourselves, and that is the way to recover whatever we
think we have lost. By honouring God's mercy in
Christ, we come to have the Spirit of Christ; therefore, when the waters of sanctification are troubled
and muddy: let us run to the witness of blood. God
seems to walk sometimes contrary to himself; he
seems to discourage, when secretly he doth encourage, as the *woman of Canaan;* but faith can find
out these ways of God, and untie these knots, by looking to the free promise and merciful nature of God.
Let our sottish and rebellious flesh murmur as much
as it will, *who art thou? and what is thy worth?* yet
a Christian *knows whom he believes.* Faith hath
learned to set God against all.

Again, we must go on to *add grace to grace.* A
growing and fruitful Christian is always a comfortable Christian; the oil of grace brings forth the oil of
gladness. Christ is first a king of righteousness, and
then a king of peace, Heb. vii. 2; the righteousness
that he works by his Spirit brings a peace of sanctification, whereby though we are not freed from sin,
yet we are enabled to combat with it, and to get the
victory over it. Some degree of comfort follows every
good action, as heat accompanies fire, and as beams
and influences issue from the sun; which is so true,
that very heathens upon the discharge of a good conscience, have found comfort and peace answerable;
this is a reward before our reward.

Another thing that hinders the comfort of Christians is, that they forget what a gracious and merciful covenant they live under, wherein the perfection
that is required is to be found in Christ. Perfection in
us is sincerity: what is the end of faith but to bring

us to Christ? Now imperfect faith, if sincere, knits to Christ, in whom our perfection lies.

God's design in the covenant of grace is to exalt the riches of his mercy, above all sin and unworthiness of man; and we yield him more glory of his mercy by believing, than it would be to his justice to destroy us. If we were perfect in ourselves, we should not honour him so much, as when we labour to be found in Christ, having his righteousness upon us.

There is no one portion of Scripture oftener used to fetch up drooping spirits than this, *Why art thou cast down O my soul?* it is figurative, and full of rhetoric, and all little enough to persuade the perplexed soul quietly *to trust in God:* which without this retiring into ourselves and checking our hearts, will never be brought to pass. Chrysostom brings in a man laden with troubles, coming into the Church, where, when he heard this passage read, he presently recovered himself, and becomes another man. As David therefore did acquaint himself with this form of dealing with his soul, so let us, demanding a reason of ourselves *Why we are cast down:* which will at least check and put a stop to the distress, and make us fit to consider more solid grounds of true comfort.

Of necessity the soul must be something calmed and staid before it can be comforted. Whilst the humours of the body rage in a great distemper, there is no giving of physic: so when the soul gives way to passion, it is unfit to entertain any counsel, therefore it must be stilled by degrees, that it may hear reason; and sometimes it is fitter to be moved with ordinary reason, (as being more familiar unto it) than with higher reasons fetched from our supernatural condition in Christ, as from the condition of man's nature

subject to changes, from the uncomeliness of yielding
to passion for that, which it is not in our power to
mend, &c.; these and such like reasons have some
use to stay the fit for a while, but they leave the core
untouched, which is sin, the trouble of all troubles.
Yet when such considerations are made spiritual by
faith on higher grounds, they have some operation
upon the soul, as the influence of the moon having
the stronger influence of the sun mingled with it becomes more effectual upon these inferior bodies.   A
candle light being ready at hand, is sometimes as useful as the sun itself.

But our main care should be to have evangelical
grounds of comfort near to us, *reconciliation with
God,* whereby all things else are reconciled to us,
adoption and communion with Christ, &c., which is
never sweeter than under the cross.   Philip Lans-
grave of Hesse, being a long time prisoner under
Charles the Fifth, was demanded what upheld him
all that time? who answered that *he felt the divine
comforts of the Martyrs:* there be divine comforts
which are felt under the cross, and not at other times.

Besides personal troubles, there are many much
dejected with the present state of the Church, seeing
the blood of so many saints to be shed, and the enemies
oft to prevail; but God hath stratagems, as Joshua, at
Ai, he seems sometimes to retire that he may come
upon his enemies with the greater advantage; the
end of all these troubles will no doubt be the ruin
of the anti-christian faction; and we shall see the
Church in her more perfect beauty when the enemies
shall be in that place which is fittest for them, the
lowest, that is, the *footstool of Christ;* the Church as
it is the highest in the favour of God, so it shall be

the highest in itself. *The mountain of the Lord shall be exalted above all mountains.* In the worst condition, the Church hath two faces, one towards heaven and Christ, which is always constant and glorious; another toward the world, which is in appearance contemptible and changeable. But God will in the end give her beauty for ashes, and glory double to her shame, and she shall in the end prevail: in the mean time, the power of the enemies is in God's hand: the Church of God conquers when it is conquered: even as our head Christ did, who overcame by patience as well as by power. Christ's victory was upon the cross. The spirit of a Christian conquers when his person is conquered.

The way is, instead of discouragement, to search all the promises made to the Church in these latter times, and to turn them into prayers, and press God earnestly for the performance of them. Then we shall soon find God both cursing his enemies, and blessing his people out of Zion, by the faithful prayers that ascend up from thence.

In all the promises we should have special recourse to God in them. In all storms there is sea room enough in the infinite goodness of God, for faith to be carried with full sail.

And it must be remembered that, in all places where God is mentioned, we are to understand God in the promised Messiah, typified out so many ways unto us. And to put the more vigour into such places in the reading of them, we in this latter age of the Church must think of God shining upon us in the face of Christ, and our father in him. If they had so much confidence in so little light, it is a shame for us, not to be confident in good things, when so strong a light shines round about us: when we profess to believe *a crown of righteousness is laid up for all those that love his appearing.* Presenting these things to the soul by faith setteth the soul in such a pitch of resolution, that no discouragements are able to seize upon it. *We faint not,* saith St. Paul: wherefore doth he not faint? because *these light and short afflictions procure an exceeding weight of glory.*

Luther when he saw Melancthon, a godly and learned man, too much dejected for the state of the Church in those times, falls a chiding of him as David doth here his own soul, *I strongly hate those miserable cares,* saith he, *whereby thou writest thou art even spent. It is not the greatness of the cause, but the greatness of our incredulity. If the cause be false, let us revoke it. If true, why do we make God in his rich promises a liar? Strive against thyself, the greatest enemy: why do we fear the conquered world, that have the conquerer himself on our side?*

Now to speak something concerning the publishing of this treatise. I began to preach on the text about twelve years since in the city, and afterwards finished the same at Grays-Inn. After which some having gotten imperfect notes, endeavoured to publish them without my privity. Therefore to do myself right, I thought fit to reduce them to this form. There is a pious and studious gentleman of Grays-Inn, that hath of late published observations upon the whole psalm: and another upon this verse very well: and very many others, by treatises of faith and such like, have furthered the spiritual peace of Christians much. It were to be wished that we would all join to do that which the apostles gloried in, *to be helpers of the joy of God's people.* 2. Cor i. ult.   Some will be ready to deprave the labours of other men; but so good may be done, let such ill disposed persons be what they are, and what they will be unless God turn their hearts: and so I commend thee and this poor treatise to God's blessing.

R. SIBBES.

GRAYS-INN, *July* 1, 1635.

THE SOUL'S CONFLICT.

WITH ITSELF.

Why art thou cast down, O my soul? and why art thou disquieted within me? Hope thou in God; for I shall yet praise him, who is the health of my countenance, and my God.—PSALM xlii.

THE Psalms are, as it were, the anatomy of a holy man, which lay the inside of a truly devout man outward to the view of others. If the Scriptures be compared to a body, the Psalms may well be the heart, they are so full of sweet affections, and passions. For in other portions of Scripture God speaks to us; but in the Psalms holy men speak to God and their own hearts: as

In this Psalm we have *the passionate passages of a broken and troubled spirit.*

At this time David was a banished man, banished from his own house, from his friends, and, which troubled him most, from the house of God, upon occasion of Saul's persecution, who hunted him as a partridge upon the mountains. See how this works upon him.

1. *He lays open his desire springing from his love.* Love being the prime and leading affection of the soul, from whence grief springs, from being crossed in that we love. For the setting out of which his affection to the full, he borroweth an expression from the hart; no hart, being chased by the hunters, *panteth more after the waters*, than my heart doth *after thee, O God*, ver. 1: though he found God present with him in exile, yet there is a sweeter presence of him in his ordinances, which now he wanted and took

2

to heart: places and conditions are happy or miserable, as God vouchsafeth his gracious presence more
or less; and therefore, *When, O when shall it be,
that I appear before God?*

2. Then after his strong desire, *he lays out his
grief,* which he could not contain, but must needs
give a vent to it in tears: and he had such a spring
of grief in him, as fed his *tears day and night,* ver. 3;
all the ease he found was to dissolve this cloud of
grief into the shower of tears.

But, *why gives he this way to his grief?*

Because together with his exiling from God's house,
he was upbraided by his enemies, with his religion:
where is now thy God? ver. 3. Grievances come not
alone, but, as Job's messengers, follow one another.
These bitter taunts, together with the remembrance
of his former happiness in communion with God in
his house, made deep impressions in his soul, when
he *remembered how he went with the multitude into
the house of God,* ver. 4, and led a goodly train with
him, being willing, as a good magistrate and master
of a family, not to go to the house of God alone, nor
to Heaven alone, but to carry as many as he could
with him; oh! the remembrance of this made him
pour forth (not his words or his tears only, but) his
very soul. *Former favours and happiness make
the soul more sensible of all impressions to the contrary;* hereupon, finding his soul over sensible, he
expostulates with himself, *Why art thou cast down,
O my soul? and why art thou disquieted within
me?* &c.

But though the remembrance of the former sweetness of God's presence did somewhat stay him, yet
his grief would not so be stilled, and therefore it
gathers upon him again; *one grief called upon another,* as one deep wave follows another, ver. 7, without intermission, until his soul was almost over-
whelmed under these waters; yet he recovers himself
a little with looking up to God, who he expected
would with speed and authority send forth *his loving
kindness* with command to raise him up and comfort

him, and give him matter of *songs in the night,* ver. 8.
For all this, his unruly grief will not be calmed, but
renews assaults upon the return of the reproach of
his enemies. Their words were *as swords,* ver. 10,
unto him, and his heart being made very tender and
sensible of grief, these sharp words enter too deep;
and thereupon he hath recourse to his former remedy,
as being the most tried to chide his soul, and charge
it to trust in God.

CHAPTER I.

GENERAL OBSERVATIONS UPON THE TEXT.

HENCE in general we may observe; that *Grief gathered to a head will not be quieted at the first.* We
see here passions intermingled with comforts, and
comforts with passions, and what bustling there is
before David can get the victory over his own heart:
you have some short spirited Christians, that if they
be not comforted at the first, they think all labour
with their hearts is in vain, and thereupon give way
to their grief. But we see in David, as distemper
ariseth upon distemper, so he gives check upon check,
and charge upon charge to his soul, until at length he
brought it to a quiet temper.

Again: In general observe in David's spirit, that *a
gracious and living soul is most sensible of the want
of spiritual means.*

The reason is because spiritual life has answerable
taste and hunger and thirst after spiritual helps.

We see in nature, that those things press hardest
upon it, that touch upon the necessities of nature,
rather than those that touch upon delights, for these
further only our comfortable being; but necessities
uphold our being itself: we see how famine wrought
upon the patriarchs to go into Egypt: where we may
see what to judge of those who willingly excommunicate themselves from the assemblies of God's people, where the Father, Son, and Holy Ghost are present, where the prayers of holy men meet together in

one, and as it were bind God, and pull down God's blessing. No private devotion hath that report of acceptance from Heaven.

A third general point is, that *a godly soul, by reason of the life of grace, knows when it is well with it, and when it is ill, when it is a good day with it, and when a bad;* when God shines in the use of means then the soul is as it were in heaven; when God withdraws himself, then it is in darkness for a time. Where there is but only a principle of nature without sanctifying grace, there men go plodding on and keep their rounds, and are at the end where they were at the beginning; not troubled with changes, because there is nothing within to be troubled; and therefore dead means, quick means, or no means, all is one with them, an argument of a dead soul. And so we come more particularly and directly to the words, *Why art thou cast down, O my soul? and why art thou disquieted within me?* &c.

The words imply, 1. David's state wherein he was; and 2. express his carriage in that state.

His state was such that in regard of outward condition, he was in variety of troubles; and that in regard of inward disposition of spirit, he was first *cast down*, and then *disquieted*.

Now for his carriage of himself in this condition, and disposition, he dealeth roundly with himself: David reasoneth the case with David, and first checketh himself for being too much *cast down*, and then for being too much *disquieted*.

And then layeth a charge upon himself *to trust in God;* wherein we have the duty he chargeth upon himself, which is to *trust in God*, and the grounds of the duty;

First, from confidence of better times to come, which would yield him matter of *praising God.*

And then by a representation of God unto him, as a saving God in all troubles, nay, as salvation itself, an open glorious Saviour in the view of all, *The salvation of my countenance*, and all this enforced from David's interest in God, *He is my God.*

Whence observe, first, from the state he was now in, that *since guilt and corruption hath been derived by the fall, into the nature of man, it hath been subjected to misery and sorrow, and in that all conditions from the king that sitteth on the throne to him that grindeth at the mill.* None ever hath been so good or so great, as could raise themselves so high as to be above the reach of *troubles.*

And that choice part of mankind, the first fruits and excellency of the rest, (which we call the Church,) more than others, which appears by consideration both of the *head*, the *body*, and *members* of the Church. For the *head* Christ, he took our flesh as it was subject to misery after the fall, and was, in regard of that which he endured, both in life and death, a man of sorrows.

For the *body* the Church, it may say from the first to the last as it is Psal. cxxix. *From my youth up they have afflicted me.* The Church begun in blood, hath grown up by blood, and shall end in blood, as it was redeemed by blood.

For the members, they are all predestinated to a conformity to Christ their Head, as in grace and glory, so in abasement, Rom. viii. 29. Neither is it a wonder for those who are born soldiers to meet with conflicts, for travellers to meet with hard usage, for seamen to meet with storms, for strangers in a strange country, (especially amongst their enemies,) to meet with strange entertainment.

A Christian is a man of another world, and here from home, which he would forget, (if he were not exercised here,) and would take his passage for his country. But though all Christians agree and meet in this, that *through many afflictions we must enter into heaven*, Acts xiv. 22; yet according to the diversity of place, parts, and grace, there is a different cup measured to every one.

And therefore it is but a plea of the flesh, to except against the cross, *Never was poor creature distressed as I am:* this is but self-love, for it was not the case both of head, body, and members, as we see here in

David a principal member? When he was brought to this case, thus to reason the matter with himself, *Why art thou cast down, O my soul? and why art thou disquieted within me?*

From the frame of David's spirit under these troubles, we may observe, that as the case is thus with all God's people, to be exercised with troubles, *They are sensible of them oftentimes, even to casting down and discouraging.* And the reason is, they are flesh and blood, subject to the same passions, and made of the same mould, subject to the same impressions from without as other men; and their nature is upheld with the same supports and refreshings as others, the withdrawing and want of which affecteth them. And besides those troubles they suffer in common with other men, by reason of their new advancement, and their new disposition they have in and from Christ their head, they are more sensible in a peculiar manner of those troubles that any way touch upon that blessed condition, from a new life they have in and from Christ, which will better appear if we come more particularly to a discovery of the more special causes of this distemper: some of which are, 1. *Without us.* 2. *Some within us.*

CHAPTER II.

OF DISCOURAGEMENTS FROM WITHOUT.

1. God himself: who sometimes withdraws the beams of his countenance from his children, whereupon the soul even of the strongest Christian is disquieted; when together with the cross, God himself seems to be an enemy unto them. The child of God, when he seeth that his troubles are mixed with God's displeasure, and perhaps his conscience tells him that God hath a just quarrel against him, because he hath not renewed his peace with his God, then this anger of God puts a sting into all other troubles, and adds to the disquiet. There were some ingredients of this divine temptation, (as we call it,) in holy David at this

time: though most properly a divine temptation be, when God appears unto us as an enemy, without any special guilt of any particular sin, as in Job's case.

And no marvel if Christians be from hence disquieted, when as the Son of God himself, having always before enjoyed the sweet communion with his Father, and now feeling an estrangement, that he might be a curse for us, complained in all his torments of nothing else, but *My God, my God, why hast thou forsaken me?* Matt. xxvii. 46. It is with the godly in this case, as with vapours drawn up by the sun, which (when the extracting force of the sun leaves them,) fall down again to the earth from whence they are drawn. So when the soul, raised up and upheld by the beams of his countenance, is left of God, it presently begins to sink. We see when the body of the sun is partly hid from us, (for totally it cannot in an eclipse by the body of the moon,) that there is a drooping in the whole frame of nature: so it is in the soul, when there is any thing that comes between God's gracious countenance and it.

Besides, if we look down to inferior causes, the soul is oft cast down by Satan, who is all for casting down, and for disquieting. For being a cursed spirit, cast and tumbled down himself from heaven, where he is never to come again, he is hereupon full of disquiet, carrying a hell about himself, whereupon all that he labours for is to cast down and disquiet others, that they may be (as much as he can procure,) in the same cursed condition with himself. He was not ashamed to set upon Christ himself with this temptation of casting down, and thinks Christ's members never low enough, till he can bring them as low as himself.

By his envy and subtlety we were driven out of Paradise at the first, and now he envies us the paradise of a good conscience: for that is our paradise until we come to Heaven; into which no serpent shall ever creep to tempt us. When Satan seeth a man strongly and comfortably walk with God, he cannot endure that a creature of meaner rank by creation than himself should enjoy such happiness. Herein, like (some peevish men which are his instruments) men too contentious, and bred up therein (as the salamander in the fire) who when they know the cause to be naught, and their adversaries to have the better title; yet, out of malice, they will follow them with suits and vexations, though they be not able to disable their opposites' title: if their malice have not a vent in hurting some way, they will burst for anger.

It is just so with the devil when he seeth men will to Heaven, and that they have good title to it, then he follows them with all dejecting and uncomfortable temptations that he can; it is his continual trade and course to seek his rest in our disquiet, he is by beaten practice and profession, a tempter in this kind.

Again, what Satan cannot do himself by immediate suggestions, that he labours to work by his instruments, who are all for casting down of those who stand in their light, as those in the Psalm, who cry, *Down with him, down with him, even to the ground;* a character and stamp of which men's dispositions we have in the verse before this text, *Mine enemies* (saith David) *reproach me.* As sweet and as compassionate a man as he was, to *pray* and *put on sackcloth* for them, yet he had enemies, and such *enemies,* as did not suffer their malice only to boil and concoct in their own breasts, but out of the abundance of their hearts, they reproached him in words. There is nothing the nature of man is more impatient of, than of reproaches; for there is no man so mean, but thinks himself worthy of some regard, and a reproachful scorn shows an utter disrespect, which issues from the very superfluity of malice.

Neither went they behind his back, but were so impudent to say *it to his face:* a malicious heart and a slandering tongue go together, and though shame might have suppressed the uttering of such words, yet their insolent carriage spake as much *in David's heart:* Psalm xxxix. 1. We may see by the language of men's carriage what their heart saith, and what their tongue would vent if they dared.

And this their malice *was unwearied,* for they said *daily* unto him, as if it had been fed with a continual spring: malice is an unsatiable monster, it will minister words, as rage ministers weapons. But what was that they said so reproachfully? and said daily? *Where is now thy God?* ver. 3, they upbraid him with his singularity, they say not now, *Where is God?* but, *Where is thy God,* that thou dost boast so much on, as if thou hadst some special interest in Him? Where we see that the scope of the devil and wicked men is to shake the godly's faith and confidence in their God: as Satan laboured to divide betwixt Christ and his Father, *If thou beest the Son of God, command that these stones be made bread,* Matth. ii. 4, so he labours to divide betwixt Father and Son and us: they labour to bring God in jealousy with David, as if God had neglected him, bearing himself so much upon God. They had some colour of this, for God at this time had veiled himself from David, as he does oft from his best children, for the better discovery of the malice of wicked men: and doth not Satan tip the tongues of the enemies of religion now, to insult over the Church now lying bleeding?* *What becomes of their reformation, of their gospel?* Nay, rather what's become of your eyes, we may say unto them? For God is nearest to his children when he seems farthest off. *In the mount of the Lord it shall be seen,* Gen. xxii. 14, God is with them, and in them, though the wicked be not aware of it; it is all one, as if one should say betwixt the space of the new and old moon, Where is now the moon? when as it is never nearer the sun than at that time.

Where is now thy God?

In heaven, in earth, in me, every where but in the heart of such as ask such questions, and yet there they shall find him too in his time, filling their consciences with his wrath; and then, Where is their God? where are their great friends, their riches, their

* This was preached in the beginning of the troubles of the *Church,* (about A. D. 1630.)

honours, which they set up as a god? what can they avail them now?

But how was David affected with these reproaches? their words were as swords, *as with a sword in my bones*, &c. ver. 10, they spake daggers to him, they cut him to the quick when they touched him in his God, as if he had neglected his servants, when as the devil himself regards those who serve his turn; touch a true godly man in his religion, and you touch his life and his best freehold, he lives more in his God than in himself; so that we may see here, there is a murder of the tongue, a wounding tongue, as well as a healing tongue: men think themselves freed from murder, if they kill none, or if they shed no blood, whereas they cut others to the heart with bitter words. It is good to extend the commandment to awake the conscience the more, and breed humility, when men see there is a murdering of the tongue. We see David therefore upon this reproach to be presently so moved, as to fall out with himself for it, *Why art thou so cast down and disquieted, O my soul?* This bitter taunt ran so much in his mind, that he expresseth it twice in this Psalm; he was sensible that they struck at God through his sides; what they spake in scorn and lightly, he took heavily. And indeed, when religion suffers, if there be any heavenly fire in the heart, it will rather break out, than not discover itself at all. We see by daily experience, that there is a special force in words uttered from a subtle head, a false heart and a smooth tongue, to weaken the hearts of professors, by bringing an evil report upon the strict profession of religion: as the *cunning* and false *spies* did upon the *good land,* Judges i. 24, as if it were not only in vain, but dangerous to appear for Christ in evil times. If the example of such as have faint spirits will discourage in an army, (as we see in Gideon's history, Judges vii.) then what will speech enforced both by example and with some show of reason do?

To let others pass, we need not go further than ourselves, for to find causes of discouragement, there is a seminary of them within us. Our flesh, an enemy so much the worse, by how much the nearer, will be ready to upbraid us within us, *Where is now thy God?* why shouldst thou stand out in profession that finds no better entertainment?

CHAPTER III.

OF DISCOURAGEMENTS FROM WITHIN.

BUT to come to some particular causes within us. There is cause oft in the body of those in whom a melancholy temper prevaileth, darkness makes men fearful: melancholy persons are in a perpetual darkness, all things seem black and dark unto them, their spirits as it were dyed black. Now to him that is in darkness, all things seem black and dark, the sweetest comforts are not lightsome enough unto those that are deep in melancholy. It is, without great watchfulness, Satan's bath; which he abuseth as his own weapon to hurt the soul, which by reason of its sympathy with the body is subject to be misled: as we see where there is a suffusion of the eye by reason of distemper of humours, or where things are presented through a glass to the eye; things seem to be of the same colour: so, whatsoever is presented to a melancholy person, comes in a dark way to the soul. From whence it is, that their fancy being corrupted, they judge amiss, even of outward things, as that they are sick of such and such a disease, or subject to such and such a danger, when it is nothing so; how fit are they then to judge of things removed from sense, as of their spiritual estate in Christ?

To come to causes more near the soul itself, as when there is want of that which should be in it, as of *knowledge* in the *understanding*, &c. Ignorance (being darkness) is full of false fears. In the night time men think every bush a thief; our forefathers in time of ignorance were frighted with every thing; therefore it is the policy of popish tyrants, taught

them from the prince of darkness, to keep the people
in darkness, that so they might make them fearful,
and then abuse that fearfulness to superstition; that
they might the better rule in their consciences for their
own ends: and that so having entangled them with
false fears, they might heal them again with false
cures.

Again, though the soul be not ignorant, yet if it be
forgetful and mindless, if, as Heb. xii. the Apostle
saith, *You have forgot the consolation that speaks
unto you*, &c.   We have no more present actual comfort, than we have remembrance: help a godly man's
memory, and help his comfort; like unto charcoal
which having once been kindled, is the more easy to
take fire.   He that hath formerly known things, takes
ready acquaintance of them again, as old friends:
things are not strange to him.

And further, *want of setting due price upon comforts;* as the Israelites were taxed for setting nothing
by the pleasant land.   It is a great fault, when (as
they said to Job) *the consolation of the Almighty
seem light, and small unto us*, Job xv. 11, unless
we have some outward comfort which we linger after.

Add unto this, *a childish kind of peevishness:*
when they have not what they would have, like children, they throw away all; which though it be very
offensive to God's Spirit, yet it seizeth often upon
men otherwise gracious.   Abraham himself, wanting
children, Gen. xvi. undervalued all other blessings.
Jonah, because he was crossed of his gourd, was
weary of his life.   The like may be said of Elias, flying from Jezebel.   This peevishness is increased by
a too much flattering of their grief, so far as to justify
it; like Jonah, *I do well to be angry even unto death,*
Jonah iv. 9, he would stand to it.   Some with Rachel
are so peremptory, that they *will not be comforted,*
Jer. xxxi. 15, as if they were in love with their grievances.   Wilful men are most vexed in their crosses:
it is not for those to be wilful that have not a great
measure of wisdom to guide their wills; for God delights to have his will of those that are wedded to

their own wills: as in Pharaoh. No men more subject to discontentments than those who would have all things after their own way.

Again, one main ground is, *false reasoning*, and error in our discourse, as that we have no grace when we feel none: feeling is not always a fit rule to judge our states by; that God hath rejected us, because we are crossed in outward things, when as this issues from God's wisdom and love. How many imagine their *failings* to be *fallings*, and their *fallings*, to be *fallings away? Infirmities* to be *presumptions:* every *sin against conscience*, to be the sin against the *Holy Ghost?* unto which misapprehensions, weak and dark spirits are subject. And Satan, as a cunning rhetorician, here enlargeth the fancy, to apprehend things bigger than they are. Satan abuseth confident spirits another contrary way; to apprehend great sins as little, and little as none. Some also think that they have no grace, because they have not so much as grown Christians: whereas, there be several ages in Christ. Some again are so desirous and enlarged after what they have not, that they mind not what they have. Men may be rich, though they have no millions, and be not emperors.

Likewise, some are much troubled, because they proceed by a false method and order in judging of their estates. They will begin with *election,* which is the highest step of the ladder; whereas they should begin from a work of grace wrought within their hearts, from God's calling them by his Spirit, and their answer to his call, and so raise themselves upwards to know their *election* by their answer to God's calling. *Give all diligence,* saith Peter, to make your *calling* and *election sure?* 2 Pet. i: your *election* by your *calling.* God descends down unto us from *election* to *calling:* and so to sanctification: we must ascend to him beginning where he ends. Otherwise it is as great folly as in removing of a pile of wood, to begin at the lowest first, and so, besides the needless trouble, to be in danger to have the rest to fall upon our heads. Which besides ignorance argues pride, appearing in

this, that they would bring God to their conceits, and
be at an end of their work before they begin.

' This great secret of God's eternal love to us in
Christ, is hidden in his breast, and doth not appear to
us, until in the use of means God by his Spirit discovereth the same to us; the Spirit letteth into the
soul so much life and sense of God's love in particular to us, as draweth the soul to Christ, from whom it
draweth so much virtue as changeth the frame of it,
and quickeneth it to duty, which duties are not grounds
of our state in grace, but issues, springing from a good
state before, and thus far they help us, in judging of
our condition, that though they be not to be rested in,
yet as streams they lead us to the spring-head of grace
from whence they arise.

And of signs, some be more apt to deceive us, as
being not so certain, as *delight and joy in hearing
the word*, Matt. xiii. 20, as appeareth in the *third
ground:* some are more constant and certain, as love
to those that are truly good, and to all such, and because they are such, &c. these as they are wrought by
the Spirit, so the same Spirit giveth evidence to the
soul of the truth of them, and leadeth us to faith
from whence they come, and faith leads us to the discovery of God's love made known to us in hearing
the word opened. The same Spirit openeth the truth
to us, and our understandings to conceive of it, and
our hearts to close with it by faith, not only as a
truth, but as a truth belonging to us.

Now this faith is manifested, either by itself reflecting upon itself the light of faith, discovering both
itself and other things, or by the cause of it, or by the
effect, or by all. Faith is oft more known to us in
the fruit of it, than in itself; as in plants, the fruits
are more apparent than the sap and root. But the
most settled knowledge is from the cause, as when I
know I believe, because in hearing God's gracious
promises opened and offered unto me, the Spirit of
God carrieth my soul to cleave to them as mine own
portion. Yet the most familiar way of knowledge of
our estates is from the effects to gather the cause, the

cause being oftentimes more remote and spiritual, the effects more obvious and visible. All the vigour and beauty in nature which we see, comes from a secret influence from the heavens which we see not: in a clear morning we may see the beams of the sun shining upon the tops of hills and houses before we can see the sun itself.

Things in the working of them, do issue from the cause, by whose force they had their being; but our knowing of things ariseth from the effect, where the cause endeth; we know God must love us before we can love him, and yet we oft *first* know that *we love him*, 1 John iv. 19; the love of God is the cause why we love our brother, and yet we know we love *our brother whom we see* more clearly, *than God whom we do not see*, ver. 20.

It is a spiritual peevishness that keeps men in a perplexed condition, that they neglect these helps to judge of their estates by, whereas God takes liberty to help us sometime to a discovery of our estate by the effects, sometimes by the cause, &c. And it is a sin to set light by any work of the Spirit, and the comfort we might have by it, and therefore we may well add this as one cause of disquietness in many, that they grieve the Spirit, by quarreling against themselves, and the work of the Spirit in them.

Another cause of disquiet is, that men by a natural kind of Popery seek for their comfort too much in sanctification, neglecting justification, relying too much upon their own performances; Paul was of another mind, *accounting all but dung and dross. compared to the righteousness of Christ.* This is that garment, wherewith being decked we please our *husband*, and wherein we get the blessing. This giveth satisfaction to the conscience, as satisfying God himself, being performed by God the Son, and approved therefore by God the Father. Hereupon the soul is quieted, and faith holdeth out this *as a shield* against the displeasure of God and temptations of Satan. Why did the apostles in their prefaces join grace and peace together, but that we should seek for our peace in the free grace and favour of God in Christ?

No wonder why Papists maintain doubting, who hold salvation by works; because Satan joining together with our consciences, will always find some flaw. even in our best performances; hereupon the doubting and misgiving soul comes to make this absurd demand, as *Who shall ascend to Heaven?* Psal. xxiv. 3, which is all one as to fetch Christ from Heaven, and so bring him down to suffer on the cross again. Whereas if we believe in Christ, we are as sure to come to Heaven as Christ is there: Christ ascending and descending with all that he hath done is ours. So that *neither height nor depth can separate us from God's love in Christ.* Rom. viii. 39.

But we must remember, though the main pillar of our comfort be in the free forgiveness of our sins; yet if there be a neglect in growing in holiness, the soul will never be soundly quiet, because it will be prone to question the truth of justification, and it is as proper for sin to raise doubts and fears in the conscience, as for rotten flesh and wood to breed worms. And therefore we may well join this as a cause of disquietness, *the neglect of keeping a clear conscience.* Sin, like Achan, or Jonah in the ship, is that which causeth storms within and without; where there is not a pure conscience, there is not a pacified conscience, and therefore though some thinking to save themselves whole in justification, neglect the cleansing of their natures, and ordering of their lives: yet in time of temptation, they will find it more troublesome than they think. For a conscience guilty of many neglects, and of allowing itself in any sin, to lay claim to God's mercy, is to do as we see mountebanks sometimes do, who wound their flesh to try conclusions upon their own bodies, how sovereign the salve is; yet oftentimes they come to feel the smart of their presumption, by long and desperate wounds. So God will let us see what it is to make wounds to try the preciousness of his balm: such may go mourning to their graves. And though, perhaps, with much wrestling with God, they may get assurance of the pardon of their sins, yet their conscience will be still trembling, like as David's, though Nathan had pronounced unto him the forgiveness of his sin, Psalm li., till God at length speaks further peace, even as the water of the sea, after a storm, is not presently still, but moves and trembles a good while after the storm is over. A Christian is a new creature, and walketh by rule, and so far as he walketh *according to his rule peace is upon him.* Gal. vi. 16. Loose walkers, that regard not their way, must think to meet with sorrows instead of peace. Watchfulness is the preserver of peace. It is a deep spiritual judgment to find peace in an ill way.

Some, again, reap the fruit of their *ignorance of Christian liberty,* by unnecessary scruples and doubts. It is both unthankfulness to God, and wrong to ourselves, to be ignorant of the extent of Christian liberty, *it makes melody to Satan, to see Christians troubled with that they neither should or need.* Yet there is danger in stretching Christian liberty beyond the bounds. For a man may condemn himself in what he approves, as in not walking circumspectly in regard of circumstances, and so breed his own disquiet, and give scandal to others.

Sometimes also, God suffers men to be disquieted for want of employment, who in shunning labour, procure trouble to themselves; and by not doing that which is needful, they are troubled with that which is unnecessary. *An unemployed life is a burden to itself.* God is always working, always doing; and the nearer our soul comes to God, the more it is an action, and the freer from disquiet. Men experimentally feel that comfort in doing that which belongs unto them, which before they longed for, and went without; a heart not exercised in some honest labour, works trouble out of itself.

Again, omission of duties and offices of love often troubles the peace of good people; for even in the time of death, when they look for peace and desire it most, then looking back upon their former failings, and seeing opportunity of doing good wanting to their desire, (the parties perhaps being deceased to whom they owed more respect) are hereupon much disquieted, and so much the more, because they see now hope of the like advantages cut off.

A Christian life is full of duties, and the peace of it is not maintained without much fruitfulness and looking about us: debt is a disquieting thing to an honest mind, and *duty is debt.* Hereupon the apostle layeth the charge, *that we should owe nothing to any man but love.* Rom. xiii. 8.

Again, one special cause of too much disquiet is, *want of firm resolution in good things.* The soul cannot but be disquieted when it knows not what to cleave unto, like a ship tossed with contrary winds: halting is a deformed and troublesome gesture; so halting in religion is not only troublesome to others, and odious, but also *disquiets* ourselves. *If God be God, cleave to him.* 1 Kings xviii. 21. If the duties of religion be such as will bring peace of conscience at length, be religious to purpose, practise them in the particular passages of life. We should labour to have a clear judgment, and from thence a resolved purpose: *a wavering* minded man is inconstant in all his ways. James i. 6. God will not speak peace to a staggering spirit that hath always its religion, and its way, to choose. Uncertain men are always unquiet men: and giving too much way to passion, maketh men in particular consultations unsettled. This is the reason why in particular cases, when the matter concerns ourselves, we cannot judge so clearly as in general truths, because Satan raiseth a mist between us and the matter in question.

TWO POSITIVE CAUSES.

May be, 1. *When men lay up their comfort too much on outward things,* which being subject to much inconstancy and change, breed disquiet. Vexation always follows vanity, when vanity is not apprehended to be where it is. In that measure we are cast down in the disappointing of our hopes, as we were too much lifted up in expectation of good from them. Whence proceed these complaints: Such a friend hath failed me; I never thought to have fallen into this condition; I had settled my joy in this child, in this friend, &c., but this is to build our comfort upon things that have no firm foundation, to build castles in the air (as we use to say.) Therefore it is a good desire of the wise man Agur, to desire God, *to remove from us vanity and lies*, Prov. xxx.; that is, a vain and false apprehension pitching upon things that are vain and lying, promising a contentment to ourselves from the creature, which it cannot yield; confidence in vain things makes a vain heart, the heart becoming of the nature of the thing it relies on: we may say of all earthly things as the Prophet speaketh, *Here is not our rest*. Mic. ii. 10.

It is no wonder, therefore, that worldly men are oft *cast down* and *disquieted*, when they *walk in a vain shadow*, Psal. xxxix., as likewise that men given much to recreations should be subject to passionate distemper, because here things fall out otherwise than they looked for: recreations being about matters that are variable, which especially falls out in games of hazard, wherein they oft spare not Divine Providence itself, but break out into blasphemy.

Likewise men that grasp more business than they can discharge, must needs bear both the blame and the grief of losing or marring many businesses. It being almost impossible to do many things so well as to give content to conscience: hence it is that covetous and busy men trouble both their hearts and their houses; though some men from a largeness of parts, and a special dexterity in affairs, may turn overmuch; yet the most capacious heart hath its measure, and when the cup is full, a little drop may cause the rest to spill. There is a spiritual surfeit, when the soul is overcharged with business; it is fit the soul should have its meet burthen and no more.

As likewise, those that depend too much upon the opinions of other men: A very little matter will refresh, and then again discourage a mind that rests too

much upon the liking of others. Men that seek themselves disquieted abroad, find themselves too much at
home; even good men many times are too much
troubled with the unjust censures of other men, especially in the day of their trouble: It was Job's case;
and it is a heavy thing to have affliction added to
affliction: It was Hannah's case, who being *troubled
in spirit,* was censured by Eli, for *distemper in brain,*
1 Sam. i. 14; but for vain men who live more to reputation than to conscience, it cannot be that they
should long enjoy settled quiet, because those in
whose good opinion they desire to dwell, are ready
often to take up contrary conceits upon slender
grounds.

It is also a ground of overmuch trouble, when we
look too much and too long upon the ill in ourselves
and abroad; we may fix our eyes too long even upon
sin itself, considering that we have not only a remedy
against the hurt by sin, but a commandment *to rejoice
always in the Lord.* Philip. iv. 4.   Much more may
we err in poring too much upon our afflictions;
wherein we may find always in ourselves upon search
a cause to justify God, and always something left to
comfort us: though we naturally mind more one cross
than a hundred favours, dwelling over long upon the
sore.

So likewise, our minds may be too much taken up
in consideration of the *miseries of the times* at home
and abroad, as if Christ did not rule in the midst of
his enemies, and would not help all in due time; or
as if the condition of the church in this world were
not for the most part in an afflicted and conflicting
condition.   Indeed there is a perfect rest both for the
souls and bodies of God's people, but that is not in
this world, but is kept for hereafter, here we are·in a
sea, where what can we look for, but storms?

To insist upon no more, one cause is, that we do
usurp upon God, and take his office upon us, by
troubling ourselves in forecasting the event of things,
whereas our work is only to do our work and be
quiet, as children when they please their parents take

no further thought; our trouble is the fruit of our folly in this kind.

That which we should observe from all that hath been said is, that we be not over hasty in censuring others, when we see their spirits out of temper, for we see how many things there are that work strongly upon the weak nature of man. *We may sin more by harsh censure, than they by overmuch distemper:* as in Job's case it was a matter rather of just grief and pity, than great wonder or heavy censure.

And, for ourselves: if our state be calm for the present, yet we should labour to prepare our hearts, not only for an alteration of estate, but of spirit, unless we be marvellous careful beforehand, that our spirits fall not down with our condition. And if it befalls us to find it otherwise with our souls than at other times, we should so far labour to bear it, as that we do not judge it our own case alone, when we see here David thus to complain of himself, *why art thou cast down, O my soul?* &c.

CHAPTER IV.

OF CASTING DOWN OURSELVES, AND ESPECIALLY BY SORROW.—THE EVILS THEREOF.

To return again to the words, *Why art thou cast down, O my soul?* &c. or, *why dost thou cast down thyself?* or, *art cast down by thyself?* Whence we may further observe; *that we are prone to cast down ourselves,* we are accessory to our own trouble, and weave the web of our own sorrow, and hamper ourselves in the cords of our own twining. God neither loves nor wills that we should be too much cast down. We see our Saviour Christ how careful he was that his disciples should not be troubled, and therefore he labours to prevent that trouble which might arise by his suffering and departure from them, by a heavenly sermon; *let not your hearts be troubled,* &c. John

xiv. 1.   He was troubled himself, that we should not
be troubled: the ground therefore of our disquiet is
chiefly from ourselves, though Satan will have a hand
in it.   We see many, like sullen birds in a cage, beat
themselves to death.   This casting down of ourselves
is not from humility, but from pride; we must have
our will, or God shall not have a good look from us,
both as pettish and peevish children, we hang our
heads in our bosom, because our wills are crossed.

Therefore in all our troubles we should look first
home to our own hearts, and stop the storm there;
for we may thank our own selves, not only for our
troubles, but likewise for overmuch troubling ourselves in trouble.   It was not the troubled condition
that so disquieted David's soul, for if he had had a
quiet mind, it would not have troubled him.   But
David yielded to the discouragements of the flesh, and
the flesh (so far as it is unsubdued) is like the sea
that is always casting mire and dirt of doubts, discouragements, and murmurings in the soul: let us
therefore lay the blame where it is to be laid.

Again, we see, *it is the nature of sorrow to cast
down, as of joy to lift up.*   Grief is like lead to the
soul, heavy and bold; it sinks downwards, and carries the soul with it.   The poor publican, to show that
his soul was cast down under the sight of his sins,
hung down his head, Luke xviii. 13; the position of
his body was suitable to the disposition of his mind,
his heart and head were cast down alike.   And it is
Satan's practice to go over the hedge where it is lowest: he adds more weights to the soul, by his temptations and vexations.   His sin cast him out of Heaven,
and by his temptations, he casts us out of our Paradise, and ever since, he labours to cast us deeper into
sin, wherein his scope is, to cast us either into too
much trouble for sin, or presumption in sin, which is
but a lifting up, to cast us down into deep despair at
length, and so at last, if God's mercy stop not his
malice, he will cast us as low as himself, even into
hell itself.

The ground hereof is because *as the joy of the*

Lord doth strengthen, so doth sorrow weaken the soul. How doth it weaken?

1. By weakening the execution of the functions thereof, because it drinketh up the spirits, which are the instruments of the soul.

2. Because it contracteth, and draweth the soul into itself from communion of that comfort it might have with God or man. And then the soul being left alone, if *it falleth,* hath none to *raise it up.* Eccl. iv. 10.

Therefore, if we will prevent casting down, let us *prevent grief, the cause of it,* and sin the cause of that. Experience proves that true which the wise man says, *Heaviness in the heart of a man makes it stoop, but a good word makes it better.* Prov. xii. 25. It bows down the soul, and therefore our blessed Saviour inviteth such unto him; *Come unto me, ye who are heavy laden with the burden of your sins.* Matt. xi. The body bends under a heavy burden, so likewise the soul hath its burden, *Why art thou cast down, O my soul? why so disquieted?* &c.

Whence we see, 1. that casting down breeds disquieting: because it springs from pride, which is a turbulent passion, when as men cannot stoop to that condition which God would have them in; this proceeds from discontentment, and that from pride. As we see, a vapour inclosed in a cloud causeth a terrible noise of thunder, whilst it is pent up there, and seeketh a vent; so all the noise within proceeds from a discontented swelling vapour. It is air inclosed in the bowels of the earth which shakes it, which all the four winds cannot do.

No creature under heaven so low cast down as Satan, none more lifted up in pride, none so full of discord; the impurest spirits are the most disquiet and stormy spirits, troublesome to themselves and others; for when the soul leaves God once, and looks downwards, what is there to stay it from disquiet? Remove the needle from the pole star, and it is always stirring and trembling, never quiet till it be right again. So, displace the soul by taking it from God, and it will never be quiet. The devil cast out of Heaven and out of the Church, keeps ado; so do unruly spirits led by him.

Now I come to the remedies,

1. *By expostulation with himself.*

2. *By laying a charge upon himself:*

(*Trust in God.*)

It is supposed here, that there is no reason, which the wisdom from above allows to be a reason, why men should be discouraged although the wisdom from beneath, which takes part with our corruption, will seldom want a plea. Nay, there is not only no reason for it, but there are strong reasons against it, there being a world of evil in it.

For, 1. It indisposes a man to all good duties, it makes him like an instrument out of tune, and like a body out of joint, that moveth both uncomely and painfully. It unfits for duties to God, who loves a *cheerful giver,* and especially a *thanksgiver.* Whereupon the apostle joins them both together, *In all things be thankful,* and *rejoice evermore.* 1 Thess. v. In our communion with God in the sacraments, joy is a chief ingredient. So in duties to men, if the spirit be dejected, they are unwelcome, and lose the greatest part of their life and grace; a cheerful and a free spirit in duty is that which is most accepted in duty. We observe not so much what, as from what affection a thing is done.

2. It is a great wrong to God himself, and it makes us conceive black thoughts of him, as if He were an enemy. ·What an injury is it to a gracious father, that such whom he hath followed with many gracious evidences of his favour and love, should be in so ill a frame, as once to call it into question?

3. So, it makes a man forgetful of all former blessings, and stops the influence of God's grace, for the time present, and for that to come.

4. So again, for receiving of good: It makes us unfit to receive mercies; a quiet soul is the seat of wisdom. Therefore, *meekness* is required for the *receiving of that engrafted word which is able to save*

our souls. James, i. 21. Till the spirit of God *meek-ens* the soul, say what you will, it minds nothing, the soul is not empty and quiet enough to receive the seed of the Word. It is ill sowing in a storm; so a stormy spirit will not suffer the Word to take place. *Men are deceived when they think a dejected spirit to be an humble spirit.* Indeed it is so when we are cast down in the sense of our own unworthiness, and then as much raised up in the confidence of God's mercy. But when we cast ourselves down sullenly, and neglect our comforts, or undervalue them, it proceeds from pride, for it controls, as much as in us lies, the wisdom and justice of God, when we think with ourselves, why should it be so with us? as if we were wiser to dispose of ourselves than God is. It disposeth us for entertaining any temptation. Satan hath never more advantage than upon discontent.

5. Besides, it keeps off beginners from coming in, and entering into the ways of God, bringing an ill report upon religion, causing men to charge it falsely for an uncomfortable way, when as men never feel what true comfort meaneth till they give up themselves to God. And it damps likewise the spirits of those that walk the same way with us, when as we should (as good travellers) cheer up one another both by word and example. In such a case, the wheels of the soul are taken off, or else (as it were) want oil, whereby the soul passeth on very heavily, and no good action comes off from it as it should, which breeds not only uncomfortableness but unsettledness in good courses. For a man will never go on comfortably and constantly in that which he heavily undertakes. That is the reason why uncheerful spirits seldom hold out as they should. Peter knew this well, and therefore he willeth that there should be *quietness and peace betwixt husband and wife, that their prayers be not hindered,* 1 Pet. iii.; insinuating that their prayers are hindered by family breaches. For by that means, those two, that should be one flesh and spirit, are divided, and so made two, and when

they should mind duty, their mind is taken up with wrongs done by the one to the other.

There is nothing more required for the performing of holy duties than uniting of spirits; and therefore God would not have the sacrifice brought to the altar, before reconciliation with our brother. Matt. v. 24. He esteems peace so highly, that he will have his own service stay for it. We see when Moses came to deliver the *Israelites out of bondage,* their mind was so taken up with their grief, that there was nobody within to give Moses an answer, their souls went altogether after their ill usage.

Therefore we should all endeavour and labour for a calmed spirit, that we may the better serve God in praying to him, and praising of him; and serve one another in love, that we may be fitted to do and receive good: that we may make our passage to Heaven more easy and cheerful, without drooping and hanging the wing. So much as we are quiet and cheerful upon good grounds, so much we live, and are as it were in Heaven. So much as we yield to discouragement, we lose so much of our life and happiness, cheerfulness being, as it were, that life of our lives, and the spirit of our spirits, by which they are more enlarged to receive happiness and to express it.

CHAPTER V.

REMEDIES OF CASTING DOWN: TO CITE THE SOUL, AND PRESS IT TO GIVE
AN ACCOUNT.

But to come to some helps:

First, in that he expostulates with himself, we may observe, that *One way to raise a dejected soul is, to cite it before itself, and as it were to reason the case.* God hath set up a court in man's heart, wherein the conscience hath the office, both of *informer, accuser, witness,* and *judge;* and if matters were well carried within ourselves, this prejudging would be a prevention of future judging. It is a great mercy of God, that the credit and comfort of man are so provided for, that he may take up matters in himself, and so prevent public disgrace. But if there be not a fair despatch and transaction in this inferior court within us, there will be a review in a higher court. Thereby by slubbering over our matters, we put God and ourselves to more trouble than needs. For a judgment must pass first or last, either within us or without us, upon all unwarrantable distempers. We must not only be ready to give an account of our *faith*, upon what grounds we believe; but of all our *actions*, upon what grounds we do what we do; and of our *passions*, upon what ground we are passionate: as in a well governed state, uproar and sedition is never stirred, but account must be given. Now in a mutiny, the presence and speech of a venerable man compose the minds of the disordered multitude; so likewise in a mutiny of the spirit, the authority that God hath put into reason, as a beam of himself, commands silence, and puts all in order again.

And there is good reason for it, for man is an understanding creature, and hath a rule given him to live by, and therefore is to be accountable of every *thought, word, action, passion.* Therefore the first way to quiet the soul, is, to ask a reason of the tumult raised, and then many of our distempers for shame will not appear, because, though they rage in silent darkness, yet they can say nothing for themselves, being summoned before strength of judgment and reason. Which is the reason why passionate men are loath that any court should be kept within them; but labour to stop judgment all they can. If men would but give themselves leave to consider better of it, they would never yield to such unreasonable motions of the soul: if they could but gain so much of their unruly passions, as to reason the matter within themselves, to hear what their consciences can tell them in secret, there would not be such offensive breakings out. And therefore, if we be ashamed to hear others upbraiding us, let us for shame hear ourselves: and if no reason can be given, what an un-

, reasonable thing is it for a man endowed with reason to act contrary to his own principles? and to be carried as a beast without reason; or if there be any reason to be given, then this is the way to scan it, see whether it will hold water or not. We shall find some reasons, if they may be so called, to be so corrupt and foul, that (if the judgment be not corrupted by them) they dare not be brought to light, but always appear under some colour and pretext; for sin, like the devil, is afraid to appear in its own likeness, and men seek out fair glosses for foul intentions. The hidden secret reason is one, the open is another: the heart being corrupt sets the wit to work, to satisfy corrupt will; such kind of men are afraid of their own consciences, as Ahab of Michaiah, 1 Kings xxii., because they fear it would deal truly with them: and therefore they take either present order for their consciences, or else (as Felix put off Paul, Acts xxiv. 25,) they adjourn the court for another time. Such men are strangers at home, afraid of nothing more than themselves, and therefore in a fearful condition, because they are reserved for the *judgment of the great day*, if God doth not before that set upon them in this world. If men carried away with their own lusts would give but a little check, and stop themselves in their posting to hell, and ask, *What have I done? What am I now about? Whither will this course tend? How will it end?* &c. Undoubtedly men would begin to be wise. Would the blasphemer give away his soul for nothing (for there is no engagement of profit or pleasure in this, as in other sins, but it issues merely out of irreverence, and a superfluity of profaneness;) would he, I say, draw so heavy a guilt upon himself for nothing, if he would but make use of his reason? would an old man, when he is very near his journey's end, make longer provision for a short way, if he would ask himself a reason? But indeed covetousness is an unreasonable vice.

If those also of the *younger sort* would ask of themselves, *Why God should not have the flower and marrow of their age? and why they should give their strength to the devil?* It might a little take them off from the devil's service. But sin is a work of darkness, and therefore shuns not only the light of grace, but even the light of reason. Yet sin seldom wants a seeming reason. *Men will not go to hell without a show of reason.* But such be sophistical fallacies, not reasons; and therefore sinners are said to play the sophisters with themselves: *Satan could not deceive us, unless we deceived ourselves first, and are willingly deceived:* wilful sinners are blind, because they put out the light of reason, and so think God, like themselves, blind too, Psalm l.; and therefore they are deservedly termed *mad men and fools;* for, did they but make use of that spark of reason, it would teach them to reason thus; *I cannot give an account of my ways to myself: what account shall I, or can I, give then to the Judge of all flesh ere it be long.*

And as it is a ground of repentance, in stopping our course to ask, *What have I done?* So likewise of faith and new obedience, to ask, *what shall I do for the time to come?* and then upon settling, the soul in way of thanks will be ready to ask of itself, *What shall I return to the Lord?* &c. So that the soul by this dealing with itself, promoteth itself to all holy duties till it come to Heaven.

The reason why we are thus backward to the keeping of this court in ourselves, is *self-love;* we love to flatter our own affections, *but this self-love is but self-hatred in the end;* as the wise man says, he that regards not this part of wisdom, *hates his own soul, and shall eat the fruits of his own ways.*

2. As likewise it issues from an irksomeness of labour, which makes us rather willing to seem base and vile to ourselves and others, than to take pains with our own hearts to be better, as those that are weary of holding the reins give them up unto the horse's neck, and so are driven whither the rage of the horse carrieth them: *sparing a little trouble at first, doubles it in the end;* as he who will not take the pains to

cast up his books, his books will cast up him in the end. *It is a blessed trouble that brings sound and long peace.* 1 Cor. xi. 31. This labour saves God a labour, for therefore he *judgeth us,* because we would not take pains with ourselves before.

3. And *pride* also, with a desire of liberty, makes men think it to be a diminishing of greatness and freedom either to be curbed, or to curb ourselves: We love to be absolute and independent; but this, as it brought ruin upon our nature in Adam, so it will upon our persons. Men, as Luther was wont to say, are born with a pope in their belly, they are loath to give an account, although it be to themselves, their wills are instead of a kingdom to them.

Let us therefore, when any lawless passions begin to stir, deal with our souls as God did with Jonah, *Doest thou well to be angry?* Jonah iv., to fret thus? This will be a means to make us quiet: for, alas! what weak reasons have we often of strong motions; such a man gave me no respect, such another looked more kindly upon another man than upon me, &c. You have some of Haman's spirit, Esther v., that for a little neglect would ruin a whole nation. Passion presents men that are innocent as guilty to us; and because we will not seem to be mad without reason, *pride* commands the wit to justify anger, and so one passion maintains and feeds another.

Neither is it sufficient to *cite the soul before itself; but it must be pressed to give an account,* as we see here, David doubles and trebles the expostulation; as oft as any distemper did arise, so oft did he labour to keep it down. If passions grow too insolent, Eli's mildness will do no good. 1 Sam. ii. 24. It would prevent much trouble in this kind, to subdue betimes, in ourselves and others, the first beginnings of any unruly passions and affections; which, if they be not well tutored and disciplined at the first, prove as headstrong, unruly, and ill natured children, who, being not chastened in time, take such a head, that it is oft above the power of parents to bring them in order. A child set at liberty (saith Solomon) *breeds shame, at length, to his parents.* Prov. xxix. 15. Adonia's example shows this. The like may be said of the affections set at liberty; it is dangerous to redeem a litttle quiet by yielding to our affections, which is never safely gotten but by mortification of them.

Those that are in great place are most in danger, by yielding to themselves, to lose themselves; for they are so taken up with the person for a time put upon them, that they, both in look and speech, and carriage, often show that they forget both their natural condition as men, and much more their supernatural as Christians; and therefore are scarce counselable by others or themselves, in those things that concern their severed condition that concerneth another world. Whereas it were most wisdom so to think of their place they bear, whereby they are called *gods*, Psal. lxxxii. 6, 7, as not to forget they must lay their person aside, and *die like men*, 2 Sam. xxiv. 4: David himself that in his afflicted condition could advise with himself, and check himself, yet in his free and flourishing estate neglected the counsel of his friends. Agur was in jealousy of a full condition, and lest instead of saying, What have I done? why am I thus cast down? &c., he should say, *Who is the Lord?* Prov. xxx. 9.

Meaner men in their lesser sphere often show what their spirits would be, if their compass were enlarged.

It is a great fault in breeding youth, for fear of taking down of their spirits, not to take down their pride, and get victory of their affections; whereas a proud unbroken heart raiseth us more trouble often than all the world beside. Of all troubles, the trouble of a proud heart is the greatest. It was a great trouble to Haman to lead Mordecai's horse, Esth. vi. 1, which another man would not have thought so; the moving of a straw is troublesome to proud flesh. And therefore it is good to *bear the yoke from our youth*, Lam. iii. 27: it is better to be taken down in youth, than to be broken in pieces by great crosses in age. First or last, self-denial and victory over ourselves is absolutely necessary; otherwise *faith*, which is a grace that requireth self-denial, will never be brought into the soul, and bear rule there.

But, *what if pressing upon our souls will not help?*

Then speak to God, to Jesus Christ by prayer, that as he rebuked the winds and the waves, and went upon the sea, so he would walk upon our souls, and command a calm there. It is no less power to settle a peace in the soul, than to command the seas to be quiet. It is God's prerogative to rule in the heart, as likewise to give it up to itself, which (next to hell) is the greatest judgment; which should draw us to the greater reverence and fear of displeasing God. It was no ill wish of him, that desired God to free him from an ill man, himself.

CHAPTER VI.

OTHER OBSERVATIONS OF THE SAME NATURE.

MOREOVER we see that a *godly man can cast a restraint upon himself,* as David here stays himself in falling. There is a principle of grace, that stops the heart, and pulls in the reins again when the affections are loose. A carnal man, when he begins to be cast down, sinks lower and lower, until he sinks into despair, as lead sinks into the bottom of the sea. *They sunk, they sunk, like lead in the mighty waters.* Exod. xv. 5. A carnal man sinks as a heavy body to the centre of the earth, and stays not, if it be not stopped: there is nothing in him to stay him in falling, as we see in Ahitophel and Saul, 2 Sam. xvii. 23: who (wanting a support) found no other stay, but the sword's point. And the greater their parts and places are, the more they entangle themselves; and no wonder, for they are to encounter with God and his deputy, conscience, who is King of kings, and Lord of lords. When Cain was cast out of his father's house, his heart and countenance was always cast down; for he had nothing in him to lift it upwards. But a godly man, though he may give a little way to passion, yet (as David) he recovers himself. Therefore as we would have any good evidence, that we have a better spirit in us than our own, greater than the flesh or the world, let us (in all troubles we meet with) gather up ourselves, that the stream of our own affections carry us not away too far.

There is an art or skill of bearing troubles, if we could learn it, without overmuch troubling of ourselves; as in bearing of a burthen there is a way so to poise it, that it weigheth not over heavy: if it hangs all on one side, it poises the body down. The greater part of our troubles we pull upon ourselves, by not parting our care so, as to take upon us only the care of duty, and leave the rest to God; and by mingling our passions with our crosses; and, like a foolish patient, chewing the pills which we should swallow down. We dwell too much upon the grief, when we should remove the soul higher. We are nearest neighbours unto ourselves; when we suffer grief, like a canker, to eat into the soul, and like a fire in the bones, to consume the marrow and drink up the spirits, we are accessory to the wrong done both to our bodies and souls: we waste our own candle, and put out our light.

We see here again, that *a godly man can make a good use of privacy.* When he is forced to be alone he can talk with his God and himself; one reason whereof is, that his heart is a treasury and storehouse of divine truths, whence he can speak to himself, by way of check, or encouragement of himself: he hath a spirit over his own spirit, to teach him to make use of that store he hath laid up in his heart, the spirit is never nearer him than when by way of witness to his spirit he is thus comforted; wherein the child of God differs from another man, who cannot endure solitariness because his heart is empty; he was a stranger to God before, and God is a stranger to him now; so that he cannot go to God as a friend. And for his conscience, that is ready to speak to him, that which he is loath to hear: and therefore he counts himself a torment to himself, especially in privacy.

We read of great princes, who after some bloody designs were as terrible to themselves,* as they were formerly to others, and therefore could never endure to be awaked in the night, without music, or some like diversion. It may be, we may be cast into such a condition, where we have none in the world to comfort us, as in contagious sickness, when none may come near us, we may be in such an estate wherein no friend will own us. And therefore let us labour now to be acquainted with God and our own hearts, and acquaint our hearts with the comforts of the Holy Ghost; then, though we have not so much as a book to look on, or a friend to talk with, yet we may look with comfort into the book of our own heart, and read what God hath written there by the finger of his Spirit; all books are written to amend this one book of our heart and conscience: by this means we shall never want a divine to comfort us, a physician to cure us, a counsellor to direct us, a musician to cheer us, a controller to check us. because, by help of the word and Spirit, we can be all these to ourselves.

Another thing we see here, that God hath made every man a governor over himself. The poor man, that hath none to govern, yet may he be a king in himself. It is the natural ambition of man's heart to desire government, as we see in the *bramble*. Judg. ix. Well then, let us make use of this disposition to rule ourselves. Absalom had high thoughts; O, if I were a king, I would do so and so! So our hearts are ready to promise, If I were as such and such a man in such and such a place, I would do this and that.

But how dost thou manage thine own affections? how dost thou rule in thine house? in thyself? do not passions get the upper hand, and keep reason under foot? When we have learned to rule over our own spirits well, then we may be fit to rule over others. *He that is faithful in a little, shall be set over more.* Matt. xxv. 21. *He that can govern himself,* in the wise man's judgment, *is better than he that can govern a city.* Prov. xvi. 32. He that cannot,

* As Charles IX. after the massacre in France.

is like a city without a wall, where those that are in may go out, and the enemies without may come in at their pleasure. So where there is not a government set up, there sin breaks out, and Satan breaks in without control.

See again, the *excellency of the soul, that can reflect upon itself, and judge of whatsoever comes from it:* a godly man's care and trouble is especially about his soul, as David here looks principally to that, because all outward troubles are for to help that; when God touches our bodies, our estates, or our friends, he aims at the soul in all. God will never remove his hand, till something be wrought upon the soul, as *David's moisture was as the drought in summer,* Psal. xxxii., so that he roared, and carried himself unseemly for so great and holy a man, till his heart was subdued to deal without all guile with God in confessing his sin; and then God forgave him the iniquity thereof, and healed his body too. In sickness, or in any other trouble, it is best the divine should be before the physician: and that men begin where God begins. In great fires men look first to their jewels, and then to their lumber; so our soul is our best jewel: a carnal worldly man is called, and well called, a fleshly man, because his very soul is flesh, and there is nothing but the world in him. And, therefore, when all is not well within, he cries out, My *body* is troubled, my *state* is broken, my friends fail me, &c., but all this while there is no care for the poor soul to settle a peace in that.

The possession of the soul is the richest possession, no jewel so precious; the account for our own souls, and the souls of others, is the greatest account, and therefore the care of souls should be the greatest care. What an indignity is it that we should forget such souls to satisfy our lusts? to have our wills? to be vexed with any; who by their judgment, example, or authority stop as we suppose our courses? Is it not the greatest plot of the world; first to have their lusts satisfied: secondly, to remove either by fraud or violence whatsoever standeth in their way: and third-

ly, to put colours and pretences upon this to delude
the world and themselves, employing all their carnal
wit and worldly strength for their carnal aims, and
fighting for that which fights against their own souls?
For what will be the issue of this but certain destruction?

Of this mind are not only the dregs of people, but
many of the more refined sort, who desire to be eminent in the world; and to have their own desires
herein, give up the liberty of their own judgments
and consciences, to the desires and lusts of others;
to be above others they will be beneath themselves,
having those men's persons in admiration for hope of
advantage, whom otherwise they despise, and so sub-
stituting in their spirits, man in the place of God, lose
heaven for earth, and bury that divine spark, their
souls, capable of the divine nature, and fitter to be a
sanctuary and temple for God to dwell in, than by
closing with baser things to become base itself. We
need not wonder that others seem base to carnal men,
who are base both in and to themselves. It is no
wonder they should be cruel to the souls of others,
who are cruel to their own souls; that they should
neglect and starve others, that give away their own
souls in a manner for nothing. Alas! upon what
poor terms do they hazard that, the nature and worth
whereof is beyond man's reach to comprehend!
Many are so careless in this kind, that if they were
thoroughly persuaded that they had souls that should
live for ever, either in bliss or torment, we might the
more easily work upon them. But as they live by
sense, as beasts, so they have no more thoughts of
future times than beasts, except at such times as conscience is awaked by some sudden judgment, whereby God's wrath is revealed from heaven against
them. But happy were it for them, if they might
die like beasts, whose misery dies with them.

To such an estate hath sin brought the soul, that
it willingly drowneth itself in the senses, and becomes
in some sort incarnate with the flesh.

We should therefore set ourselves to have most

care of that, which God cares most for: which he breathed into us at first, set his own image upon, gave so great a price for, and values above all the world besides. Shall all our study be to satisfy the desires of the flesh, and neglect this?

Is it not a vanity to prefer the casket before the jewel, the shell before the pearl, the gilded potsherd before the treasure? and is it not much more vanity, to prefer the outward condition before the inward? The soul is that which Satan and his hath most spite at, for in troubling our bodies or estates, he aims at the vexation of our souls. As in Job i. his aim was to abuse that power God had given him over his children, body, and goods, to make him out of a disquieted spirit blaspheme God. It is an ill method to begin our care in other things, and neglect the soul, as Ahitophel, who set his house in order, when he should have set his soul in order first. 2 Sam. xvii. 23. Wisdom begins at the right end. If all be well at home, it comforts a man, though he meets with troubles abroad. Oh, saith he, I shall have rest at home, I have a loving wife and dutiful children; so whatsoever we meet withal abroad, if the soul be quiet, thither we can retire with comfort. See that all be well within, and then all troubles from without cannot much annoy us.

Grace will teach us to reason thus, God hath given mine enemies power over my liberty and condition, but shall they have power and liberty over my spirit? It is that which Satan and they most seek for: but never yield, O my soul! and thus a godly man will become more than a conqueror; when in appearance he is conquered, the cause prevails, his spirit prevails, and is undaunted. A Christian is not subdued till his spirit be subdued. Thus Job prevailed over Satan and all his troubles at length. This tormenteth proud persons to see godly men enjoy a calm and resolute frame of mind in the midst of troubles; when their enemies are more troubled in troubling them, than they are in being troubled by them.

We see likewise here, *how to frame our complaints:*

David complains not of God, nor of his troubles, nor of others, but of his own soul: He complains of himself to himself; as if he should say, *Though all things else be out of order, yet, O my soul, thou shouldst not trouble me too: thou shouldst not betray thyself unto troubles, but rule over them.* A godly man complains to God, but not of God, but of himself; a carnal man is ready to justify himself and complain of God, he complains not to God, but of God, at the least, in secret murmuring, he complains of others that are but God's vials; he complains of the grievance that lies upon him, but never regards what is amiss in himself within: Openly he cries out upon fortune, yet secretly he striketh at God, under that idol of fortune, by whose guidance all things come to pass; whilst he quarrels with that which is nothing, he wounds him that is the cause of all things; like a gouty man that complains of his shoe, and of his bed; or an aguish man of his drink, when the cause is from within. So men are disquieted with others, when they should rather be disquieted and angry with their own hearts.

We condemn Jonas for contending with God, and justifying his unjust anger, but yet the same risings are in men naturally, if shame would suffer them to give vent to their secret discontent; their heart speaks what Jonas' tongue spake. Oh, but here we should lay our hand upon our mouth, and adore God, and command silence to our souls.

No man is hurt but by himself first: We are drawn to evil, and allured from a true good to a false by our own lusts, *God tempts no man.* Jam. 1. 13. Satan hath no power over us further than we willingly lie open to him; Satan works upon our affections, and then our affections work upon our will. He doth not work immediately upon the will; we may thank ourselves in willingly yielding to our own passions, for all that ill Satan or his instruments draws us unto; Saul was not vexed with an *evil spirit.* 1 Sam. xvi, till he gave way to his own *evil spirit of envy* first. The devil entered not into Judas, Matt. xxvii. 3, until his covetous heart made way for him. The apostle strengtheneth his conceit against rash and lasting anger from hence, that by this we give way to the devil. Eph. iv. It is a dangerous thing to pass from God's government, and come under Satan's.

Satan mingleth himself with our own passions, therefore we should blame ourselves first, be ashamed of ourselves most, and judge ourselves most severely. But self-love teacheth us the contrary method, to translate all upon others; it robs us of a right judgment of ourselves. Though we desire to know all diseases of the body by their proper names, yet we will conceive of sinful passions of the soul under milder terms; as *lust* under *love*, *rage* under *just anger*, *murmuring* under *just displeasure*, &c., thus whilst we flatter our grief, what hope of cure! Thus sin hath not only made all the creatures enemies to us, but ourselves the greatest enemies to ourselves, and therefore we should begin our complaints against ourselves, and discuss ourselves thoroughly; how else shall we judge truly of other things without us, above us, or beneath us? The sun when it rises enlightens first the nearest places, and then the more remote; so where true light is set up, it discovers what is amiss within first.

Hence also we see, that *as in all discouragements a godly man hath most trouble with his own heart, so he knows how to carry himself therein,* as David doth here.

For the better clearing of this, we must know there be divers kinds and degrees of conflicts in the soul of man, whilst it is united to the body.

First, between one corrupt passion and another, as between covetousness and pride; pride calls for expense, covetousness for restraint; oft passions fight not only against God and reason, to which they owe a homage, but one against another; sin fights against sin, and a lesser sin is oftentimes overcome by a greater. The soul in this case is like the sea tossed with contrary winds; and like a kingdom divided, wherein the subjects fight both against their prince, and one against another.

Secondly, There is a natural conflict in the affections, whereby nature seeks to preserve itself, as betwixt anger and fear; anger calls for revenge, fear of the law binds the soul to be quiet. We see in the creatures, fear makes them abstain from that which their appetites carry them unto. A wolf comes to a flock with an eagerness to prey upon it, but seeing the shepherd standing in defence of his sheep, returns and doth no harm; and yet for all this, as he came a wolf, so he returns a wolf.

A natural man may oppose some sin from an obstinate resolution against it, not from any love of God, or hatred of sin, as sin, but because he conceives it a brave thing to have his will. As one hard weapon may strike at another, as a stone wall may beat back an arrow; but this opposition is not from a contrariety of nature, as is betwixt fire and water.

Thirdly, There is a conflict of a higher nature, as between some sins and the light of reason helped by a natural conscience. The heathen could reason from the dignity of the soul, to count it a base thing to prostitute themselves to beastly lusts, so as it were degrading and unmanning themselves. Natural men desirous to maintain a great opinion of themselves, and to awe the inferior sort by gravity of deportment in carriage, will abstain from that, which otherwise their hearts carry them unto, lest yielding should render them despised, by laying themselves too much open; as because passion discovers a fool as he is, and makes a wise man thought meaner than he is; therefore a prudent man will conceal his passion. Reason refined and raised by education, example, and custom, doth break in some degree the force of natural corruption, and brings into the soul, as it were, another nature, and yet no true change; as we see in such as have been inured to good courses, they feel conscience checking them upon the first discontinuance and alteration of their former good ways, but this is usually from a former impression of their breeding, as the boat moves some little time upon the water by virtue of the former stroke, yet at length we see corruption prevailing over education, as in Joas, who was awed by the reverent respect he bare to his uncle Jehoiada, he was good *all his uncle's days.* 2 Kings xii. 2. And in Nero, in whom the goodness of his education prevailed over the fierceness of his nature, for the first five years.

Fourthly, but in the Church, where there shineth a light above nature, as there is a discovery of more sins, and some strength, with the light, to perform more duty; so there is a further conflict than in a man that hath no better than nature in him. By a discovery of the excellent things of the Gospel, there may be some kind of joy stirred up, and some degree of obedience: whence there may be some degree of resistance against the sins of the Gospel, as obstinate unbelief, desperation, profaneness, &c. A man in the Church may do more than another out of the Church, by reason of the enlargement of his knowledge; whereupon such cannot sin at so easy a rate as others that know less, and, therefore, meet with less opposition from conscience.

Fifthly, there is yet a further degree of conflict betwixt the sanctified powers of the soul, and the flesh, not only as it is seated in the baser parts, but even in the best faculties of the soul, and as it mingles itself with every gracious performance: as in David, there is not only a conflict betwixt sin and conscience, enlightened by a *common work* of the *Spirit;* but between the commanding powers of the soul *sanctified,* and itself *unsanctified,* between reasons of the *flesh* and reasons of the *Spirit,* between *faith* and *distrust,* between the true light of knowledge, and false light. For it is no question but the flesh would play its part in David, and muster up all the strength of reason it had. And usually *flesh,* as it is more ancient than the *Spirit,* we being first natural, then spiritual, so it will put itself first forward in devising shifts, as Esau comes out of the womb first before

Jacob; yet hereby the *spirit* is stirred up to a present examination and resistance, and in resisting, as we see here, at length the godly gets the victory. As in the conflict between the higher parts of the soul with the lower, it clearly appears, that the soul doth not rise out of the temper of the body, but is a more noble substance, commanding the body by reasons fetched from its own worth; so in this spiritual conflict, it appears there is something better than the soul itself, that hath superiority over it.

CHAPTER VII.

DIFFERENCE BETWEEN GOOD MEN AND OTHERS IN CONFLICTS WITH SIN.

But how doth it appear that this combat in David was a *spiritual combat?*

First, a natural conscience is troubled for sins against the light of *nature* only, but David for inward and secret corruptions, as discouragement and disquietness arising from faint trusting in God.

David's conflict was not only with the sensual lower part of his soul, which is carried to ease and quiet, and love of present things, but he was troubled with a mutiny in his understanding, between *faith* and *distrust;* and therefore he was forced to rouse up his soul so oft to *trust* in God, which shows that carnal reason did solicit him to discontent, and had many colourable reasons for it.

Secondly, a man endowed with *common* grace, is rather a patient than an agent in conflicts; the *light* troubles him against his will, as discovering and reproving him, and hindering his sinful contentments, his heart is more biased another way if the *light* would let him; but a godly man labours to help the *light*, and to work his heart to an opposition against sin; he is an agent as well as a patient. As David here doth not suffer disquieting, but is *disquieted* with himself for being so. A godly man is an *agent* in opposing his corruption, and a *patient* in enduring of it! whereas a natural man is a secret *agent* in and for his corruptions, and a *patient* in regard of any help against them; a good man suffers evil and doth good, a natural man suffers good and doth evil.

Thirdly, a conscience guided by *common* light, withstands distempers most by outward means, but David here fetcheth help from the Spirit of God in him, and from trust in God. Nature works from within, so doth the new nature; David is not only something *disquieted*, and something troubled for being disquieted, but sets himself thoroughly against his distempers; he complains, and expostulates, he censures, and chargeth his soul. The other, if he doth any thing at all, yet it is faintly; he seeks out his corruption as a coward doth his enemy, loath to find him, and more loath to encounter with him.

Fourthly, David withstands sin *constantly*, and gets ground. We see here, he gives not over at the first, but presseth again and again. Nature works constantly, so doth the new nature. The conflict in the other is something forced, as taking part with the worser side in himself; good things have a weak, or rather no party in him, bad things a strong; and therefore he soon gives over in this holy quarrel.

Fifthly, David is not discouraged by his foils, but sets himself afresh against his corruptions, with confidence to bring them under. Whereas he that hath but a common work of the Spirit, after some foils, lets his enemy prevail more and more, and so despairs of victory, and thinks it better to sit still, than to rise and take a new fall; by which means his latter end is worse than his beginning; for *beginning in the Spirit, he ends in the flesh.* A godly man, although upon some foil, he may for a time be discouraged, yet by holy indignation against sin, he renews his force, and sets afresh upon his corruptions, and gathers more strength by his falls, and groweth into more acquaintance with his own heart, and Satan's malice, and God's strange ways in bringing light out of darkness.

Sixthly, An ordinary Christian may be disquieted

for being disquieted, as David was, but then it is only as disquiet hath vexation in it; but David here striveth against the unquietness of his spirit, not only as it brought vexation with it, but as it hindered communion with his God.

In sin there is not only a *guilt* binding over the soul to God's judgment, and thereupon filling the soul with inward fears and terrors; but in sin likewise there is, 1. a contrariety to God's holy nature; and 2. a contrariety to the divine nature and image stamped upon ourselves; 3. a weakening and disabling of the soul from good; and 4. a hindering of our former communion with God, sin being in its nature a leaving of God, the fountain of all strength and comfort, and cleaving to the creature; hereupon the soul having tasted the sweetness of God before, is now grieved, and this grief is not only for the guilt and trouble that sin draws after it, but from an inward antipathy and contrariety betwixt the sanctified soul and sin. It hates sin as sin, as the only bane and poison of renewed nature, and the only thing that breeds strangeness betwixt God and the soul. And this hatred is not so much from discourse and strength of reason, as from nature itself rising presently against its enemy; the lamb presently shuns the wolf from a contrariety; antipathies wait not for any strong reason, but are exercised upon the first presence of a contrary object.

Seventhly, hereupon ariseth the last difference; that because the soul hateth sin as sin, therefore it opposeth it universally and eternally, in all the powers of the soul, and in all actions inward and outward issuing from those powers; *David regarded no iniquity in his heart, but hated every evil way,* Psal. lxvi. 18, the desires of his soul were, *that it might be so directed that he might keep God's law.* Psal. cxix. 5. And if there had been no binding law, yet there was such a sweet sympathy and agreement betwixt his soul and God's truth, that he *delighted in it* above all natural *sweetness;* hence it is that John saith, *He that is born of God cannot sin,*

1 John iii. 9, that is, so far forth as he is *born of God;* his *new* nature will not suffer him, he cannot lie, he cannot deceive, he cannot be earthly minded, he cannot but love and delight in the persons and things that are good. There is not only a light in the understanding, but a new life in the will, and all other faculties of a godly man; what good his knowledge discovereth, that his will makes choice of, and his heart loveth; what ill his understanding disco vers, that his will hateth and abstains from. But in a man not thoroughly converted, the will and affections are bent otherwise, he loves not the good he doth, nor hates the evil he doth not.

Therefore let us make a narrow search into our souls upon what grounds we oppose sin, and fight God's battles. A common Christian is not cast down, because he is disquieted in God's service, or for his inward failings, that he cannot serve God with that liberty and freedom he desires, &c. But a godly man is troubled for his distempers, because they hinder the comfortable intercourse betwixt God and his soul, and that spiritual composedness, and sabbath of spirit which he enjoyed before, and desires to enjoy again. He is troubled that the waters of his soul are troubled so, that the image of Christ shines not in him as it did before. It grieves him to find an abatement in affection, in love to God, a distraction or coldness in performing duties, any doubting of God's favour, any discouragement from duty, &c. A godly man's com forts and grievances are hid from the world; natural men are strangers to them. Let this be a rule of discerning our estates, how we stand affected to the distempers of our hearts; if we find them troublesome, it is a ground of comfort unto us that our *spirits* are ruled by a *higher Spirit;* and that there is a principle of that life in us, which cannot brook the most secret corruption, but rather casts it out by a holy complaint, as strength of nature doth poison, which seeks its destruction. And let us be in love with that work of grace in us, which makes us out of love with the least stirring that hinders our best condition.

See again, *We may be sinfully disquieted for that which is not a sin to be disquieted for.*   David had sinned if he had not been somewhat troubled for the banishment from God's house, and the blasphemy of the enemies of the Church; but yet, we see, he stops himself, and sharply takes up his soul for being disquieted: he did well in being disquieted, and in checking himself for the same; there were good grounds for both: he had wanted spiritual life if he had not been disquieted: he abated the vigour and liveliness of his life, by being overmuch disquieted.

CHAPTER VIII.

OF UNFITTING DEJECTION: AND WHEN IT IS EXCESSIVE.—WHAT IS THE RIGHT TEMPER OF THE SOUL HEREIN.

§ 1. *Then, how shall we know when a man is cast down and disquieted, otherwise than is befitting?*

There is a threefold miscarriage of inward trouble.

1. *When the soul is troubled for that it should not be vexed for*, as Ahab, when he was crossed in his will for Naboth's vineyard.

2. *In the ground*, as when we grieve for that which is good, and for that which we should grieve for; but it is with too much reflecting upon our own particular.

As in the troubles of the state or Church, we ought to be affected; but not because these troubles hinder any liberties of the flesh, and restrain pride of life, but from higher respects; as that by these troubles God is dishonoured, the public exercises of religion hindered, and the gathering of souls thereby stopped; as the states and commonwealth, which should be harbours of the Church, are disturbed; as lawless courses and persons prevail; as religion and justice is triumphed over, and trodden under.   Men usually are grieved for public miseries from a spirit of self-love only, because their own private is embarked in the public.   There is a depth of deceit of the heart in this matter.

3. So for the measure, when we trouble ourselves (though not without cause) yet without bounds.

The spirit of man is like unto moist elements, as air and water, which have no bounds of their own to contain them in, but those of the vessel that keeps them: water is spilt and lost without something to hold it; so it is with the spirit of man, unless it be bounded with the Spirit of God. Put the case, a man be disquieted for sin, for which not to be disquieted is a sin, yet we may look too much, and too long upon it, for the soul hath a double eye, one to look to sin, another to look up to God's mercy in Christ. Having two objects to look on, we may sin in looking too much on the one, with neglect of the other.

§ II. *Seeing then, disquieting and dejection for sin is necessary, how shall we know when it exceeds measure?*

First, *when it hinders us from holy duties, or in the performance of them*, by distraction or otherwise; whereas they are given to carry us to that which is pleasing to God, and good to ourselves.

Grief is ill when it taketh off the soul from minding that it should, and so indisposeth us to the duties of our callings. Christ upon the cross was grieved to the utmost, yet it did not take away his care for his mother: so the good thief, Luke xxiii. 42, in the midst of his pangs laboured to gain his fellow, and to save his own soul, and to glorify Christ. If this be so in grief of body, which taketh away the free use of reason, and exercise of grace more than any other grief, then much more in grief from more remote causes; for in extremity of body the sickness may be such, as all that we can perform to God is a quiet submission, and a desire to be carried unto Christ by the prayers of others; we should so mind our grief as not to forget God's mercy, or our own duty.

Secondly, when we forget the grounds of comfort, and suffer our mind to run only upon the present grievance, it is a sin to dwell on sin, and turmoil our thoughts about it, when we are called to thankfulness.

A physician in good discretion forbids a dish at some times to prevent the nourishment of some disease, which another time he gives way unto. So we may and ought to abstain from too much feeding our thoughts upon our corruptions in case of discouragement, which at other times is very necessary. It should be our wisdom in such cases to change the object, and labour to take off our minds, and give them to that which calls more for them. Grief oft presseth unseasonably upon us, when there is cause of joy, and when we are called to joy; as Joab justly found fault with David for grieving too much, when God had given him the victory, and rid him and the state of a traitorous son. God hath made some days for joy, and joy is the proper work of those days. *This is the day which the Lord hath made.* Psalm cxviii. 24. Some in a sick distemper desire that which increaseth their sickness; so some that are deeply cast down, desire a wakening ministry, and whatever may cast them down more; whereas they should meditate upon comforts, and get some sweet assurance of God's love. Joy is the constant temper which the soul should be in. *Rejoice evermore,* 1 Thes. v. 16, saith the apostle. If a sink be stirred, we stir it not more, but go into a sweeter room. So we should think of that which is comfortable, and of such truths as may raise up the soul, and sweeten the spirit.

Thirdly, Grief is too much, when it inclines the soul to any inconvenient courses: for if it be not looked to, it is an ill counsellor, when either it hurts the health of our bodies, or draws the soul, for to ease itself, to some unlawful liberty. When grief keeps such a noise in the soul, that it will not hear what the messengers of God, or the still voice of the Spirit saith; as in combustions, loud cries are scarce heard: so in such cases the soul will neither hear itself nor others. The fruit of this overmuch trouble of spirit is increase of trouble.

§ III. Another question may be, *What that sweet*

and holy temper is the soul should be in, that it may neither be faulty in the defect, nor too much abound in grief and sorrow?

1. The soul must be raised to a right grief.

2. The grief that is raised, though it be right, yet it must be bounded. Before we speak of raising grief in the godly, we must know there are some who are altogether strangers to any kind of spiritual grief or trouble at all; such must consider, that the way to prevent everlasting trouble, is to desire to be troubled with a preventing trouble. Let those that are not in the way of grace think with themselves what cause they have not to take a minute's rest while they are in that estate. For a man to be in debt both body and soul, subject every minute to be arrested and carried prisoner to hell, and not to be moved: for a man to have the wrath of God ready to be poured out upon him, and hell gape for him, nay, to carry a hell about him in conscience, if it were awake, and to have all his comfort here hanging upon a weak thread of this life ready to be cut and broken off every moment, and to be cursed in all those blessings that he enjoys; and yet not to be disquieted, but continually treasuring up wrath against the day of wrath, by running deeper into God's books: for a man to be thus, and not to be disquieted, is but the devil's peace, whilst the strong man holds possession. *A burning ague is more hopeful than a lethargy:* The best service that can be done to such men, is to startle and rouse them, and so with violence to pull them out of the fire, as Jude speaks, verse 23, or else they will another day curse that cruel mercy that lets them alone now. In all their jollity in this world, they are but as a book fairly bound, which when it is opened is full of nothing but tragedies. So when the book of their consciences shall be once opened, there is nothing to be read but lamentations and woes. Such men were in a way of hope, if they had but so much apprehension of their estates, as to ask themselves, *What have I done?* If this be true that there are such fearful things prepared for sin-

5

ners, *why* am I not *cast down?* Why am I no more
troubled and discouraged for my wicked courses?
Despair to such is the beginning of comfort; and
trouble the beginning of peace. A storm is the way
to a calm, and hell the way to heaven.

But for raising of a right grief in the soul of a holy
man, *look what is the state of the soul in itself, in
what terms it is with God:* whether there be any
sin hanging on the file unrepented of. If all be not
well within us, then here is place for inward trouble,
whereby the soul may afflict itself.

God saw this grief so needful for his people, that
he appointed certain days for afflicting them, Lev.
xvi. 29; because it is fit that sin contracted by joy
should be dissolved by grief; and sin is so deeply invested into the soul, that a separation betwixt the
soul and it cannot be wrought without much grief;
when the soul hath smarted for sin, it sets then the
right price upon reconciliation with God in Christ,
and it feeleth what a bitter thing sin is, and therefore
it will be afraid to be too bold with it afterward; it
likewise aweth the heart so, that it will not be so
loose towards God as it was before; and certainly
that soul that hath felt the sweetness of keeping
peace with God, cannot but take deeply to heart,
that there should be any thing in us that should divide betwixt us and the fountain of our comfort, that
should stop the passage of our prayers and the current of God's favours both towards ourselves and
others, it is such an ill as is the cause of all other ill,
and damps all our comforts.

2. We should look out of ourselves also, considering whether for troubles at home and abroad, God
calls not to mourning or troubling of ourselves; grief
of compassion is as well required as grief of contri-
tion.

It is a dead member that is not sensible of the state
of the body. Jeremy, for fear he should not weep
enough for the distressed estate of the Church, desired
of God *that his eyes might be made a fountain of
tears.* Jer. ix. 1. A Christian, as he must not be

proud flesh, so neither must he be dead flesh; none more truly sensible either of sin or of misery, so far as misery carries with it any sign of God's displeasure, than a true Christian: which issues from the life of grace, which, where it is in any measure, is lively, and therefore sensible: for God gives motion and senses for the preservation of life. As God's bowels are tender towards us, so God's people have tender bowels towards *him*, his *cause*, his *people*, and his *Church*. The fruit of this sensibleness, is earnest prayer to God. As Melancthon said well, *If I cared for nothing, I would pray for nothing.*

2. Grief being thus raised, must, as we said before, be bounded and guided.

1. God hath framed the soul, and planted such affections in it, as may answer all his dealing towards his children; that when he enlargeth himself towards them, then the soul should enlarge itself to him again; when he opens his hand, we ought to open our hearts; when he shows any token of displeasure, we should grieve; when he troubles us, we should trouble and grieve ourselves. As God any way discovereth himself, so the soul should be in a suitable pliableness. Then the soul is as it should be, when it is ready to meet God at every turn, to joy when he calls for it, to mourn when he calls for that, to labour to know God's meaning in every thing.

Again, God has made the soul for a communion with himself, which communion is especially placed in the affections, which are the springs of all spiritual worship. Then the affections are well ordered, when we are fit to have communion with God, to *love, joy, trust*, to *delight* in him above all things. The affections are the inward movings of the soul which then move best when they move us to God, not from him. They are the feet of the soul, whereby we walk with, and before God. When we have our affections at such command, that we can take them off from any thing in the world, at such times as we are to have more near communion with God in *heaven* or *prayer*, &c. Gen. xxii. 5. As Abraham when he was to sacrifice, left whatsoever might hinder him at the *bottom of the Mount*. When we let our affections so far into the things of the world, as we cannot take them off when we are to deal with God; it is a sign of spiritual intemperancy. It is said of the Israelites that they brought Egypt with them into the wilderness; so many bring the world into their hearts with them, when they come before God.

But because our affections are never well ordered without judgment, as being to follow, not to lead; it is an evidence that the soul is in a fit temper, when there is such a harmony in it, as that we judge of things as they are, and affect as we judge, and execute as we affect. This harmony within breeds uniformity and constancy in our resolutions, so that there is, as it were, an even thread drawn through the whole course and tenor of our lives, when we are not off and on, up and down. It argues an ill state of body when it is very hot, or very cold, or hot in one part, and cold in another: so unevenness of spirit argues a distemper; a wise man's life is of one colour like itself. The soul bred from heaven, so far as it is heavenly minded, desires to be, like heaven, above all storms, uniform, constant; not as things under the sun, which are always in changes, constant only in inconstancy. Affections are as it were the wind of the soul, and then the soul is carried as it should be, when it is neither so becalmed that it moves not when it should, nor yet tossed with tempests to move disorderly. When it is so well balanced that it is neither lifted up, nor cast down too much, but keeps a steady course. Our affections must not rise to become unruly passions, for then as a river that overfloweth the banks, they carry much slime and soil with them. Though affections be the wind of the soul, yet unruly passions are the storms of the soul, and will overturn all, if they be not suppressed. The best, as we see in David here, if they do not steer their hearts aright, are in danger of sudden gusts. A Christian must neither be a dead sea, nor a raging sea.

Our affections are then in best temper, when they

become so many graces of the Spirit; as when love is turned to a love of God; joy, to a delight in the best things; fear, to a fear of offending him more than any creature; sorrow, to a sorrow for sin, &c.

They are likewise in good temper, when they move us to all duties of love and mercy towards others; when they are not shut where they should be open, nor open where they should be shut.

Yet there is one case wherein exceeding affection is not over exceeding; as in an ecstasy of zeal upon a sudden apprehension of God's dishonour, and his cause trodden under foot. It is better in this case, rather scarce to be our own men, than to be calm or quiet. It is said of Christ and David, that their hearts were eaten up with a holy zeal for God's house. In such a case Moses, unparalleled for meekness, was turned into a holy rage. The greatness of the provocation, the excellency of the object, and the weight of the occasion, bears out the soul, not only without blame, but with great praise, in such seeming distempers. It is the glory of a Christian to be carried with full sail, and as it were with a spring-tide of affection. So long as the stream of affection runneth in the due channel, and if there be great occasions for great motions, then it is fit the affections should rise higher, as to burn with zeal, to be *sick of love*, Cant. ii. 5, to be *more vile* for the Lord, as David; to be counted *out of our wits* with Paul, to further the cause of Christ and the good of souls.

Thus we may see the life of a poor Christian in this world. 1. He is in great danger, if he be not troubled at all. 2. When he is troubled, he is in danger to be over-troubled. 3. When he hath brought his soul in tune again, he is subject to new troubles. Betwixt this ebbing and flowing there is very little quiet. Now because this cannot be done without a great measure of God's Spirit, our help is to make use of that promise of giving *the Holy Ghost to them that ask it.* John xi. 13. To teach us when, how long, and how much to grieve: and when, and how long, and how much to rejoice; the Spirit must teach the heart this, who as he moved upon the waters before the creation, so he must move upon the waters of our souls, for we have not the command of our own hearts. Every natural man is carried away with his flesh and humours, upon which the devil rides, and carries him whither he list; he hath no better counsellors than flesh and blood, and Satan counselling with them. But a godly man is not a slave to his carnal affections, but (as David here) labours to bring into captivity the first motions of sin in his heart.

CHAPTER IX.

OF THE SOUL'S DISQUIETS, GOD'S DEALINGS, AND POWER TO CONTAIN OUR-
SELVES IN ORDER.

MOREOVER we see, that *the soul hath disquiets pro-per to itself, besides those griefs of sympathy that arise from the body;* for here the soul complains of the soul itself, as when it is out of the body it hath torments and joys of its own. And if these troubles of the soul be not well cured, then by way of fellow-ship and redundance they will affect the outward man, and so the whole man shall be enwrapt in misery.

From whence we further see, that *God, when he will humble a man, need not fetch forces from with-out,* if he let but our own hearts loose, we shall have trouble and work enough, though, we were as holy as David, God did not only exercise him with a re-bellious son out of his own loins, but with rebellious risings out of his own heart. If there were no enemy in the world, nor devil in hell, we carry that within us, that, if it be let loose, will trouble us more then all the world besides. Oh that the proud creature should exalt himself against God, and run into a vo-luntary course of provoking him, who cannot only raise the humours of our bodies against us, but the passions of our minds also to torment us! Therefore it is the best wisdom not to provoke the great God, for *are we stronger than he*, 1 Cor. x. 22, that can raise ourselves against ourselves? and work wonders not only in the great world, but also in the little world, our souls and bodies, when he pleases?

We see likewise hence a *necessity of having something in the soul above itself, it must be partaker of a diviner nature than itself;* otherwise, when the most refined part of our souls, the very spirit of our minds is out of frame, what shall bring it in again? Therefore we must conceive in a godly man, a double self, one which must be denied, the other which must deny; one that breeds all the disquiet, and another that stilleth what the other hath raised. The way to still the soul, as it is under our corrupt self, is not to parley with it, and divide government for peace sake, as if we should gratify the flesh in some things, to redeem liberty to the spirit in other things; for we shall find the flesh will be too encroaching. We must strive against it, not with subtlety and discourse so much, as with peremptory violence silence it and vex it; an enemy that parleys will yield at length. Grace is nothing else but that blessed power, whereby as spiritual we gain upon ourselves as carnal. Holy love is that which we gain of self-love; and so joy, and delight, &c. Grace labours to win ground of the old man, until at length it be all in all; indeed we are never ourselves perfectly, till we have wholly put off ourselves; nothing should be at a greater distance to us, than ourselves. This is the reason why carnal men that have nothing above themselves but their corrupt self, sink in great troubles, having nothing within to uphold them, whereas a good man is wiser than himself, holier than himself, stronger than himself, there is something in him more than a man. There be evils that the spirit of man alone out of the goodness of nature cannot bear, but the spirit of man assisted with a higher spirit, will support and carry him through. It is a good trial of a man's condition to know what he esteems to be himself. A godly man counts the inner man, the sanctified part, to be himself, whereby he stands in relation to Christ and a better life. Another man esteems his contentment in the world, the satisfaction of his carnal desires, the respect he finds from men by reason of his parts, or something without him, that he is master of, this he counts himself, and by this he values himself, and to this he makes his best thoughts and endeavours serviceable; and of crosses in these things he is most sensible, and so sensible, that he thinks himself undone if he seeth not a present issue out of them.

That which most troubles a good man in all troubles is himself, so far as he is unsubdued; he is more disquieted with himself, than with all troubles out of himself; when he hath gotten the better once of himself, whatsoever falls from without, is light; where the spirit is enlarged, it cares not much for outward bondage; where the spirit is lightsome, it cares not much for outward darkness; where the spirit is settled, it cares not much for outward changes; where the spirit is one with itself, it cannot bear outward breaches; where the spirit is sound, it can bear outward sickness. Nothing can be very ill with us, when all is well within. This is the comfort of a holy man, that though he be troubled with himself, yet by reason of the spirit in him, which is his better self, he works out by degrees whatever is contrary. As spring-water being clear of itself, works itself clean, though it be troubled by something cast in; as the sea will endure no poisonous thing, but casts it upon the shore. But a carnal man is like a spring corrupted, that cannot work itself clear, because it is wholly tainted; his eye and light is darkness, and therefore no wonder if he seeth nothing. Sin lieth upon his understanding, and hinders the knowledge of itself; it lies close upon the will, and hinders the striving against itself.

True self that is worth the owning, is when a man is taken into a higher condition, and made one with Christ, and esteems neither of himself nor others, as happy for any thing according to the flesh. 1. He is under the law and government of the Spirit, and so far as he is himself, works according to that principle.

2. He labours more and more to be transformed into the likeness of Christ, in whom he esteemeth that he hath his best being. 3. He esteems of all things that befall him, to be good or ill, as they further or hinder his best condition. If all be well, for that, he counts himself well, whatsoever else befalls him.

Another man when he doth any thing that is good, acts not his own part; but a godly man when he doth good, is in his proper element; what another man doth for by-ends and reasons, that he doth from a new nature; which if there were no law to compel, yet would move him to that which is pleasing to Christ. If he be drawn aside by passion or temptation, that he judgeth not to be himself, but taketh a holy revenge on himself for it, as being redeemed and taken out from himself; he thinks himself no debtor, nor to owe any service to his corrupt self. That which he plots and projects and works for is, that Christ may rule every where, and especially in himself, for he is not his own but Christ's, and therefore desires to be more and more emptied of himself, that Christ might be *all in all* in him.

Thus we see what great use there is of dealing with ourselves, for the better composing and settling of our souls. Which though it be a course without glory and ostentation in the world, as causing a man to retire inwardly into his own breast, having no other witness but God and himself; and though it be likewise irksome to the flesh, as calling the soul home to itself, being desirous naturally to wander abroad, and be a stranger at home: yet it is a course both good in itself, and makes the soul good.

For by this means the judgment is exercised and rectified, the will and affections ordered, the whole man put into a holy frame fit for every good action. By this the tree is made good and the fruit cannot but be answerable; by this the soul itself is set in tune, whence there is a pleasant harmony in our whole conversation. Without this we may do that which is outwardly good to others, but we can never be good ourselves. The first justice begins within, when there is a due subjection of all the powers of the soul to the spirit, as sanctified and guided by God's Spirit; when justice and order is first established in the soul, it will appear from thence in all our dealings. He that is at peace in himself, will be peaceable to others, peaceable in his family, peaceable in the church, peaceable in the state; the soul of a wicked man is in perpetual sedition; being always troubled in itself, it is no wonder if it be troublesome to others. Unity in ourselves is before union with others.

To conclude this first part, concerning intercourse with ourselves. As we desire to enjoy ourselves, and to live the life of men and of Christians, which is, to understand our ways: as we desire to live comfortably, and not to be accessory of yielding to that sorrow which causeth death: as we desire to answer God and ourselves, when we are to give an account of the inward tumults of our souls; as we desire to be vessels prepared for every good work, and to have strength to undergo any cross: as we desire to have healthy souls, and to keep a sabbath within ourselves: as we desire not only to do good, but to be good in ourselves: so let us labour to quiet our souls, and often ask a reason of ourselves, *Why we should not be quiet?*

CHAPTER X.

MEANS NOT TO BE OVERCHARGED WITH SORROW.

To help us further herein, besides that which hath been formerly spoken,

1. We must take heed of building an ungrounded confidence of happiness for time to come: which makes us when changes come, 1. Unacquainted with them; 2. Takes away expectation of them; 3. And preparation for them. When any thing is strange and sudden, and lights upon us unfurnished and unfenced, it must needs put our spirits out of frame. It

is good therefore to make all kind of troubles familiar to us, in our thoughts at least, and this will break the force of them. It is good to fence our souls beforehand against all assaults, as men use to keep out the sea, by raising banks; and if a breach be made, to repair it presently.

We had need to maintain a strong garrison of holy reasons against the assaults of strong passions; we may hope for the best, but fear the worst, and prepare to bear whatsoever. We say that a set diet is dangerous, because variety of occasions will force us upon breaking of it: so in this world of changes we cannot resolve upon any certain condition of life, for upon alteration the mind is out of frame. We cannot say this or that trouble shall not befall, yet we may, by help of the Spirit, say, nothing that doth befall shall make me do that which is unworthy of a Christian.

That which others make easy by suffering, that a wise man maketh easy by thinking of beforehand. If we expect the worst, when it comes, it is no more than we thought of: if better befalls us, then it is the sweeter to us, the less we expected it. Our Saviour foretells the worst: *In the world you shall have tribulation*, John xvi. 33, therefore look for it, but then he will not leave us. Satan deludes with many promises: but when the contrary falls out, he leaves his followers in their distresses. We desire peace and rest, but we seek it not in its own place; *There is a rest for God's people*, Heb. iv. 9, but that is not here, nor yet; but it remains for them; *they rest from their labours*, Rev. xiv. 13, but that is after they are *dead in the Lord*. There is no sound rest till then. Yet this caution must be remembered, that we shape not in our fancies such troubles as are never likely to fall out. It comes either from weakness or guiltiness, to fear shadows. We shall not need to make crosses, they will, as we say of foul weather, come before they be sent for. How many evils do people fear, from which they have no further hurt than what is bred only by their causeless fears? Nor yet, if they be probable, must we think of them so as to be altogether so affected, as if undoubtedly they would come, for so we give certain strength to an uncertain cross, and usurp upon God, by anticipating that which may never come to pass. It was rashness in David to say, *I shall one day perish by the hand of Saul.* 1 Sam. xxvii. 1.

If they be such troubles as will certainly come to pass, as parting with friends and contentments, at least, by death; then 1. *Think* of them so as not to be much dismayed, but furnish thy heart with strength before hand, that they may fall the lighter. 2. *Think* of them so as not to give up the bucklers to passion, and lie open as a fair mark for any uncomfortable accident to strike to the heart; nor yet so think of them as to despise them, but to consider of God's meaning in them, and how to take good by them. 3. *Think* of the things we enjoy, so as to moderate our enjoying of them, by considering there must be a parting, and therefore how we shall be able to bear it when it comes.

2. *If we desire* not to be overcharged with sorrow, when that which we fear is fallen upon us, we must then beforehand look that our love to any thing in this world shoot not so far as that, when the time of severing cometh, we part with so much of our hearts by that rent. Those that love too much will always grieve too much. It is the greatness of our affections which causeth the sharpness of our afflictions. He that cannot abound without pride and high mindedness will not want without too much dejectedness. Love is planted for such things as can return love; and make us better by loving them, wherein we shall satisfy our love to the full. It is pity so sweet an affection should be lost; so sorrow is for sin, and for other things as they make sin the more bitter to us. The life of a Christian should be a meditation how to unloose his affections from inferior things; he will easily die that is dead before in affection. But this will never be unless the soul seeth something better than all things in the world, upon which it may

bestow itself. In that measure our affections die in
their excessive motion to things below, as they are
taken up with the love and admiration of the best
things. He that is much in heaven in his thoughts is
free from being tossed with tempests here below; the
top of those mountains that are above the middle
region, are so quiet as that the lightest things, as
ashes, lie still and are not moved. The way to
mortify *earthly members,* that bestir themselves in
us, is to *mind things above,* Col. iii. 1, 5. The more
the ways of wisdom lead us on high, the more we
avoid the snares below.

In the uncertainty of all events here, labour to
frame that contentment in and from our own selves,
which the things themselves will not yield; frame
peace by freeing our hearts from too much fear, and
riches by freeing our hearts from covetous desires.
Frame a sufficiency out of contentedness; if the soul
itself be out of tune, outward things will do no more
good than a fair shoe to a gouty foot.

And seek not ourselves abroad out of ourselves in
the conceits of other men. A man shall never live
quietly that hath not learned to be set light by of
others. He that is little in his own eyes will not be
troubled to be little in the eyes of others. Men that
set too high a price upon themselves, when others
will not come to their price, are discontent. Those
whose condition is above their worth, and their pride
above their condition, shall never want sorrow; yet
we must maintain our authority and the image of
God in our places, for that is God's and not ours;
and we ought so to carry ourselves as we approve
ourselves to their consciences, though we have not
their good words; *Let none despise thy youth,* saith
Paul to Timothy; that is, *walk so before them as
they shall have no cause.* It is not in our own
power what other men think or speak, but it is in our
power, by God's grace, to live so that none can think
ill of us, but by slandering, and none believe ill but
by too much credulity.

3. When any thing seizeth upon us, we must take

heed we mingle not our own passions with it; we must neither bring sin to, nor mingle sin with the suffering; for that will trouble the spirit more than the trouble itself. We are more to deal with our own hearts than with the trouble itself. We are not hurt till our souls be hurt. God will not have it in the power of any creature to hurt our souls, but by our own treason against ourselves.

Therefore we should have our hearts in continual jealousy, for they are ready to deceive the best. In sudden encounters, some sin doth many times discover itself, the seed whereof lieth hid in our natures, which we think ourselves very free from. Who would have thought the seeds of murmuring had lurked in the meek nature of Moses? That the seeds of murther had lurked in the pitiful heart of David? 2 *Sam.* xii. 9. That the seeds of denial of Christ, *Matt.* xxvi. 72, had lien hid in the zealous affection of Peter towards Christ? If passions break out from us, which we are not naturally inclined unto, and over which by grace we have got a great conquest, how watchful need we be over ourselves in those things, which by temper, custom, and company, we are carried unto? and what cause have we to fear continually that we are worse than we take ourselves to be?

There are many unruly passions lie hid in us, until they be drawn out by something that meeteth with them; either 1. by way of opposition, as when the truth of God spiritually unfolded meets with some beloved corruption, it swelleth bigger; the force of gunpowder is not known until some spark light on it; and oftentimes the stillest natures, if crossed, discover the deepest corruptions. Sometimes it is drawn out by dealing with the opposite spirits of other men. Oftentimes retired men know not what lies hid in themselves.

2. Sometimes by crosses, as many people whilst the freshness and vigour of their spirits last, and while the flower of age, and a full supply of all things continue, seem to be of a pleasing and calm disposition; but afterwards, when changes come, like Job's wife,

they are discovered. Then that which in nature is unsubdued, openly appears.

3. Temptations likewise have a searching power to bring that to light in us which was hidden before. Satan hath been a winnower and a sifter of old, Luke xxii. 3: he thought if Job had been but touched in his body, he would have cursed God to his face. Job i.

Some men out of policy conceal their passion, until they see some advantage to let it out; as Esau smothered his hatred until his father's death. When the restraint is taken away, men, as we say, show themselves in their pure naturals; unloose a tiger or a lion, and you know what he is.

4. Further, let us see more every day into the state of our own souls; what a shame is it that so nimble and swift a spirit as the soul is, that can mount up to heaven, and from thence come down into the earth in an instant, should, whilst it looks over all other things, overlook itself? that it should be skilful in the story, almost, of· all times and places, and yet ignorant of the story of itself? that we should know what is done in the court and country, and beyond the seas, and be ignorant of what is done at home in our own hearts? that we should live known to others, and yet die unknown to ourselves? that we should be able to give account of any thing better than of ourselves to ourselves? This is the cause why we stand in our own light; why we think better of ourselves than others, and better than is cause. This is that which hindereth all reformation; for how can we reform that which we are not willing to see, and so we lose one of the surest evidences of our sincerity, which is, a willingness to search into our hearts, and to be searched by others. A sincere heart will offer itself to trial.

And therefore let us sift our actions, and our passions, and see what is flesh in them, and what is spirit, and so separate the precious from the vile. It is good likewise to consider what sin we were guilty of before, which moved God to give us up to excess in

any passion, and wherein we have grieved his Spirit.
Passion will be more moderate when thus it knows it
must come to the trial and censure. This course will
either make us weary of passion, or else passion will
make us weary of this strict course. We shall find
it the safest way to give our hearts no rest, till we
have wrought on them to purpose, and gotten the
mastery over them.

When the soul is inured to this dealing with itself,
it will learn the skill to command, and passions will
be soon commanded, as being inured to be examined
and checked; as we see dogs, and such like domes-
tic creatures, that will not regard a stranger, yet
will be quieted in brawls presently, by the voice of
their master, to which they are accustomed. This
fits us for service. Unbroken spirits are like unbroken
horses, unfit for any use, until they be thoroughly
subdued.

5. And it were best to prevent, as much as in us
lieth, the very first risings, before the soul be overcast; passions are but little motions at the first, but
grow as rivers do, greater and greater, the further
they are carried from the spring. The first *risings*
are the more to be looked unto, because there is most
danger in them, and we have least care over them.
Sin, like rust, or a canker, will by little and little *eat
out* all the graces of the soul. There is no staying
when we are once down the hill, till we come to the
bottom. *No sin but is easier kept out, than driven
out.* If we cannot prevent wicked thoughts, yet we
may deny them lodging in our hearts. It is our
giving willing entertainment to sinful motions, that
increaseth guilt, and hindereth our peace. It is that
which moveth God to give us up to a further degree
of evil affections. Therefore what we are afraid to
do before men, we should be afraid to think before
God. It would much further our peace to keep our
judgments clear, as being the eye of the soul, whereby
we may discern in every action and passion, what is
good, and what is evil; as likewise to preserve tenderness of heart, that may check us at the first, and

not brook the least evil being discovered. When the heart begins once to be kindled, it is easy to smother the smoke of passion, which otherwise will fume up into the head, and gather into so thick a cloud, as we shall lose the sight of ourselves, and what is best to be done. And therefore David here labours to take up his heart at the first; his care was to crush the very first insurrections of his soul, before they came to break forth into open rebellion: storms we know rise out of little gusts. Little risings neglected cover the soul before we are aware. If we would check these risings and stifle them in their birth, they would not break out afterwards to the reproach of religion, to the scandal of the weak, to the offence of the strong, to the *grief of God's Spirit* in us, to the disturbance of our own spirits in doing good, and to the disheartening of us in troubling of our inward peace, and thereby weakening our assurance. Therefore let us stop beginnings as much as may be; and so soon as they begin to rise let us begin to examine what raised them, and whither they are about to carry us. Psalm iv. The way to be still, is to examine ourselves first; and then censure what stands not with reason. As David doth, when he had given way to unbefitting thoughts of God's providence, *So foolish*, saith he, *was I, and as a beast before thee.* Psalm lxxiii. 22.

Especially, then look to these sinful stirrings when thou art to deal with God. I am to have communion with a God of peace; what then do turbulent thoughts and affections in my heart? I am to deal with a patient God, why should I cherish revengeful thoughts? Abraham drove away the *birds* from the *sacrifice*. Gen. xv. 11. Troublesome thoughts like birds will come before they be sent for, but they should find entertainment accordingly.

6. In all our grievances let us look to something that may comfort us, as well as discourage: look to that we enjoy, as well as that we want. As in prosperity God mingles some crosses to diet us; so in all crosses there is *something to comfort us.* As there is a vanity lies hid in the best *worldly good*, so there

is a blessing lies hid in the worst *worldly evil.* God usually maketh up that with some advantage in another kind, wherein we are inferior to others. Others are in greater place, so they are in greater danger. Others be richer, so their cares and snares be greater; the *poor in the world* may be *richer in faith* than they. James ii. 5. The soul can better digest and master a low estate than a prosperous, and if under some abasement, it is in a less distance from God. Others are not so afflicted as we, then they have less experience of God's gracious power than we. Others may have more healthy bodies, but souls less weaned from the world. We would not change conditions with them, so as to have their spirits with their condition. For one half of our lives, the meanest are as happy and free from cares, as the greatest monarch : that is, whilst both sleep ; and usually the sleep of the one is sweeter than the sleep of the other. What is all that the earth can afford us, if God deny health? and this a man in the meanest condition may enjoy. That wherein one man differs from another, is but title, and but for a little time ; death leveleth all.

There is scarce any man, but the good he receives from God is more than the ill he feels, if our unthankful hearts would suffer us to think so. Is not our health more than our sickness ? do we not enjoy more than we want, I mean, of the things that are necessary ; are not our good days more than our evil ? but we would go to heaven upon roses, and usually one cross is more taken to heart, than a hundred blessings. So unkindly we deal with God. Is God indebted to us ? doth he owe us any thing ? those that deserve nothing, should be content with any thing.

We should look to others as good as ourselves, as well as to ourselves, and then we shall see it is not our own case only ; who are we that we should look for an exempted condition from those troubles which God's dearest children are addicted unto ?

Thus when we are surprised contrary to our looking for and liking, we should study rather how to exercise some grace, than give way to any passion.

Think now is a time to exercise our patience, our wisdom, and other graces. By this means we shall turn that to our greatest advantage; which Satan intendeth greatest hurt to us by. Thus we shall not only master every condition, but make it serviceable to our good. If nature teach bees, not only to gather honey out of sweet flowers, but out of bitter, shall not grace teach us to draw even out of the bitterest condition something to better our souls? we learn to tame all creatures, even the wildest, that we may bring them to our use; and why should we give way to our own unruly passions?

7. It were good to have in our eye the beauty of a well ordered soul, and we should think that nothing in this world is of sufficient worth to put us out of frame. The sanctified soul should be like the sun in this, which though it worketh upon all these inferior bodies, and cherisheth them by light and influence; yet is not moved nor wrought upon by them again, but keepeth its own lustre and distance: so our spirits, being of a heavenly breed, should rule other things beneath them, and not be ruled by them. It is a holy state of soul to be under the power of nothing beneath itself. Are we stirred? then consider, is this matter worth the loss of my quiet? What we esteem, that we love, what we love, we labour for; and therefore let us esteem highly of a clear calm temper, whereby we both enjoy our God and ourselves, and know how to rank all things else. It is against nature for inferior things to rule that, which the wise disposer of all things hath set above them. We owe the flesh neither suit nor service, we are no debtors to it.

The more we set before the soul that quiet estate in heaven, which the souls of perfect men now enjoy, and itself ere long shall enjoy there, the more it will be in love with it, and endeavour to attain unto it. And because the soul never worketh better, than when it is raised up by some strong and sweet affection; let us look upon our nature, as it is in Christ, in whom it is pure, sweet, calm, meek, every way lovely. This sight is a changing sight, love is an affection of imitation, we affect a likeness to him we love. Let us *learn of Christ to be humble and meek,* and then we *shall find rest to our souls.* Matt. xi. 29. The setting of an excellent idea and platform before us, will raise and draw up our souls higher, and make us sensible of the least moving of spirit, that shall be contrary to that, the attainment whereof we have in our desires. He will hardly attain to mean things, that sets not before him higher perfection. Naturally we love to see symmetry and proportion, even in a dead picture, and are much taken with some curious piece. But why should we not rather labour to keep the affections of the soul in due proportion? seeing a meek and well ordered soul is not only lovely in the sight of men and angels, but is much set by, by the great God himself. But now the greatest care of those that set highest price upon themselves is, how to compose their outward carriage in some graceful manner, never studying how to compose their spirits; and rather how to cover the deformity of their passions than to cure them. Whence it is that the foulest inward vices are covered with the fairest vizards, and to make this the worse, all this is counted the best breeding.

The Hebrews placed all their happiness in peace, and when they would comprise much in one word, they would wish peace. This was that the angels brought news of from Heaven, at the birth of Christ. Now peace riseth out of quietness and order, and God that is *the God of peace, is the God of order* first. 1 Cor. xiv. 33. What is health, but when all the members are in their due posture, and all the humours in a settled quiet? Whence ariseth the beauty of the world, but from that comely order wherein every creature is placed; the more glorious and excellent creatures above, and the less below? So it is in the soul; the best constitution of it is when by the Spirit of God it is so ordered, as that all be in subjection to the law of the mind. What a sight were it for the feet to be where the head is, and the earth to be where the heaven is, to see all turned upside down?

And to a spiritual eye it seems as great a deformity, to see the soul to be under the rule of sinful passions.

Comeliness riseth out of the fit proportion of divers members to make up one body, when every member hath a beauty in itself, and is likewise well suited to other parts; a fair face and a crooked body, comely upper parts, and the lower parts uncomely, suit not well; because comeliness stands in oneness, in a fit agreement of many parts to one; when there is the head of a man, and the body of a beast, it is a monster in nature; and is it not as monstrous for to have an understanding head, and a fierce untamed heart? It cannot but raise up a holy indignation in us against these risings, when we consider how unbeseeming they are; what do these base passions in a heart dedicated to God, and given up to the government of his Spirit? What an indignity is it for princes to go afoot, and servants on horseback? for those to rule, whose place is to be ruled? as being good attendants, but bad guides. It was Ham's curse to be a *servant of servants.*

8. This must be strengthened with a strong selfdenial, without which there can be no good done in religion.

There be two things that most trouble us in the way to heaven; corruption within us, and the cross without us: that which is within us must be denied, that that which is without us may be endured. Otherwise we cannot follow him by whom we look to be saved. The gate, the entrance of religion, is narrow; we must strip ourselves of ourselves before we can enter; if we bring any ruling lust to religion, it will prove a bitter root of some gross sin, or of apostasy and final desperation.

Those that sought the *praise of men, more than the praise of God,* John xii. 43, could not believe, because that lust of ambition would, when it should be crossed, draw them away. The young man thought it better for Christ to lose a disciple, than that he should lose his *possession,* Matt. xix. 22, and therefore *went away* as he came; Matt. xiii. 25. The *third ground* came to nothing, because the plough had not gone deep enough to break up the roots, whereby their hearts were fastened to earthly contentments. This self-denial we must carry with us through all the parts of religion, both in our active and passive obedience; for in obedience there must be a subjection to a superior; but corrupt self, *neither is subject, nor can be*, Rom. viii.; it will have an oar in every thing, and maketh every thing, yea, religion serviceable to itself. It is the idol of the world, or rather the god that is set highest of all in the soul; and so God himself is made but an idol. It is hard to deny a friend who is another self, harder to deny a wife that lieth in the bosom, but most hard to deny ourselves. Nothing so near us as ourselves to ourselves, and yet nothing so far off. Nothing so dear, and yet nothing so malicious and troublesome. Hypocrites would part with the *fruit of their body*, Mic. vi., sooner than *the sin* of their souls.

CHAPTER XI.

SIGNS OF VICTORY OVER OURSELVES, AND OF A SUBDUED SPIRIT.

BUT *how shall we know, whether we have by grace got the victory over ourselves or not?*

I answer; 1. If in good actions we stand not so much upon the credit of the action, as upon the good that is done. What we do as unto God, we look for acceptance from God. It was Jonah's fault to stand more upon his own reputation, than the glory of God's mercy. It is a prevailing sign, when though there be no outward encouragements, nay, though there be discouragements, yet we can rest in the comfort of a good intention. For usually inward comfort is a note of inward sincerity. Jehu must be *seen*, or else all is lost. 2 Kings x. 16.

2. It is a good evidence of some prevailing, when upon religious grounds we can cross ourselves in those things unto which our hearts stand most affected; this showeth we reserve God his own place in our hearts.

3. When being privy to our own inclination and

temper, we have gotten such a supply of spirit, as that the grace which is contrary to our temper appears in us. As oft we see, none more patient, than those that are naturally inclined to intemperancy of passion, because natural proneness makes them jealous over themselves. Some out of fear of being overmuch moved, are not moved so much as they should be: this jealousy stirreth us up to a careful use of all helps, where grace is helped by nature, there a little grace will go far; but where there is much untowardness of nature, there much grace is not so well discerned. *Sour wines need much sweetening;* and that is most spiritual which hath least help from nature, and is won by prayer and pains.

4. When we are not partial when the things concern ourselves. David could allow himself another man's wife, and yet judgeth another man worthy of death for taking away a *poor man's lamb.* 2 Sam. xii.

4. Men usually favour themselves too much, when they are chancellors in their own cause, and measure all things by their private interest. He hath taken a good degree in Christ's school, that hath learned to forget himself here.

5. It is a good sign, when upon discovery of self-seeking we can gain upon our corruption; and are willing to search and to be searched, what our inclination is, and where it faileth. That which we favour, we are tender of, it must not be touched. A good heart, when any corruption is discovered by a searching ministry, is affected as if it had found out a deadly enemy. Touchiness and passion argues guilt.

6. This is a sign of a man's victory over himself, when he loves health and peace of body and mind, with a supply of all needful things, chiefly for this end, that he may with more freedom of spirit serve God in doing good to others. So soon as grace entereth into the heart, it frameth the heart to be in some measure public: and thinks it hath not its end, in the bare enjoying of any thing, until it can improve what it hath for a further end. Thus to seek ourselves is to deny ourselves, and thus to deny ourselves is truly to seek

ourselves. It is no self-seeking, when we care for no more than that, without which we cannot comfortably serve God. When the soul can say unto God, Lord, as thou wouldst have me serve thee in my place, so grant me such a measure of health and strength, wherein I may serve thee.

But what if God thinks it good, that I shall serve him in weakness, and in want, and suffering?

Then, it is a comfortable sign of gaining over our own wills, when we can yield ourselves to be disposed of by God, as knowing best what is good for us. There is no condition but therein we may exercise some grace, and honour God in some measure. Yet because some enlargement of condition is ordinarily that estate wherein we are best able to do good in; we may in the use of means desire it, and upon that, resign up ourselves wholly unto God, and make his will our will, without exception or reservation, and care for nothing more than we can have with his leave and love. This Job had exercised his heart unto; whereupon in that great change of condition, *he sinned not*, Job ii., that is, fell not into the sins incident to that dejected and miserable state; into sins of rebellion and discontent. He carried his crosses comely, with that staidness and resignedness, which became a holy man.

7. It is further a clear evidence of a spirit subdued, when we will discover the truth of our affection towards God and his people though with censure of others. David was content to endure the censure of neglecting the state and majesty of a king, out of joy for settling the ark. Nehemiah could not dissemble his grief for the ruins of the church, though in the king's presence. Neh. ii. 3. It is a comfortable sign of the wasting of self-love, when we can be at a point what becomes of ourselves, so it go well with the cause of God and the church.

Now the way to prevail still more over ourselves, as when we are to do or suffer any thing, or withstand any person in a good cause, &c. is, not to think that we are to deal with men, yea, or with devils so much as with ourselves. The saints resisted their enemies to death, by resisting their own corruptions first: if we once get the victory over ourselves, all other things are conquered to our ease. All the hurt Satan and the world do us, is by correspondency with ourselves. All things are so far under us, as we are above ourselves.

For the further subduing of ourselves, it is good to follow sin to the first hold and castle, which is corrupt nature; the streams will lead us to the spring head: indeed the most apparent discovery of sin is in the outward carriage; we see it in the fruit before in the root; as we see grace in the expression before in the affection; but yet we shall never hate sin thoroughly, until we consider it in the poisoned root from whence it ariseth.

That which least troubles a natural man, doth most of all trouble a true Christian; a natural man is sometimes troubled with the fruit of his corruption, and the consequents of guilt and punishment that attend it; but a true-hearted Christian, with corruption itself; this drives him to complain with St. Paul, *O wretched man that I am, who shall deliver me*, not from the members only, but *from this body of death?* Rom. vii.; which is as noisome to my soul, as a dead carrion is to my senses; which together with the members, is marvellously nimble and active; and hath no days, or hours, or minutes of rest; always laying about it to enlarge itself, and like spring water, which the more it issueth out, the more it may.

It is a good way, upon any particular breach of our inward peace, presently to have recourse to that which breeds and foments all our disquiet. Lord! what do I complain of this my unruly passion? I carry a nature about me subject to break out continually upon any occasion; Lord! strike at the root, and dry up the fountain in me. Thus David doth arise from the guilt of those two foul sins, of *murder* and *adultery*, Psalm li. to the sin of his nature, the root itself; as if he should say, Lord! it is not these actual sins that defile me only; but if I look back to my first conception, I was tainted in the spring of my nature.

This is that which put David's soul so much out of frame; for from whence was this contradiction? and whence was this contradiction so unwearied, in making head again and again against the checks of the Spirit in him? Whence was it that corruption would not be said nay? Whence were these sudden and unlooked for objections of the flesh? but from the remainder of old Adam in him, which like a Michal within us is either scoffing at the ways of God; or as Job's wife, fretting and thwarting the motions of God's Spirit in us; which prevails the more, because it is homebred in us: whereas holy motions are strangers to most of our souls. Corruption is loath that a new comer in should take so much upon him as to control: as the Sodomites thought much that Lot being a stranger should intermeddle amongst them. Gen. xix. 9. If God once leave us as he did Hezekiah to try what is in us, what should he find but darkness, rebellion, unruliness, doubtings, &c. in the best of us? this flesh of ours hath principles against all God's principles, and laws against all God's laws, and reasons against all God's reasons. Oh! if we could but one whole hour seriously think of the impure issue of our hearts, it would bring us down upon our knees in humiliation before God. But we can never whilst we live, so thoroughly as we should, see into the depth of our deceitful hearts, nor yet be humbled enough for what we see; for though we speak of it and confess it, yet we are not so sharpened against this corrupt flesh of ours, as we should. How should it humble us, that the seeds of the vilest sin, even of the *sin against the Holy Ghost*, are in us? and no thank to us that they break not out. It should humble us to hear of any great enormous sin in another man, considering what our own nature would proceed unto if it were not restrained. We may see our own nature in them as *face answering face;* if God should take his Spirit from us, there is enough in us to defile a whole world; and although we be ingrafted into Christ, yet we carry about us a relish of the old stock still. David was a man of a good natural constitution; and for grace a man after God's own heart, and had got the better of himself in a great measure, and had learned to overcome himself in matter of revenge, as in Saul's case, 1 Sam. xxiv. 6: yet now we see the vessel is shaken a little, and the dregs appear that were in the bottom before. Alas! we know not our own hearts, till we plough with God's heifer, till his Spirit bringeth a light into our souls. It is good to consider how this impure spring breaks out diversly, in the divers conditions we are in; there is no estate of life, nor no action we undertake, wherein it will not put forth itself to defile us: it is so full of poison that it taints whatsoever we do, both our natures, conditions, and actions. In a prosperous condition, like David, we think we *shall never be moved.* Psalm xxx. 6. Under the cross the *soul is troubled,* and drawn to murmur, and to be sullen, and sink down in discouragement, to be in a heat almost to blasphemy, to be weary of our callings, and to quarrel with every thing in our way. See the folly and fury of most men in this, for us silly worms to contradict the great God: and to whose peril is it? Is it not our own? let us gather ourselves with all our wit and strength together. Alas! what can we do but provoke him, and get more stripes? we may be sure he will deal with us, as we deal with our children, if they be froward and unquiet for lesser matters, we will make them cry and be sullen for something: refractory, stubborn horses are the more spurred, and yet shake not off the rider.

CHAPTER XII.

OF ORIGINAL RIGHTEOUSNESS, NATURAL CORRUPTION, SATAN'S JOINING WITH IT, AND OUR DUTY THEREUPON.

§ I. But here mark a plot of spiritual treason; Satan joining with our corruption, setteth the wit on work to persuade the soul, that this inward rebellion is not so bad, because it is natural to us, as a condition of nature rising out of the first principles in our creation, and was curbed in by the bridle of original righteousness, which they would have accessary and supernatural, and therefore allege that concupiscence is less odious and more excusable in us, and so no great danger in yielding and betraying our souls into it, and by that means persuading us that that which is our deadliest enemy, hath no harm in it, nor meaneth any to us.

This rebellion of lusts against the understanding is not natural, as our nature came out of God's hands at the first. Gen. i.   For this being evil and the cause of evil, could not come from God who is good, and the cause of all good, and nothing but good: who upon the creation of all things pronounced them *good*, and after the creation of man pronounced of all things that they were *very good*.   Now that which is ill and very ill, cannot be seated at the same time in that which is *good* and *very good:* God created man at the first, *right*, he of himself *sought out many inventions.*   As God beautified the heaven with stars, and decked the earth with variety of plants, and herbs, and flowers; so he adorned man, his prime creature here below, with all those endowments that were fit for a happy condition, and original righteousness was fit and due to an original and happy condition.   Therefore as the angels were created with all angelical perfections, and as our bodies were created in an absolute temper of all the humours; so the soul was created in that sweet harmony wherein there was no discord, as an instrument in tune fit to be moved to any duty ; as a clean neat glass the soul represented God's image and holiness.

§ II. Therefore it is so far, that concupiscence should be natural, that the contrary to it, namely, righteousness, wherein Adam was created, was natural to him; though it were planted in man's nature by God, and so in regard of the cause of it, was supernatural, yet because it was agreeable to that happy condition, without which he could not subsist, in that · respect it was natural, and should have been derived, if he had stood, together with his nature, to his posterity. As heat in the air, though it hath its first impression from the heat of the sun, yet is natural, because it agreeth to the nature of that element: though man be compounded of a spiritual and earthly substance, yet it is natural that the baser earthly part should be subject to the superior, because where there is different degrees of worthiness, it is fit there should be a subordination of the meaner to that which is in order higher. The body naturally desires food and bodily contentments, yet in a man endued with reason this desire is governed so as it becomes not inordinate: a beast sins not in its appetite, because it hath no power above to order it. A man that lives in a solitary place far remote from company, may take his liberty to live as it pleaseth him; but if he comes to live under the government of some well ordered city, then he is bound to submit to the laws, and customs of that city, under penalty, upon any breach of order: so the risings of the soul, howsoever in other creatures they are not blamable, having no commander in themselves, above them, yet in man they are to be ordered by reason and judgment.

Therefore it cannot be, that concupiscence should be natural, in regard of the state of creation; it was Adam's sin which had many sins in the womb of it, that brought this disorder upon the soul; Adam's person first corrupted our nature, and nature being corrupted, corrupts our persons, and our persons being corrupted, increase the corruption of our nature, by custom of sinning, which is another nature in us; as a stream the further it runs from the spring head, the more it enlargeth its channel, by the running of lesser rivers into it, until it empties itself into the sea; so corruption, till it be overpowered by grace, swelleth bigger and bigger, so that though this disorder was not natural, in regard of the first creation, yet since the fall it is become natural, even as we call that which is common to the whole kind, and propagated from parents to their children, to be natural, so that it is both natural and against nature, natural now, but against nature in its first perfection.

And because corruption is natural to us, therefore
1. We delight in it, whence it comes to pass, that our
souls are carried along in an easy current, to the
committing of any sin without opposition. 2. Because it is natural, therefore it is unwearied and restless, as light bodies are not wearied in their motion
upwards, nor heavy bodies in their motion downwards, nor a stream in its running to the sea, because
it is natural: hence it is that the *old man* is never
tired in the *works of the flesh;* nor never drawn dry.
When men cannot act sin, yet they will love sin, and
act it over again by pleasing thoughts of it, and by
sinful speculation suck out the delight of sin; and
are grieved, not for their sin, but because they want
strength and opportunity to commit it; if sin would
not leave them, they would never leave sin. This
corruption of our nature is not wrought in us by reason and persuasions, for then it might be satisfied
with reasons, but it is in us by way of a natural inclination, as iron is carried to the loadstone; and till
our natures be altered, no reason will long prevail,
but our sinful disposition, as a stream stopped for a
little while, will break out with greater violence. 3.
Being natural, it needs no help, as the earth needs no
tillage to bring forth weeds. When our corrupt nature is carried contrary to that which is good, it is
carried of itself. As when Satan lies or murders, it
comes from his own cursed nature; and though Satan joineth with our *corrupt nature,* yet the proneness to sin, and the consent unto it, is of ourselves.

§ III. But how shall we know, that Satan joins
with our nature, in those actions unto which nature
itself is prone?

Then Satan adds his help, when our nature is carried more eagerly than ordinary to sin; as when a
stream runs violently, we may know that there is
not only the tide, but the wind that carrieth it.

So in sudden and violent rebellions, it is Satan that
pusheth on nature left to itself of God. A stone falls
downwards by its own weight, but if it falls very
swiftly, we know it is thrown down by an outward

mover. Though there were no devil, yet our corrupt nature would act Satan's part against itself, it would have a supply of wickedness (as a serpent doth poison) from itself, it hath a spring to feed it.

But that man whilst he lives here is not altogether excluded from hope of happiness, and hath a nature not so large and capable of sin as Satan's; whereupon he is not so obstinate in hating God, and working mischief as he, &c. Otherwise there is for kind the same cursed disposition, and malice of nature against true goodness in man, which is in the devils and damned spirits themselves.

It is no mitigation of sin, to plead it is natural, for natural diseases, as leprosies, that are derived from parents, are most dangerous, and least curable; neither is this any excuse, for because as it is natural, so it is voluntary, not only in Adam, in whose loins we were, and therefore sinned; but likewise in regard of ourselves, who are so far from stopping the course of sin either in ourselves or others, that we feel and strengthen it, or at least give more way to it, and provide less against it than we should, until we come under the government of grace; and by that means, we justify Adam's sin, and that corrupt state that followeth upon it, and show that if we had been in Adam's condition ourselves, we would have made that ill choice which he made. And though this corruption of our nature be necessary to us, yet it is no violent necessity from an outward cause, but a necessity that we willingly pull upon ourselves, and therefore ought the more to humble us; for the more necessarily we sin, the more voluntarily, and the more voluntarily, the more necessarily; the will putting itself voluntary into these fetters of sin. Necessity is no plea, when the will is the immediate cause of any action; men's hearts tell them they might rule their desires if they would; for tell a man of any dish which he liketh, that there is poison in it, and he will not meddle with it; so tell him that death is in that sin which he is about to commit, and he will abstain if this must be done by the light and teaching of God's Spirit, who knows us and all the turnings and windings and byways of our souls, better than we know ourselves. We must see it as the most odious and loathsome thing in the world, making our natures contrary to God's pure nature, and of all other duties making us most indisposed to spiritual duties, wherein we should have nearest communion with God; because it seizeth on the very spirits of our minds.

2. We should look upon it as worse than any of those filthy streams that come from it, nay, than all the impure issues of our lives together; there is more fire in the furnace than in the sparkles; there is more poison in the root than in all the branches; for if the stream were stopped, and the branches cut off, and the sparkles quenched, yet there would be a perpetual supply; as in good things, the cause is better than the effect; so in ill things, the cause is worse. Every fruit should make this poison root more hateful to us, and the root should make us hate the fruit more, as coming from so bad a root, as being worse in the cause, than in itself; the affection is worse than the action, which may be forced or counterfeited. We cry out upon particular sins, but are not humbled as we should be for our impure dispositions; without the sight of which there can be no *sound repentance* arising from the deep and thorough consideration of sin; no desire to be *new moulded,* without which we can never enter into so holy a place as heaven; no self-denial till we see the best things in us are enmity against God; no high prizing of Christ, without whom our natures, our persons, and our actions are abominable in God's sight; nor any solid peace settled in the soul; which peace ariseth not from the ignorance of our corruption, or compounding with it, but from sight and hatred of it, and strength against it.

3. Consider the spiritualness and large extent of the law of God, together with the curse annexed, which forbids not only particular sins, but all the kinds, degrees, occasions, and furtherances of sin in the whole breadth and depth of it, and our very nature

itself so far as it is corrupted ; for want of which we see many *alive without the law*, Rom. vii. 2, jovial and merry from ignorance of their misery, who if they did but once see their natures and lives in *that glass*, it would take away that liveliness and courage from them, and make them vile in their own eyes ; men usually look themselves into the laws of the state wherein they live, and think themselves good enough ; if they are free from the danger of penal statutes ; this glass discovers only foul spots, gross scandals, and breakings out ; or else they judge of themselves by parts to nature, or common grace, or by outward conformity to religion, or else by that light they have to guide themselves in the affairs of this life, by their fair and civil carriage, &c., and thereupon live and die without any sense of the *power of godliness*, which begins in the right knowledge of ourselves, and ends in the right knowledge of God. The spiritualness and purity of the law should teach us to consider the purity and holiness of God ; the bringing of our souls into whose presence will make us to *abhor ourselves*, with Job, *in dust and ashes*, Job xlii. 6.; contraries are best seen by setting one near the other ; whilst we look only on ourselves, and upon others amongst whom we live, we think ourselves to be somebody. It is an evidence of some sincerity wrought in the soul, not to shun that light which may let us see the foul corners of our hearts and lives.

4. The consideration of this likewise should enforce us to carry a double guard over our souls: David was very watchful, yet we see here he was surprised unawares by the sudden rebellion of his heart; we should observe our hearts as governors do rebels and mutinous persons: observation awes the heart; we see to what an access sin groweth in those that deny themselves nothing, nor will be denied in any thing; who if they may do what they will, will do what they may; who turn liberty into license, and make all their abilities and advantages to do good, contributary to the commands of overruling and unruly lusts.

Were it not that God partly by his power suppress-

eth, and partly by his grace subdueth the disorders of man's nature for the good of society, and the gathering of a Church upon earth; corruption would swell to that excess, that it would overturn and confound all things together with itself. Although there be a common corruption that cleaves to the nature of all men in general, as men (as distrust in God, self-love, a carnal and worldly disposition, &c.) yet God so ordereth it, that in some there is an ebb and decrease, in others (God justly leaving them to themselves) a flow and increase of sinfulness, even beyond the bounds of ordinary corruption, whereby they become worse than themselves, either like beasts in sensuality, or like devils in spiritual wickedness; though all be blind in spiritual things, yet some are more blinded: though all be hard-hearted, yet some are more hardened : though all be corrupt in evil courses, yet some are more corrupted: and sink deeper into rebellion than others.

Sometimes God suffers this corruption to break out in civil men, yea, even in his own children, that they may know themselves the better, and because sometimes corruption is weakened not only by smothering, but by having a vent, whereupon grace stirs up in the soul a fresh hatred and revenge against it; and lets us see a necessity of having whole Christ, not only to pardon sin, but to purge and cleanse our sinful natures. But yet that which is ill in itself, must not be done for the good that comes by it by accident; this must be a comfort after our surprisals, not an encouragement before.

5. And because the Divine nature, wrought in us by divine truth, together with the Spirit of God, is the only counter-poison against all sin, and whatsoever is contrary to God in us, therefore we should labour that the truth of God may be grafted in our hearts, that so all the powers of our souls may relish of it, that there may be a sweet agreement betwixt the soul and all things that are spiritual, that truth being engrafted in our hearts, we may be engrafted into Christ, and grow up in him, and put him on more

and more, and be changed into his likeness. Nothing in heaven or earth will work out corruption, and change our dispositions, but the Spirit of Christ, clothing divine truths, with a divine power to this purpose.

6. When corruption rises, pray it down, as Paul did, and to strengthen thy prayer, claim the promise of the new covenant, that God would *circumcise our hearts*, and *wash us with clean water*, that he would *write his law in our hearts*, and give us his *holy Spirit* when we *beg it;* and look upon Christ as a public *fountain* open for *Judah* and *Jerusalem to wash in*. Herein consists our comfort, 1. That Christ hath all fulness for us, and that our nature is perfect in him; 2. That Christ in our nature hath satisfied divine justice, not only for the sin of our lives, but for the sin of our nature. And, 3. That he will never give over until by his Spirit he hath made our nature holy and pure as his own, till he hath taken away not only the reign, but the very life and being of sin out of our hearts. 4. That to this end he leaves his Spirit and truth in the church to the end of the world, that the seed of the Spirit may subdue the *seed of the serpent* in us, and that the Spirit may be a never failing spring of all holy thoughts, desires, and endeavours in us, and dry up the contrary issue and spring of corrupt nature.

And Christians must remember when they are much annoyed with their corruptions, that it is not their particular case alone, but the condition of all God's people, lest they be discouraged by looking on the ugly deformed visage of old Adam: which affrighteth some so far, that it makes them think, *no man's nature is so vile as theirs;* which were well if.it tended to humiliation only; but Satan often abuseth it towards discouragement and desperation. Many out of a misconceit think that corruption is greatest when they feel it most, whereas indeed, the less we see it and lament it, the more it is. Sighs and groans of the soul are like the pores of the body, out of which in diseased persons sick humours break forth and so become less. The more we see and grieve for pride, which is an immediate issue of our corrupted nature, the less it is, because we see it by a contrary grace; the more sight the more hatred, the more hatred of sin, the more love of grace, and the more love the more life, which the more lively it is, the more it is sensible of the contrary: upon every discovery and conflict, corruption loses some ground, and grace gains upon it.

CHAPTER XIII.

OF IMAGINATION, SIN OF IT, AND REMEDIES FOR IT.

§ 1. AND amongst all the faculties of the soul most of the disquiet and unnecessary trouble of our lives arise from the vanity and ill government of that power of the soul which we call imagination and opinion, bordering between the senses and our understanding; which is nothing else but a shallow apprehension of good or evil taken from the senses: now because outward good or evil things agree or disagree to the senses, and the life of sense is in us before the use of reason, and the delights of sense are present, and pleasing, and suitable to our natures: thereupon the imagination setteth a great price upon sensible good things; and the judgment itself since the fall, until it hath a higher light and strength, yieldeth to our imagination; hence it comes to pass that the best things, if they be attended with sensible inconveniences, as want, disgrace in the world, and such like, are misjudged for evil things; and the very worst things, if they be attended with respect in the world, and sensible contentments, are imagined to be the greatest good: which appears not so much in men's words, (because they are ashamed to discover their hidden folly and atheism,) but the lives of people speak as much, in that particular choice which they make. Many there are who think it not only a vain but a dangerous thing to serve God, and a base thing to be awed with religious respects; they count the ways that God's people take, no better than madness, and that course which God takes in bringing men to heaven by a plain publishing of heavenly truths, to be nothing but foolishness, and those people that regard it, are esteemed, as the Pharisees esteemed them that heard Christ, ignorant, base, and despicable persons; hence arise all those false prejudices against the ways of holiness, as they in the Acts were shy in entertaining the truth, because it was *a way every where spoken against*. Acts xxviii. 22. The doctrine of the cross hath the cross always following it, which imagination counteth the most odious and bitter thing in the world.

This imagination of ours is become the seat of vanity, and thereupon of vexation to us, because it apprehends a greater happiness in outward good things than there is, and a greater misery in outward evil things than indeed there is; and when experience shows us that there is not that good in those things which we imagine to be, but contrarily, we find much evil in them which we never expected, hereupon the soul cannot but be troubled. The life of many men, and those not the meanest, is almost nothing else but a fancy; that which chiefly sets their wits to work, and takes up most of their time, is how to please their own imagination, which setteth up an excellency within itself, in comparison of which it despiseth all true excellency, and those things that are of most necessary consequence indeed. Hence springs ambition, and the vein of being great in the world; hence comes an unmeasurable desire of abounding in those things which the world esteems highly of, there is in us naturally a competition and desire of being equal or above others, in that which is generally thought to make us happy and esteemed amongst men; if we be not the only men, yet we will be somebody in the world, something we will have to be highly esteemed for, wherein if we be crossed, we count it the greatest misery that can befall us.

And which is worse, a corrupt desire of being great

in the opinion of others, creeps into the profession of religion, if we live in those places wherein it brings credit or gain; men will sacrifice their very lives for vain glory : it is an evidence a man lives more to opinion and reputation of others, than to conscience, when his grief is more for being disappointed of that approbation which he expects from men, than for his miscarriage towards God. It mars all in religion, when we go about heavenly things with earthly affections, and seek not Christ in Christ, but the world. What is popery but an artificial frame of man's brain to please men's imaginations by outward state and pomp of ceremonies, like that golden image of Nebuchadnezzar, wherein he pleased himself so that to have uniformity in worshipping the same, he compelled all under pain of *death* to *fall down* before it : *Dan.* iii. 6; this makes superstitious persons always cruel, because superstitious devices are the brats of our own imagination, which we strive for more than for the purity of God's worship : hence it is likewise that superstitious persons are restless, as the woman of Samaria, in their own spirits, as having no bottom but fancy instead of faith.

§ II. Now the reason why imagination works so upon the soul, is, because it stirs up the affections answerable to the good or ill which it apprehends, and our affections stir the humours of the body, so that oftentimes both our souls and bodies are troubled hereby.

Things work upon the soul in this order: 1. Some object is presented. 2. Then it is apprehended by imagination as good and pleasing, or as evil and hurtful. 3. If good, the desire is carried to it with delight : if evil, it is rejected with distaste, and so our affections are stirred up suitably to our apprehension of the object. 4. Affections stir up the spirits. 5. The spirits raise the humours, and so the whole man becomes moved and oftentimes distempered; this falleth out by reason of the sympathy between the soul and body, whereby what offendeth one redoundeth to the hurt of the other.

And we see conceived troubles have the same effect upon us, as true. Jacob was as much troubled with the imagination of his son's death, as if he had been dead indeed; imagination, though it be an empty windy thing, yet it hath real effects. Superstitious persons are as much troubled for neglecting any voluntary service of man's invention, as if they had offended against the direct commandment of God: thus superstition breeds false fears, and false fear brings true vexation; it transforms God to an idol, imagining him to be pleased with whatsoever pleases ourselves, when as we take it ill that those who are under us should take direction from themselves, and not from us, in that which may content us, superstition is very busy, but all in vain, *in vain they worship me*, Matt. xv. 9, saith God; and how can it choose but vex and disquiet men, when they shall take a great deal of pains *in vain*, and which is worse, to displease most in that wherein they think to please most. God blasteth all devised service with one demand, *Who required these things at your hands?* Isaiah i. 12. It were better for us to ask ourselves this question before-hand, *Who required this? Why do we trouble ourselves about that which we shall have no thanks for?* We should not bring God down to our own imaginations, but raise our imaginations up to God.

Now imagination hurteth us, 1. By false representations. 2. By preventing reason, and so usurping a censure of things, before our judgments try them, whereas, the office of imagination is to minister matter to our understanding to work upon, and not to lead it, much less mislead it in any thing. 3. By forging matter out of itself without ground, the imaginary grievances of our lives are more than the real. 4. As it is an ill instrument of the understanding to devise vanity and mischief.

§ III. The way to cure this malady in us, is, 1. To labour to bring these risings of our souls into the obedience of God's truth and spirit; for *imagination* of itself, *if ungoverned*, is a *wild* and a *ranging thing*,

2 Cor. x. 5; it wrongs not only the frame of God's work in us, setting the baser part of a man above the higher, but it wrongs likewise the work of God in the creatures and every thing else, for it shapes things as itself pleaseth, it maketh evil good, if it pleaseth the senses; and good evil, if it be dangerous and distasteful to the outward man; which cannot but breed an unquiet and an unsettled soul. As if it were a god, it can tell good and evil at its pleasure, it sets up and pulls down the price of what it listeth: by reason of the distemper of imagination, the life of many is little else but a dream; many good men are in a long dream of misery, and many bad men in as long a dream of happiness, till the time of awaking come, and all because they are too much led by appearances; and as in a dream men are deluded with false joys, and false fears; so here, which cannot but breed an unquiet and an unsettled soul; therefore it is necessary that God by his word and Spirit should erect a government in our hearts to captivate and order this licentious faculty.

2. Likewise it is good to present real things to the soul, as the true riches, and true misery of a Christian, the true honour and dishonour, true beauty and deformity, the true nobleness and debasement of the soul; whatever is in the world, are but shadows of things in comparison of those true realities which religion affords; and why should we vex ourselves about a *vain shadow?* Psalm xxxix. 6.

The Holy Ghost to prevent further mischief by these outward things, gives a dangerous report of them, calling them *vanity, unrighteous mammon,* Luke xvi. 9, *uncertain riches, thorns,* yea *nothing;* because though they be not so in themselves, yet, our imagination overvaluing them, they prove so to us upon trial: now knowledge that is bought by trial is often dear bought, and therefore God would have us prevent this by a right conceit of things beforehand, lest trusting to vanity we vanish ourselves, and trusting to nothing we become nothing ourselves, and which is worse, worse than nothing.

3. Oppose serious consideration against vain imagination, and because our imagination is prone to raise false objects, and thereby false conceits, and discourses in us; our best way herein is to propound true objects of the mind to work upon; as, 1. To consider the greatness and goodness of Almighty God, and his love to us in Christ. 2. The joys of heaven, and the torments of hell. 3. The last and strict *day of account.* 4. The vanity of all earthly things. 5. The uncertainty of our lives, &c. From the meditation of these truths, the soul will be prepared to have right conceits of things, and to discourse upon true grounds of them, and think with thyself, that if these things be so indeed, then I must frame my life suitable to these principles; hence arise true affections in the soul, true fear of God, true love and desire after the best things, &c.

4. Moreover, to the well ordering of this unruly faculty, it is necessary that our nature itself should be changed; for as men are, so they *imagine,* as the *treasure of the heart is,* Matt. xii. 35, such is that which comes from it; an evil heart cannot think well: before the heart be changed our judgment is depraved in regard of our last end, we seek our happiness where it is not to be found; *wickedness comes from the wicked,* 1 Sam. xxiv. 13, as the proverb is. If we had as large and as quick apprehensions as Satan himself, yet if the relish of our will and affections be not changed, they will set the imagination to work, to devise satisfaction to themselves. For there is a mutual working and reflux betwixt the will and the imagination; the imagination stirs up the will, and as the will is affected, so imagination worketh.

When the *Law* of God by the Spirit is *so written in our hearts,* that the law and our hearts become agreeable one to the others, then the soul is inclined and made pliable to every good thought: when the heart is once *taught of God* to love, it is the nature of this sweet affection, as the Apostle saith, to *think no evil,* 1 Cor. xiii. 5, either of God or man, and not only so, but it carries the bent of the whole soul with it to good, so that we *love God* not only *with all our heart,* but *with all our mind,* Matt. xxii. 37, that is, both with our understanding and imagination.   Love is an affection full of inventions, and sets the wit to work to devise good things; therefore our chief care should be, that our hearts may be circumcised and purified so, as they may be filled with the *love of God,* and then we shall find this duty not only easy but delightful unto us.   The Prophet *healed* the *waters* by *casting salt* into the *spring,* 2 Kings ii. 20, so the seasoning of the spring of our actions seasons all. And indeed what can be expected from man whilst he is vanity but *vain imaginations ?*   What can we look for from a *viper* but *poison ?*   Isaiah lix. 5.   A man naturally is either *weaving spiders' webs,* or *hatching cockatrices' eggs,* that is, his heart is exercised eitheir in vanity or mischief, for not only the frame of the heart, but what the heart frameth is evil continually.   A wicked man that is besotted with false *conceits,* will admit of no good thoughts to enter. Gen. vi. 5.

5.   Even when we are good and devise good things, yet there is still some sickness of fancy remaining in the best of us, whereby we work trouble to ourselves, and therefore it is necessary we should labour to restrain and limit our fancy, and *stop these waters* at the *beginning,* giving no not the least way thereunto. If it begins to grow wanton, tame the wildness of it by fastening it to the cross of Christ, *whom we have pierced with our sins,* Zach. xii. 10, and amongst other, with these sins of our spirits, who hath *redeemed* us from our *vain* thoughts and *conversations,* 1 Pet. i. 18, set before it the consideration of the wrath of God, of death, and judgment, and the woful estate of the damned, &c., and take it not off till thy heart be taken off from straying from God; when it begins once to run out to impertinencies, confine it to some certain thing, and then upon examination we shall find it bring home some honey with it; otherwise it will bring us nothing but a sting from the bitter remembrance of our former mispent thoughts and time,

which we should *redeem* and fill up, with things that most *belong to our peace.* Luke xix. 47. Idleness is the hour of temptation, wherein Satan joins with our imagination, and sets it about his own work, for the soul as a mill either grinds that which is put into it, or else works upon itself. Imagination is the first wheel of the soul, and if that move amiss, it stirs all the inferior wheels amiss with it; it stirs itself, and other powers of the soul are stirred by its motion; and therefore the well ordering of this is of the greater consequence; for as the imagination conceiveth, so usually the judgment concludeth, the will chooseth, the affections are carried, and the members execute.

If it break loose, (as it will soon run riot,) yet give no consent of the will to it; though it hath defiled the memory, yet let it not defile the will; though it be the *first born* of the soul, yet let it not defile that which should be kept pure for the Spirit of Christ; resolve to act nothing upon it, but cross it before it moves to the execution and practice of any thing: as in sickness, many times we imagine (by reason of the corruption of our taste) physic to be ill for us, and those meats which *nourish the disease* to be good, yet care of health makes us cross our own conceits, and take that which fancy abhors: so if we would preserve sound spirits, we must conclude against groundless imagination, and resolve that whatsoever it suggests cannot be so, because it crosses the grounds both of religion and reason: and when we find imagination to deceive us in sensible things, as melancholy persons are subject to mistake, we may well gather, that it will much more deceive us in our *spiritual condition;* and indeed such is the incoherence, impertinency, and unreasonableness of imagination, that men are often ashamed and angry with themselves afterwards for giving the least way to such thoughts; and it is good to chastise the soul for the same, that it may be more wary for time to come; whilst men are led with imagination, they work not according to right rules prescribed to men, but as other baser creatures, in whom phantasy is the chief ruling power, and therefore those whose will is guided by their fancies live more like beasts than men.

We allow a horse to prance and skip in a pasture, which if he doth when he is once backed by the rider, we count him unruly and unbroken: so howsoever in other creatures we allow liberty of fancy, yet we allow it not in man to frisk and rove at its pleasure, because in him it is to be bridled with reason.

6. Especially take heed of those cursed imaginations out of which, as of mother roots, others spring forth; as questioning God's providence, and care of his children, his justice, his disregarding of what is done here below, &c., thoughts of putting off our amendment for time to come, and so *blessing ourselves* in an evil way; thoughts against the necessity of exact and *circumspect walking* with God, &c. Eph. v. 15. When these and such like principles of Satan's and the *flesh's divinity* take place in our hearts, they block up the soul against the entrance of *soul-saving* truths, and taint our whole conversation, which is either good or evil, as the principles are by which we are guided and as our imagination is, which lets in all to the soul.

The Jews in Jeremiah's time were forestalled with vain imaginations against sound repentance, and therefore his counsel is, *wash thine heart, O Jerusalem, how long shall vain thoughts lodge within thee?* Jer. iv. 14.

7. Fancy will the better be kept within its due bounds, if we consider the principal use thereof; sense and imagination is properly to judge what is comfortable or uncomfortable, what is pleasing or displeasing to the outward man, not what is morally or spiritually good or ill, and thus far by the laws of nature and civility we are bound to give fancy contentment both in ourselves and others, as not to speak or do any thing uncomely, which may occasion a loathing or distaste in our converse with men: and it is a matter

of conscience to make our lives as comfortable as may be; as we are bound to love, so we are bound to use all helps that may make us lovely, and endear us into the good affections of others: as we are bound to give no offence to the conscience of another, so to no power or faculty either of the outward or inward man of another: some are taken off in their affection by a fancy, whereof they can give but little reason; and some are more careless in giving offence in this kind, than stands with that Christian circumspection and mutual respect which we owe one to another; the Apostle's rule is of large extent, *Whatsoever things are not only true, and honest, and just,* but *whatsoever things are lovely, and of good report, &c. think of these things.* Phil. iv. 8.   Yet our main care should be to manifest ourselves rather to men's consciences than to their imaginations.

8. It should be our wisdom likewise to place ourselves in the best conveniency of all outward helps which may have a kind working upon our fancy; and to take heed of the contrary, as time, place, and objects, &c.   There be good hours and good messengers of God's sending, golden opportunities wherein God uses to give a meeting to his children, and breathes good thoughts into them.   Even the wisest and holiest men, as David and Solomon, &c., had no further safety than they were careful of well-using all good advantages, and sequestering themselves from such objects as had a working power upon them; by suffering their souls to be led by their fancies, and their hearts to run after their eyes, they betrayed and robbed themselves of much grace and comfort, thereupon Solomon cries out with grief and shame from his own experience, *Vanity of vanities,* &c. Eccles. i. 2. Fancy will take fire before we be aware.   Little things are seeds of great matters; Job knew this, and therefore *made a covenant with his eyes.* Job xxxi. 1: but *a fool's eyes* are in the *corners of the earth,* saith Solomon. Prov. xvii. 34.

Sometimes the ministering of some excellent thought from what we hear or see, proves a great advantage of spiritual good to the soul: whilst Austin out of curiosity delighted to hear the eloquence of Ambrose, he was taken with the matter itself, sweetly sliding together with the words into his heart. Of later times, whilst Galeaceus Caracciolus, an Italian marquis, and nephew to Pope Paul V., was hearing Peter Martyr reading upon 1 Corinthians, and showing the deceivableness of man's judgment in spiritual things, and the efficacy of divine truth in those that belong unto God, and further using a similitude to this purpose; "If a man be walking afar off, and see people dancing together, and hear no noise of the music, he judges them fools and out of their wits; but when he comes nearer and hears the music, and sees that every motion is exactly done by art; now he changes his mind, and is so taken up with the sweet agreement of the gesture, and the music, that he is not only delighted therewith, but desirous to join himself in the number: so it falls out, saith he, with men; whilst they look upon the outward carriage and conversation of God's people, and see it differing from others, they think them fools; but when they look more narrowly into their courses, and see a gracious harmony betwixt their lives and the Word of God, then they begin to be in love with the *beauty of holiness,* and join in conformity of holy obedience with those they scorned before." This similitude wrought so with this nobleman, that he began from that time forward to set his mind to the study of heavenly things.

One seasonable truth falling upon a prepared heart, hath oftentimes a sweet and strong operation; Luther confesseth that having heard a grave divine Staupicius say, that *that is kind repentance which begins from the love of God,* ever after that time the practice of repentance was sweeter to him. This speech of his likewise took well with Luther that in doubts of *predestination we should begin from the wounds of Christ,* that is from the sense of God's love to us in Christ, we should arise to the grace given us in *election before the world was.* 2 Tim. i. 9.

The putting of lively colours upon common truths hath oft so strong working both upon the fancy, and our will and affections; the spirit is refreshed with fresh things, or old truths refreshed; this made *the preacher seek to find out pleasing and acceptable words*, Eccl. xii. 10; and our Saviour Christ's manner of teaching was by a lively representation to men's fancies to teach them heavenly truths in an earthly sensible manner; and indeed what do we see or hear but will yield matter to a holy heart to raise itself higher?

We should make our fancy serviceable to us in spiritual things, and take advantage by any pleasure, or profit, or honour which it presents our thoughts with, to think thus with ourselves, What is this to the true honour, and to those enduring pleasures? &c. And seeing God hath condescended to represent heavenly things to be under earthly terms we should follow God's dealing herein: God represents heaven to us under the term of a *banquet*, and of a *kingdom*, &c. Luke x. 32; our *union* with Christ under the term of a *marriage*, yea, Christ himself, under the name of whatsoever is lovely or comfortable in heaven or earth. So the Lord sets out hell to us by whatsoever is terrible or tormenting. Here is a large field for our imagination to walk in, not only without hurt, but with a great deal of spiritual gain; if the wrath of a king be as the roaring of a lion, what is the wrath of the *King of kings?* If fire be so terrible what is hell fire? If a dark dungeon be so loathsome what is that eternal dungeon of darkness? If a feast be so pleasing, what is the *continual feast of a good conscience?* Prov. xxv. 15. If the meeting of friends be so comfortable, what will our meeting together in heaven be. The Scripture by such like terms would help our faith and fancy both at once; a sanctified fancy will make every creature a *ladder to heaven*. And because childhood and youth are ages of fancy, therefore it is a good way to instil into the hearts of children betimes, the loving of good, and the shunning of evil, by such like representations as agree with their fancies, as to hate hell under the representation of fire and darkness, &c. Whilst the soul is joined with the body, it hath not only a necessary but a holy use of imagination, and of sensible things whereupon our imagination worketh; what is the use of the sacraments, but to help our souls by our senses, and our faith by imagination? as the soul receives much hurt from imagination, so it may have much good thereby.

But yet it ought not to invent or devise what is good and true in religion, here fancy must yield to faith, and faith to divine revelation; the *things we believe* are such, as neither *eye hath seen, nor ear heard*, neither *come into the heart of man*, 1 Cor. ii. 9, by imagination stirred up from any thing which we have seen or heard; they are above not only imagination, but reason itself, in men and angels: but after God hath revealed spiritual truths, and faith hath apprehended them, then imagination hath use while the soul is joined with the body, to colour divine truths, and make lightsome what faith believes; for instance, it doth not devise either heaven or hell, but when God hath revealed them to us; our fancy hath a fitness of enlarging our conceits of them, even by resemblance from things in nature, and that without danger; because the joys of heaven, and the torments of hell are so great, that all the representations which nature affords us, fall short of them.

Imagination hath likewise some use in religion by putting cases to the soul, as when we are tempted to any unruly action, we should think with ourselves, What would I do if some holy grave person whom I much reverence should behold me? Whereupon the soul may easily ascend higher; God sees me, and my own conscience is ready to witness against me, &c.

It helps us also in taking benefit by the example of other men; good things are best learned by others expressing of them to our view; the very sight often (nay, the very thought) of a good man doth good, as representing to our souls some good thing which we affect; which makes histories, and the lively characters and expressions of virtues and vices useful to us. The sight, yea, the very reading of the suffering of the martyrs hath wrought such a hatred of that persecuting church, as hath done marvellous good; the sight of justice executed upon malefactors, works a greater hatred of sin in men than naked precepts can do; so outward pomp and state in the world, doth further that awful respect due to authority, &c.

Lastly, it would much avail for the well ordering of our thoughts, to set our souls in order every morning, and to strengthen and perfume our spirits with some gracious meditations, especially of the chief end and scope wherefore we live here, and how every thing we do, or befalls us, may be reduced and ordered to further the main. The end of a Christian is glorious, and the oft thoughts of it will raise and enlarge the soul, and set it on work to study how to make all things serviceable thereunto. It is a thing to be lamented that a Christian born for heaven, having the *price of his high calling* set before him, and matters of that weight and excellency to exercise his heart upon, should be taken up with trifles, and fill both his head and heart with vanity and nothing, as all earthly things will prove ere long; and yet if many men's thoughts and discourses were distilled, they are so frothy that they would hardly yield one drop of true comfort.

§ IV. Oh but, say some, thoughts and imaginations are free, and we shall not be accountable for them.

This is a false plea, for God hath a sovereignty over the whole soul, and his law binds the whole inward and outward man; as we desire our whole man should be saved by Christ, so we must yield up the whole man to be governed by him; and it is the effect of the dispensation of the Gospel, accompanied with the Spirit, to captivate whatsoever is in man unto Christ, and to bring down all *high towering imaginations*, 2 Cor. x. 5, that exalt themselves against God's Spirit. There is a divinity in the word of God powerfully unfolded, which will convince our souls of the sinfulness of natural imaginations, as we see in the idiot, Cor. 14, who, seeing himself laid open before himself, cried out, that *God was in the speaker.* 1 Cor. xiv. 25.

There ought to be in man a conformity to the truth and goodness of things, or else, 1. We shall wrong our own souls with false apprehensions : and 2. the creature, by putting a fashion upon it otherwise than God hath made : and 3. we shall wrong God himself the author of goodness, who cannot have his true glory but from a right apprehension of things as they are ; what a wrong is it to men when we shall take up false prejudices against them without ground ; and so suffer our conceits to be envenomed against them by unjust suspicions, and by this means deprive ourselves of all that good which we might receive by them ? for our nature is apt to judge, and accept of things as the persons are, and not of persons according to the things themselves : this faculty exercises a tyranny in the soul, setting up and pulling down whom it will. Job judged his friends *altogether vain,* Job xxvii. 12 ; because they went upon a vain imagination and discourse, judging him to be a hypocrite, which could not but add much to his affliction : when men take a toy in their head against a person or place, they are ready to reason as he did, *Can any good come out of Nazareth?* John vi. 46.

It is an indignity for men to be led with surmises and probabilities, and so to pass a rash judgment upon persons and things ; oftentimes falsehood hath a fairer gloss of probability than truth ; and vices go masked under the appearance of virtue, whereupon *seeming likeness* breeds a mistake of one thing for another ; and Satan oftentimes casts a mist before our imagination, that so we might have a misshapen conceit of things ; by a spirit of illusion he makes worldly things appear bigger to us, and spiritual things less than indeed they are ; and so by sophisticating of things our affections come to be misled. Imagination is the womb, and Satan the father of all monstrous conceptions and disordered lusts, which are well called *deceitful lusts,* Eph. iv. 22 ; and *lusts of ignorance,*

1 Tim. vi. 9, foolish and noisome lusts, because they both spring from error and folly, and lead unto it.

We see even in religion itself, how the world, together with the help of *the god of the world*, is led away, if not to worship images, yet to worship the image of their own fancy; and where the truth is most professed, yet people are prone to fancy to themselves such a breadth of religion, as will altogether leave them comfortless, when things shall appear in their true colours; they will conceit to embrace truth without hatred of the world, and Christ without his cross, and a godly life without persecutions, they would pull a rose without pricks; which though it may stand with their own base ends for a while, yet will not hold out in times of change when the sickness of body and trouble of mind shall come; empty conceits are too weak to encounter real griefs.

Some think orthodox and right opinions to be a plea for a loose life, whereas there is no ill course of life but springs from some false opinion. God will not only call us to an account how we have *believed*, *disputed*, and *reasoned*, &c., but how we have lived. Our care therefore should be to build our profession not on seeming appearances, but upon sound grounds, that the gates of hell cannot prevail against. The hearts of many are so vain, that they delight to be blown up with flattery, because they would have their imaginations pleased (yea, even when they cannot but know themselves abused) and are grieved to have their windy bladder pricked, and so to be put out of their conceited happiness. Others out of a tediousness in serious and settled thoughts entertain every thing as it is offered to them at the first blush, and suffer their imaginations to carry them presently thereunto without further judging of it; the will naturally loves variety and change, and our imagination doth it service herein, as not delighting to fix long upon any thing; hereupon men are contented both in religion, and in common life to be misled with prejudices upon shallow grounds: whence it is that the best things and persons suffer much in the world, the power and practice of religion is hated under odious names, and so condemned before it is understood; whence we see a necessity of getting spiritual eye-salve, for *without true knowledge the heart cannot be good.* Prov. xix. 2.

It is just with God that those who take liberty in their thoughts should be given up to their own imaginations, to delight in them, and to be out of conceit with the best things, and so to reap the fruit of their own ways. Nay, even the best of God's people, if they take liberty herein, God will let loose their imagination upon themselves, and suffer them to be entangled and vexed with their own hearts; those that give way to their imaginations, show what their actions should be, if they dared; for if they forbear doing evil out of conscience, they should as well forbear imagining evil; for both are alike open to God and hateful to him; and therefore oft where there is no conscience of the thought, God gives men up to the deed. The greatest, and hardest work of a Christian is least in sight, which is the well ordering of his heart; some buildings have most workmanship under ground; it is our spirits *that God who is a Spirit,* John iv. 24, hath most communion withal; and the less freedom we take to sin here, the more argument of our sincerity, because there is no law to bind the inner man but the law of the Spirit of grace, whereby we are *a law to ourselves.* A good Christian begins his repentance where his sin begins, in his thoughts, which are the next issue of his heart. God counts it an honour when we regard his all-seeing eye so much, as that we will not take liberty to ourselves in that which is offensive to him, no, not in our hearts, wherein no creature can hinder us; it is an argument that the Spirit hath set up a kingdom and order in our hearts, when our spirits rise within us against any thing that lifts itself up against goodness.

§ V. Many flatter themselves, from an impossibility of ruling their imaginations, and are ready to lay all upon infirmity and natural weakness, &c.

But such must know that if we be sound Christians,

the Spirit of God will enable us to do all things
(evangelical) that we are called unto, if we give way
without check to the motions thereof; where the Spirit
is, it is such a light as discovers not only dunghills,
but motes themselves, even light and flying imaginations, and abaseth the soul for them, and by degrees
purgeth them out; and if they press (as they are as
busy as flies in summer) yet a good heart will not own
them, nor allow himself in them, but casts them off,
as hot water doth the scum, or as the stomach doth
that which is noisome unto it, they find not that entertainment here which they have in carnal hearts,
where the scum soaks in; which are stews of unclean
thoughts, shambles of cruel and bloody thoughts, ex-
changes and shops of vain thoughts, a very forge and
mint of false, politic, and undermining thoughts, yea,
often a little hell of confused and black imaginations.
There is nothing that more moveth a godly man to
renew his interest every day in the perfect righteousness and obedience of his Saviour, than these sinful
stirrings of his soul, when he finds something in himself always enticing and drawing away his heart from
God, and intermingling itself with his best performances. Even good thoughts are troublesome if they
come unreasonably, and weaken our exact performance of duty.

§ VI. But here some misconceits must be taken
heed of.

1. As we must take heed that we account not our
imaginations to be religion; so we must not account
true religion, and the power of godliness to be a matter of imagination only, as if holy men troubled themselves more than needs, when they stand upon religion and conscience, seeking to *approve* themselves
to God in all things, 1 Thes. v. 12, and endeavouring
so far as frailty will permit, to *avoid all appearances
of evil*. 1 Thes. v. 22. Many men are so serious in
vanities, and real in trifles, that they count all, which
dote not upon such outward excellencies as they do,
because the Spirit of God hath revealed to them things
of a higher nature, to be fantastic and humorous peo-

ple, and so impute the work of the Spirit to the flesh, God's work to Satan, which comes near unto blasphemy: they imagine good men to be led with vain conceits, but good men know them to be so led. Not only Paul, but Christ himself, were counted beside themselves, Acts xxvi. 24, when they were earnest for God and the souls of his people. But there is enough in religion to bear up the soul against all imputations laid upon it: the true children of wisdom are always able to justify their mother, Matt. xi. 19, and the conscionable practice of holy duties, is founded upon such solid grounds as shall hold out when heaven and earth shall vanish.

2. We must know that as there is great danger in false conceits of the way to heaven, when we make it broader than it is, for by this means we are like men going over a bridge, who think it broader than it is, but being deceived by some shadow, sink down, and are suddenly drowned; so men mistaking the strait way to life, and trusting to the shadow of their own imagination, fall into the bottomless pit of hell before they are aware. In like manner the danger is great in making the way to heaven narrower than indeed it is by weak and superstitious imaginations, making more sins than God hath made. The *wise man's* counsel is that we should not make ourselves *over-wicked*, not be *foolisher than we are*, Eccl. vii. 17, by devising more sins in our imagination than we are guilty of.

It is good, in this respect, to know our Christian liberty, which being one of the fruits of Christ's death, we cannot neglect the same, without much wrong not only to ourselves, but to the rich bounty and goodness of God. So that the due rules of limitation be observed, from authority, piety, sobriety, needless offence of others, &c., we may with better leave use all those comforts which God hath given to refresh us in the way to heaven, than refuse them; the care of the outward man binds conscience so far, as that we should neglect nothing which may help us in a cheerful serving of God, in our places, and tend to the due honour of our bodies, which are the *temples of the Holy Ghost*, 1 Cor. iii. 16, 17, and companions with our souls in all performances. So that under this pretence we take not too much liberty to satisfy the lusts of the body. Intemperate use of the creatures is the nurse of all passions: because our spirits, which are the soul's instruments, are hereby inflamed and disturbed; it is no wonder to see an intemperate man transported into any passion.

3. Some out of their high and airy imaginations (and out of their iron and flinty philosophy) will needs think outward good and ill, together with the affections of grief and delight stirred up thereby to be but opinions and conceits of good and evil only, not true and really so founded in nature, but taken up of ourselves; but though our fancy be ready to conceit a greater hurt in outward evils than indeed there is, as in *poverty, pain* of *body, death* of *friends*, &c., yet we must not deny them to be evils: that wormwood is bitter, it is not a conceit only, but the nature of the thing itself, yet to abstain from it altogether for the bitterness thereof is a hurtful conceit. That honey is sweet, it is not a conceit only, but the natural quality of it is so; yet out of a taste of the sweetness, to think we cannot take too much of it, is a misconceit paid home with loathsome bitterness. Outward good and outward evil, and the affections of delight and sorrow rising thence, are naturally so, and depend not upon our opinion. This were to offer violence to nature, and to take man out of man, as if he were not flesh but steel; universal experience, from the sensibleness of our nature in any outward grievance, is sufficient to damn this conceit.

The way to comfort a man in grief, is not to tell him that it is only a conceit of evil, and no evil indeed that he suffers; this kind of learning will not down with him, as being contrary to his present feeling; but the way is, to yield unto him that there is cause of grieving, though not of over grieving, and to show him grounds of comfort stronger than the grief he suffers. We should weigh the degrees of evil in a right balance, and not suffer fancy to make them greater than they are; so as that for obtaining the greatest outward good, or avoiding the greatest outward ill of suffering, we should give way to the least evil of sin. This is but a policy of the flesh to take away the sensibleness of evil, that so those checks of conscience and repentance for sin, which are oft occasioned thereby, might be taken away; that so men may go on enjoying a stupid happiness, never laying any thing to heart, nor afflicting their souls, until their consciences awaken in the place of the damned, and then they feel that grief return upon them for ever, which they laboured to put away when it might have been seasonable to them.

§ VII. I have stood the longer upon this, because Satan and his instruments by bewitching the imagination with false appearances, misleadeth not only the world, but troubleth the peace of men *taken out of the world,* whose estate is laid up safe in Christ, who, notwithstanding, pass their few days here in an uncomfortable, wearisome, and unnecessary *sadness of spirit,* being kept in ignorance of their happy condition by Satan's juggling and their own mistakes, and so come to heaven before they are aware. Some again pass their days in a golden dream, and drop into hell before they think of it; but it is far better to dream of ill, and when we awake to find it but a dream, than to dream of some great good, and when we awake to find the contrary.

As the distemper of the fancy disturbing the act of reason, oftentimes breeds madness in regard of civil conversation; so it breeds likewise spiritual madness, carrying men to those things, which if they were in their right wits they would utterly abhor, therefore we cannot have too much care upon what we fix our thoughts; and what a glorious discovery is there of the excellencies of religion that would even ravish an angel, which may raise up, exercise, and fill our hearts? we see our fancy hath so great a force in natural conceptions, that it oft sets a mark and impression upon that which is conceived in the womb. So likewise strong and holy conceits of things, having a divine virtue accompanying of them, transform the soul, and breed spiritual impressions answerable to our spiritual apprehensions. It would prevent many crosses, if we would conceive of things as they are; when trouble of mind, or sickness of body, and death itself cometh, what will remain of all that greatness which filled our fancies before? then we can judge soberly and speak gravely of things. The best way of happiness, is not to multiply honours or riches, &c., but to cure our conceits of things, and then we cannot be very much cast down with any thing that befalls us here.

Therefore when any thing is presented to our souls, which we see is ready to work upon us, we should ask of ourselves upon what ground we entertain such a conceit, whether we shall have the same judgment after we have yielded to it as now we have? and whether we will have the same judgment of it in sickness and death, and at the day of reckoning as we have for the present? That which is of itself evil, is always so at one time as well as another; if the time will come, when we shall think those things to be vain, which now we are so eagerly set upon, as if there were some great good in them; why should we not think so of them now, when as the reforming of our judgment may do us good : rather than to be led on with a pleasing error until that time, wherein the sight of our error will fill our hearts with horror and shame, without hope of ever changing our condition?

Here therefore is a special use of these soliloquies, to awake the soul, and to stir up reason cast asleep by Satan's charms, that so scattering the clouds through which things seem otherwise than they are, we may discern and judge of things according to their true and constant nature. Demand of thy soul, Shall I always be of this mind? Will not the time come when this will prove bitterness in the end? Shall I redeem a short contentment with lasting sorrow? Is my judge of my mind? Will not a time come when all things shall appear as they are? Is this according to the rule, &c.?

To conclude, therefore, whereas there be divers principles of men's actions, as 1. *Natural inclination,* inclining us to some courses more than others: 2. *Custom,* which is another nature in us: 3. *Imagination,* apprehending things upon shallow grounds; from whence springs affection, whereby we desire glory in things above our own strength and measure, and make show of that, the truth whereof is wanting in us. 4. *True judgment,* discerning the true reasons of things. 5. *Faith,* which is a spiritual principle planted in the soul, apprehending things above reason, and raising us up to conceive of all things as God hath discovered them. Now a sound Christian should not be lightly led with those first common grounds of natural inclination, custom, opinion, &c., but by judgment enlightened, advanced, and guided by faith. And we must take heed we suffer not things to pass suddenly from imagination to affection, without asking advice of our judgment, and faith in the way, whose office is to weigh things in God's balance, and thereupon to accept or refuse them.

CHAPTER XIV.

OF HELP BY OTHERS—OF TRUE COMFORTERS, AND THEIR GRACES—ME-
THOD—ILL SUCCESS.

§ 1. But because we are subject to favour and flatter ourselves, it is wisdom to take the benefit of a second self, that is, a well chosen friend, living or dead, (books I mean) which will speak truly without flattery of our estates. *A friend is made for the time of adversity,* Prov. xvii. 17; and two are better than one; for by this means our troubles are divided, and so more easily borne. The very presence of a true-hearted friend yields often ease to our grief: of all friends, those that by office are to speak a word to a weary soul, are most to be regarded, as speaking to us in Christ's stead. Oftentimes, especially in our own case, we are blinded and benighted with passion, and then the judgment of a

friend is clearer. Loving friends have a threefold
privilege: 1. Their advice is suitable, and fit to our
present occasion, they can meet with our grievance,
so cannot books so well: 2. What comes from a
living friend, comes lively, as helped by his spirit:
3. In regard of ourselves, what they say is apprehended with more ease, and less plodding and bent of
mind; there is scarce any thing wherein we see God
more in favour towards us, than in our friends, and
their seasonable speeches; our hearts being naturally
very false and willingly deceived. God often gives
us up to be misled by men, not according to his, but
our own naughty hearts. As men are, so are their
counsellors, for such they will have, and such God
lets them have. Men whose wills are stronger than
their wits, who are wedded to their own ways, are
more pleased to hear that which complies with their
inclinations, than a harsh truth which crosses them;
this presages ruin, because they are not counselable:
wherefore God suffers them to be led through a *fool's
paradise* to a true prison, as men that will neither
hear themselves nor others who would do them good
against their wills; it was a sign God would destroy
Eli's sons when they would hear no counsel, 1 *Sam.*
ii. 25; God fills such men with their *own ways.*
Prov. xiv. 14. Men in great place often in the
abundance of all things else, want the benefit of a
true friend, because under pretence of service of them
men carry their own ends; as they flatter themselves,
so they are flattered by others, and so robbed of the
true judgment of themselves. Of all spiritual judgments this is the heaviest, for men to be given up to
such a measure of self-willness, and to refuse spiritual
balm to heal them, usually such *perish without remedy*, Prov. xxix. 1, because to be wilfully miserable
is to be doubly miserable, for it adds to our misery,
that we brought it willingly upon ourselves.

It is a course that will have a blessing attending it,
for friends to join in league, one to watch over another,
and observe each other's ways. It is a usual course
for Christians to join together in other holy duties, as

hearing, receiving of the sacrament, prayer, &c. but this fruit of holy communion which ariseth from a mutual observing one another is much wanting; whence it is that many droop, so many are so uncheerful in the ways of God, and lie groaning under the burden of many cares, and are battered with so many temptations, &c. because they are left only to their own spirits. What an unworthy thing is it, that we should pity a beast over-loaden, and yet take no pity of a brother? whereas there is no living member of Christ but hath spiritual love infused into him, and some ability to comfort others. Dead stones in an arch uphold one another, and shall not living? It is the work of an angel to comfort, nay it is the office of the Holy Ghost to be a comforter, not only immediately, but by breathing comfort into our hearts together with the comfortable words of others; thus one friend becomes an angel, nay a God to another; and there is a sweet sight of God in the face of a friend; for though the comfort given by God's messengers be ordinarily most effectual, as the blessing of parents, who are in God's room, is more effectual that the blessing of others upon their children; yet God hath promised a blessing to the offices of communion of saints performed by one private man towards another. Can we have a greater encouragement than under God to be gainer of a soul, which is as much in God's esteem as if we should gain a world? Spiritual alms are the best alms; mercy showed to the souls of men is the greatest mercy; and wisdom in winning of souls is the greatest wisdom in the world, because the soul is especially the man, upon the goodness of which, the happiness of the whole man depends; what shining and flourishing Christians should we have if these duties were performed? As we have a portion in the communion of saints, so we should labour to have humility to take good, and wisdom and love to do good. A Christian should have feeding lips, and a healing tongue ; the leaves, the very words *of the tree of righteousness* have a curing virtue in them.

Some will show a great deal of humanity in comforting others, but little Christianity; for as kind men they will utter some cheerful words, but as Christians they want wisdom from above to speak a gracious *word in season*; nay, some there are, who hinder the saving working of any affliction upon the hearts of others, by unseasonable and unsavory discourses, either by suggesting false remedies, or else diverting men to false contentments, and so become spiritual traitors rather than friends, taking part with their worst enemies, their lusts, and wills. Happy is he that in his way to heaven meeteth with a cheerful and skilful guide and fellow-traveller, that carrieth cordials with him against all faintings of spirit; it is a part of our *wisdom to salvation* to make choice of such a one as may further us in our way; an indifferency for any company shows a dead heart; where the life of grace is, it is sensible of all advantages and disadvantages: how many have been refreshed by one short, apt, savoury speech? which hath begotten, as it were, new spirits in them.

In ancient times, as we see in the story of Job, chap ii. 12, it was the custom of friends to meet together, to comfort those that were in misery, and Job takes it for granted, that *to him that is afflicted pity should be showed from his friends,* chap vi. 14: for besides the presence of a friend which hath some influence of comfort in it; 1. The discovery of his loving affection hath a cherishing sweetness in it. 2. The expression of love in real comforts and services by supplying any outward want of the party troubled, prevails much; thus Christ made way for his comforts to the souls of men, by showing outward kindness to their bodies; love with the sensible fruits of it, prepareth for any wholesome counsel. 3. After this, wholesome words carry a special cordial virtue with them, especially when the Spirit of God in the affectionate speaker joins with the word of comfort, and thereby closeth with the heart of a troubled patient: when all these concentre and meet together in one, then is comfort *sealed* up to the soul. The *child in*

Elizabeth's womb sprang at the presence and salu-
tation of Mary, Luke i. 41 ; the speech of one hearty
friend cannot but revive the spirits of another ; sympathy hath a strange force, as we see in the strings of
an instrument, which being played upon, as they say,
the strings of another instrument are also moved with
it.   After love hath once kindled love, then the heart
being melted, is fit to receive any impression ; unless
both pieces of the iron be red hot they will not join
together ; two spirits warmed with the same heat will
easily solder together.

§ II. In him that shall stay the mind of another
there had need to be an excellent temper of many
graces; as, 1. Knowledge of the grievance, together with wisdom to speak a word in season, and to
conceal that which may set the cure backwards.
2. Faithfulness with liberty, not to conceal any thing
which may be for his good, though against present
liking.   The very life and soul of friendship stands
in freedom, tempered with wisdom and faithfulness.
3. Love with compassion and patience *to bear all,* and
hope all, and *not to be easily prvooked,* by the waywardness of him we deal with.   Short-spirited men
are not the best comforters ; God himself is said to
bear with the manners of his people in the wilder-
ness, Acts xiii. 18; it is one thing to bear with a wise
sweet moderation that which may be borne, and another thing to allow or approve that which is not to
be approved at all.   Where these graces are in the
speaker, and apprehended so to be by the person
distempered, his heart will soon embrace whatsoever
shall be spoken to rectify his judgment or affection.
A good conceit of the spirit of the speaker is of as
much force to prevail as his words.   Words especially
prevail, when they are uttered more from the bowels
than the brain, and from our own experience, which
made even Christ himself a more compassionate high
priest.   When men come to themselves again they
will be the deepest censurers of their own miscarriage.

§ III. Moreover to the right comforting of an afflicted person, special care must be had of discerning the

true ground of his grievance, the core must be searched out; if the grief ariseth from outward causes, then
it must be carried into the right channel, the course of
it must be turned another way, as in staying of blood:
we should grieve for sin in the first place, as being
the evil of all evils: if the ground be sin, then it must
be drawn to a head, from a confused grief to some
more particular sin, that so we may strike the right
vein; but if we find the spirit much cast down for
particular sins, then comfort is presently to be applied;
but if the grief be not fully ripe, then, as we use to
help nature by physic, till the sick matter be carried
away; so when conscience, moved by the Spirit, begins to ease itself by confession, it is good to help
forward the work of it, till we find the heart low
enough for comfort to be laid upon. When Paul
found the jailer cast down almost as low as hell, he
stands not now upon further hammering, and preparing of him for mercy, that work was done already,
but presently stirs him up to *believe in the Lord
Jesus Christ*, Acts xvi. 31; here being a fit place
for an interpreter to declare unto man his righteousness, and his mercy that belongs unto him after he
hath acknowledged his personal and particular sins,
which the natural guilt of the heart is extremely
backward to do, and yet cannot receive any sound
peace till it be done: if signs of grace be discerned,
here likewise is a fit place to declare unto man the
saving work of grace in his heart, which Satan labours
to hide from him. Men oft are not able to read their
own evidences without help.

In case of stiffness and standing out, it is fit the
man of God should take some authority upon him,
and lay a charge upon the souls of men in the name
of Christ, to give way to the truth of Christ, and to
forbear putting off that mercy which is so kindly offered when we judge it to be their portion; which
course will be successful in hearts awed with a reverent fear of grieving God's Spirit. Sometimes men
must be dealt roundly with, as David here deals
with his own soul, that so whilst we ask a reason of

9

their dejection, they may plainly see they have no reason to be so cast down; for oftentimes grievances are irrational, rising from mistakes; and counsel, bringing into the soul a fresh light, dissolves those gross fogs, and setteth the soul at liberty. What grief is contracted by false reason, is by true reason altered. Thus it pleaseth God to humble men by letting them see in what need they stand one of another, that so the communion of saints may be endeared; every relation wherein we stand towards others, are so many bonds and sinews whereby one member is fitted to derive comfort to another, *through love the bond of perfection,* Col. iii. 18; all must be done in this sweet affection. A member out of joint must be tenderly set in again, and bound up, which only men guided by the spirit of love seasoned with discretion are fit to do, they are taught of God to do what they should. The more of Christ is in any man, the more willingness and fitness to this duty; to which this should encourage us, that in strengthening others we strengthen ourselves, and derive upon ourselves the *blessing* pronounced on those that *consider the needy,* Psalm xli. 1, which will be our comfort here, and crown hereafter, that God hath honoured us, to be instruments of spiritual good to others. It is an injunction to *comfort the feeble minded,* 1 Thes. v. 14, and there is a heavy imputation on those that *comforted not the weak,* Ezek. xxxiv. 4, when men will not own men in trouble, but as the herd of deer forsake and push away the wounded deer from them; and those that are any ways cast down, must stoop to those ways which God hath sanctified to convey comfort; for though sometimes the Spirit of God immediately comforts the soul, *which is the sweetest,* yet for the most part the *Sun of righteousness* that hath *healing in his wings,* conveyeth the beams of his comfort by the help of others, in whom he will have much of our comfort to lie hid, and for this very end it pleaseth God to exercise his children, and ministers especially, with trials and afflictions, that so they, having felt what a troubled spirit is in themselves, might be able to comfort others in their distresses with the same comfort wherewith they have been comforted: God often suspends comfort from us to drive us to make use of our Christian friends, by whom he purposeth to do us good. Oftentimes the very opening of men's grievances, bringeth ease without any further working upon them; the very opening of a vein cools the blood. If God in the state of innocency thought it fit man should have a helper, if God thought it fit to send an angel to comfort Christ in his agonies, shall any man think the comfort of another more than needs? Satan makes every affliction, by reason of our corruption, a temptation to us, whereupon we are to encounter not only with our own corruptions, but with spiritual wickedness, and need we not then that others should join forces with us to discover the temptation, and to confirm and comfort us against it? for so reason joining with reason, and affection with affection, we come by uniting of strength to be impregnable. Satan hath most advantage in solitariness, and thereupon sets upon Christ in the *wilderness*, Matt. iv., and upon Eve single, Gen. iii., and it added to the glory of Christ's victory, that he overcame him in a single combat, and in a place of such disadvantage. Those that will be alone, at such times, do as much as in them lieth to tempt the tempter himself to tempt them. The preacher gives three reasons why *two are better than one*, Eccles. iv. 9: 1. Because if one fall, the other may lift him up: as that which is stronger shoreth up that which is weaker, so feeble minds are raised and kept up by the stronger: nay, oftentimes he that is weaker in one grace is stronger in another; one may help by his experience and meekness of love, that needs the help of another for knowledge. 2. If *two lie together*, one may warm another by kindling one another's spirits. Where two meet together upon such holy grounds and aims, there Christ by his Spirit makes up another, and this threefold cable who shall break? While Joas lived, Jehoida stood upright; while Latimer and Ridley lived, they kept up Cranmer by intercourse of letters and otherwise, from entertaining counsels of revolt. The disciples presently upon Christ's apprehension fainted, notwithstanding he laboured by his heavenly doctrine to put courage and comfort into them. 3. If any give an onset upon them, there is *two to withstand it,* spirit joining with spirit: and because there is an acquaintance of spirits as well as of persons, those are fittest to lay open our minds unto, in whom upon experience of their fidelity our hearts may most safely rely, we lose much of our strength in the loss of a true friend; which made David bemoan the loss of his friend Jonathan, *Woe is me for thee my brother Jonathan!* 2 Sam. i. 20. He lost a piece of himself, by losing him whom his heart so clave unto; Paul accounted that God had showed especial mercy to him, in the recovery of Epaphroditus. Phil. ii. 27.

§ IV. But there are divers miscarriages in those that are troubled, which make the comfort of others of none effect.

1. When the troubled party deals not directly, but doubleth with him that is to help him. Some are ashamed to acknowledge the true ground of their grievance, pretending sorrow for one thing, when their hearts tell them it ariseth from another: like the lapwings which make greatest noise furthest from their nest, because they would not have it discovered: this deceit moved our blessed Saviour (who knew what was in the hearts of men) to fit his answers many times, rather to the man than to the matter.

2. Some rely too much upon particular men. Oh if they had such a one they should do well, and mislike others (fitter perhaps to deal with them, as having more thorough knowledge of their estates) because they would have their disease rather covered than cured; or if cured, yet with soft words, whereas no plaister worketh better than that which causes smart. Some out of mere humorous fondness must have that which can hardly be got, or else nothing pleases them: David must needs have the *waters of Bethlehem,* 2 Sam. xxiii. 15, when others were nearer hand: and oftentimes when men have not only whom they desire, but

such also who are fit and dextrous in dealing with a troubled spirit, yet their souls feel no comfort because they make idols of men; whereas men at the best are but conduits of comfort, and such as God freely conveyeth comfort by, taking liberty oft to deny comfort by them, that so he may be acknowledged the *God of all comfort*.

3. Some delude themselves by thinking it sufficient to have a few good words spoken to them, as if that could cure them; not regarding to apprehend the same, and mingle it with faith, without which good words lose their working, even as wholesome physic in a dead stomach.

Besides miscarriages in comforting; times will often fall out in our lives, that we shall have none either to comfort us, or to be comforted by us, and then what will become of us unless we can comfort ourselves? Men must not think always to live upon alms, but lay up something in store for themselves, and provide oil for their own lamps, and be able to draw out something from the treasury of their own hearts. We must not go to the surgeon for every scratch. No wise traveller but will have some refreshing waters about him. Again, we are often driven to retire home to our own hearts, by uncharitable imputations of other men; even friends sometimes become miserable comforters; it was Job's case, chap. ii., his friends had honest intentions to comfort him, but erred in their manner of dealing; if he had found no more comfort by reflecting upon his own sincerity, than he received from them, who laboured to take it from him, he had been doubly miserable. We are most privy to our own intentions and aims, whence comfort must be fetched; let others speak what they can to us, if our own hearts speak not with them, we shall receive no satisfaction. Sometimes it may fall out that those which should unloose our spirits when they are bound up, mistake, the key misses the right wards, and so we lie bound still. Opening of our estate to another is not good, but when it is necessary, and it is not necessary; when we can fetch supply from our own store; God would have us tender of our reputations, except in some special cases, wherein we are to give glory to God by a free and full confession. Needless discovery of ourselves to others, makes us fear the conscience of another man, as privy to that which we are ashamed he should be privy unto, and it is neither wisdom nor mercy to put men upon the rack of confession, further than they can have no ease any other way, for by this means we raise in them a jealousy towards us, and oft without cause, which weakeneth and tainteth that love which should unite hearts in one.

CHAPTER XV.

OF FLYING TO GOD IN DISQUIETS OF SOUL: EIGHT OBSERVATIONS OUT OF
THE TEXT.

WHAT if neither the speech of others to us, nor the rebuke of our own hearts will quiet the soul; is there no other remedy left?

Yes, then look up to God, the father and fountain of comfort, as David doth here; for the more special means whereby he sought to recover himself, was by laying a charge upon his soul to *trust in God;* for having let his soul run out too much, he begins to recollect himself again, and resign up all to God.

§ I. But how came David to have the command of his own soul, so as to take it off from grief, and to place it upon God, could he dispose of his own heart himself?

The child of God hath something in him above a man, he hath the *Spirit of God* to guide his spirit: this command of David to his soul was under the command of the great commander: God commands David to *trust in him,* and at the same time infuseth strength into his soul by thinking of God's command, and trusting to God's power, to *command itself* to *trust in God:* so that this command is not only by authority, but by virtue likewise of God's command:

as the inferior orbs move as they are moved by a
higher; so David's spirit here moves as it is moved
by God's Spirit, which inwardly spake to him to speak
to himself.

David, in speaking thus to his own soul, was, as
every true Christian is, a prophet, and an instructer
to himself: it is but as if inferior officers should
charge in the name and power of the king. God's
children have a principle of life in them from the Spirit of God, by which they command themselves. To
give charge belongs to a superior; David had a double superior above him, his own spirit as sanctified,
and God's Spirit guiding that. Our spirits are the
Spirit's agents, and the Holy Spirit is a divine agent,
maintaining his right in us. As God hath made man
a free agent, so he guides him, and preserves that free
manner of working which is agreeable to man's nature.

By this it appears, that David's moving of himself,
did not hinder the Spirit's moving of him, neither did
the Spirit's moving of him hinder him from moving
himself in a free manner; for the Spirit of God
moveth according to our principles; it openeth our
understandings to see that it is best to *trust in God;*
it moveth so sweetly, as if it were an inbred principle,
and all one with our own spirits; if we should hold
our will to move itself, and not to be moved by the
Spirit, we should make a God of it, whose property
is to move other things, and not to be moved by any.

We are in some sort lords over our own speeches
and actions, but yet, under a higher lord. David
was willing to trust in God, but God wrought that
will in him: he first makes our will good, and then
works by it. It is a sacrilegious liberty that will acknowledge no dependence upon God. We are wise
in his wisdom, and strong in his strength, who saith,
Without me ye can do nothing. John xv. But the
bud of a good desire, and the blossom of a good resolution, and the fruit of a good action, all comes
from God. Indeed, the understanding is ours whereby we know what to do, and the will is ours whereby

we make choice of what is best to be done; but the light whereby we know, and the guidance whereby we choose, that is from a higher agent, which is ready to flow into us with present fresh supply, when by virtue of former strength we put ourselves forward in obedience to God. Let but David say to his soul being charged of God to trust, I charge thee, my soul, to trust in him, and he finds a present strength enabling to it. Therefore we must both depend upon God as the first mover, and withal set all the inferior wheels of our souls agoing according as the Spirit of God ministers motion unto us. So shall we be free from self-confidence, and likewise from neglecting that order of working which God hath established. David hearkened what the Lord said, before he said any thing to himself; so should we. God's commands tend to this, that we should command ourselves. God, and the minister under God, bid us *trust in him*, but all is to no purpose till grace be wrought in the soul, whereby it bids itself; our speaking to others doth no good, till they by entertaining what we say, speak the same to their own souls.

In this charge of David upon his own soul, we may see divers passages and privileges of a gracious heart in trouble.

§ II. As 1. *That a Christian, when he is beaten out of all other comforts, yet hath a God to run unto;* a wicked man beaten out of earthly comforts, is as a naked man in a storm, and an unarmed man in the field, or as a ship tossed in the sea without an anchor, which presently dashes upon rocks, or falleth upon quicksands; but a Christian, when he is driven out of all comforts below, nay, when God seems to be angry with him, he can appeal from God angry to God appeased, he can wrestle and strive with God by God's own strength, and plead with God by his own arguments. What a happy estate is this? who would not be a Christian, if it were but for this, to have something to rely on when all things else fail? the confusion and unquietness which troubles raise in the

soul, may drive it from resting in itself, but there can
never be any true peace settled, until it sees and resolves *what to stay upon.*

§ III. 2. We see here, that *there is a sanctified
use of all troubles to God's children;* first they drive
them *out of themselves,* and then draw them nearer
to God. Crosses indeed of themselves estrange us
more from God, but by an overruling work of the
Spirit, they bring us nearer to him; the soul of itself
is ready to misgive, as if God had too many contro-
versies with it, to show any favour towards it; and
Satan helpeth; because he knows nothing can stand
and prevail against God, or a soul that relieth on
him, therefore he labours to breed and increase an
everlasting division betwixt God and the soul; but
let not Christians muse so much upon their trouble,
but see whither it carries them, whether it brings
them nearer unto God, or not; it is a never failing
rule of discerning a man to be in the state of grace,
*when he finds every condition draw him nearer to
God;* for thus it appears that such love God, and are
called of him, unto whom *all things work together
for the best.* Rom. v. viii. 28.

§ IV. 3. Again, hence • we see that the Spirit of
God by these *inward speeches* doth awake the soul,
and keep it in a holy exercise, by stirring up the
grace of faith to its proper function. It is not so
much the having of grace, as grace in exercise,
that preserves the soul; therefore we should by this
and the like means *stir up the grace of God* in us,
that so it may be kept working and in vigour and
strength. It was David's manner to awake himself,
by bidding both *heart* and *harp* to *awake.* It is the
waking Christian (that hath his wit and his grace
ready about him) who is the safe Christian; grace
dormant without the exercise doth not secure us. It
is almost all one (in regard of present exigence) for
grace not to be and not to work. The soul without
action is like an instrument not played upon, or like
a ship always in the haven, motion is a preservative

of the purity of things.   Even life itself is made more
lively by action.   The Spirit of God whereby his
children are led, is compared to things of the quickest
and strongest actions; as fire and wind, &c.   God
himself is a pure act, always in acting; and every
thing the nearer it comes to God, the more it hath its
perfection in working.   The happiness of man consists chiefly in a gracious frame of spirit, and actions
suitable sweetly issuing therefrom; the very rest of
heavenly bodies is in motion in their proper places.
By this stirring up the grace of God in us, sparkles
come to be flames, and all graces are kept bright.
Troubles stir up David, and David being stirred stirs
up himself.

§ V. 4. We see likewise here a *further use of soliloquies* or *speeches to our own hearts;* when the
soul by entering into itself sees itself put out of order,
then it enjoins this duty of *trusting in God* upon it:
if we look only on ourselves and not turn to God, the
work of the soul is imperfect; then the soul worketh
as it should, when as by reflecting on itself, it gathers
some profitable conclusion, and leaveth itself with
God.   David upon reflecting on himself found nothing but discouragement, but when he looks upward
to God, there he finds rest.   This is one end why
God suffers the soul to tire and beat itself, that finding no rest in itself, it might seek to him.   David
yields not so much to his passion as that it should
keep him from God.   Therefore let no man truly
religious pretend, for an excuse, his temper or pro-.
voking occasions, &c., for grace doth raise the soul
above nature; grace doth not only stop the soul in
an evil way, but carries it to a contrary good, and
raiseth it up to God.   Though holy men be subject
to *like passions with others,* James v. 17, (as it is
said of Elias) yet they are not so enthralled to them,
as that they carry them wholly away from their God,
but they hear a voice of the Spirit within them calling them back again to their former communion with
God; and so grace takes occasion, even from sin to
exercise itself.

§ VI. 5. Observe further, that *distrust is the cause of all disquiet :* the soul suffers itself by something here below to be drawn away from God, but can find no rest till it return to him again. As Noah's dove had no place to set her *foot upon,* Gen. viii. 11, till it was received into the ark from whence it came. And it is God's mercy to us, that when we have let go our hold of God, we should find nothing but trouble and unquietness in any thing else, that so we might remember from whence we are fallen, and return home again. That is a good trouble which frees us from the greatest trouble, and brings with it the most comfortable rest; it is but an unquiet quiet, and a restless rest which is out of God. It is a deep spiritual judgment for a man to find too much rest in the creature : the soul that hath had a saving work upon it, will be always impatient until it recover its former sweetness in God: after God's Spirit hath once touched the soul, it will never be quiet until it stands pointed God-ward.

But conscience may object, *Upon any offence is God offended,* and therefore not to be *trusted?*

It is true, where faith is not above natural conscience, but a conscience *sprinkled with the blood of Christ,* is not scared from God by its infirmities and failings, but as David here is rather stirred up to run unto God by his distemper; and it had been a greater sin than his distemper not to have gone unto God. Those that have the spirit of sons in their hearts, run not further from God, after they have a little *strayed from him,* but though it be the nature of sinful passions to breed grief and shame, yet they will repair to God again, and their confidence overcomes their guilt, so well are they acquainted with God's gracious disposition.

Yet we see here, David thinks not of *trusting in God,* till first he had done justice upon his own soul, in rebuking the unruly motions thereof; censure for sin goeth before favour in pardoning sin, or boldness to ask pardon of God; those that *love God* must *hate ill,* Psalm xcvii. 10 : if our consciences condemn us of allowing any sin, we cannot have *boldness with God* who is (light and can abide no darkness and) *greater than our consciences.*

§ VII. 6. Moreover, hence we see *it is no easy thing to bring God and the heart together:* David here as he often checks his heart, so he doth often charge his heart. Doubts and troubles are still gathering upon him, and his faith still gathering upon them. As one striving to get the haven, is driven back by the waves, but recovering himself again, gets forward still, and after often beating back, at length obtains the wished haven, and then is at rest. So much ado is there to bring the soul unto God, the harbour of true comfort. It were an easy thing to be a Christian, if religion stood only in a few outward works and duties, but to take the soul to task, and to deal roundly with our own hearts, and to let conscience have its full work, and to bring the soul into spiritual subjection unto God; this is not so easy a matter, because the soul out of self-love is loath to enter into itself, lest it should have other thoughts of itself than it would have; David must bid his soul trust, and trust, and trust again before it will yield. One main ground of this difficulty, is that contrary which is in the soul by reason of contrary principles: the soul so far as it is gracious, commands, so far as it is rebellious, resists, which drew holy Austin to a kind of astonishment: *" The soul commands the body and it yields,* saith he, *it commands itself, and is resisted by itself;* it commands the hand to move, and it moveth with such an unperceivable quickness that you can discern no distance betwixt the command and the motion: Whence comes this? but because the soul perfectly wills not, and perfectly enjoins not that which is good, and so far forth as it fully wills not, so far it holds back." There should be no need of commanding the soul if it were perfect, for then it would be of itself, what it now commandeth. If David had gotten his soul at perfect freedom at the first, he needed not have repeated his charge so often upon it. But the soul naturally sinks downward, and therefore had need often to be wound up.

§ VIII. 7. We should therefore labour to bring our souls, as David doth here, to a firm and peremptory resolution, and not stand wavering, and as it were equally balanced betwixt God and other things; but enforce our souls, we shall get little ground of infidelity else; drive your souls therefore to this issue, either to rely upon God, or else to yield up itself to the present grievance; if by yielding it resolves to be miserable, there's an end; but if it desires rest, then let it resolve upon this only way, to trust in God: and well may the soul so resolve, because in God there are grounds of quieting the soul, above all that may unsettle it; in him there is both worth to satisfy, and strength to support the soul. The best way to maintain inward peace, is to settle and fix our thoughts upon that which will make us better, till we find our hearts warmed and wrought upon thereby, and then, as the prophet speaks, *God will keep us in peace: peace,* that is, *in perfect and abundant peace.* Isaiah xxvi. 3. This resolution stayed Job, that *though God should kill him,* yet he resolved *to trust in him.* Answerable to our resolution is our peace: the more resolution the more peace; irresolution of itself without any grievance is full of disquiet; it is an unsafe thing always to begin to live: to be always cheapening and paltering with God: come to this point once, *trust God* I ought, therefore *trust God* I will, come what may or will.

And it is good to renew our resolutions again and again: for every new resolution brings the soul closer to God, and gets further in him, and brings fresh strength from him; which if we neglect, our corruption joining with outward hindrances will carry us further and further backward, and this will double, yea, multiply our trouble and grief to recover ourselves again; we have both wind and tide against us; we are going up the hill, and therefore had need to arm ourselves with resolution. Since the fall, the motion of the soul upward, as of heavy bodies, is violent; in regard of corruption which weighs it downward, and therefore all enforcement is little enough: oppose therefore with David all invincible resolution, and then doubt not of prevailing; if we resolve in God's power and not our own, and be *strong in the Lord*, Eph. vi. 10, and not in ourselves, then it matters not what our troubles or temptations be either from within, or without, for *trust in God* at length will triumph.

Here is a great mercy, that when David had a little let go his hold of God, yet God would not let go his hold of him, but by a spirit of faith draws him back again to himself; God *turns us* into him, and then we return. *Turn us again*, saith the Psalmist, *cause thy face to shine upon us and we shall be saved.* Psalm lxxx. 19. When the soul leaves God once, it loses its way, and itself; and never returns till God recalls it again. If moral principles, cherished and strengthened by good education, will enable the soul against vicious inclinations, so that though some influence of the heavens work upon the air, and the air upon the spirits, and the spirits upon the humours, and these incline the temper, and that inclines the soul of a man such and such ways, yet breeding in the more refined sort of civil persons, will much prevail to draw them another way; what then may we think of this powerful grace of faith which is altogether supernatural? Will not this carry the soul above all natural inclinations whatsoever (though strengthened by outward occasions), if we resolve to put it to it. David was a king of other men, but here he shows that he was a king of himself. What benefit is it for a man to be ruler over all the world, and yet remain a slave to himself?

§ IX. 8. Again, David here doth not only *resolve*, but *presently takes up his soul before it strayed too far from God;* the further and the longer the soul wanders from God, the more it entangles itself, and the thicker darkness will cover the soul, yea, the loather it is come to God again, being ashamed to look God in the face after discontinuing of acquaintance with him; nay, the stronger the league grows betwixt sin and the soul, and the more there groweth a kind of suitableness betwixt the soul and sin; too long giving way to base thoughts and affections, discovers too much complacency and liking of sin. If we once give way, a little grief will turn into bitter sorrow, and that into a settled pensiveness and *heaviness of spirit, fear* will grow into *astonishment,* and *discouragement* into *despair;* if ever we mean to trust God, why not now? How many are taken away in their offers and essays, before they have prepared their hearts to cleave unto God? The sooner we give up ourselves to the Lord, the sooner we know upon what terms we stand, and the sooner we provide for our best security, and have not our grounds of comfort to seek when we shall stand most in need of them. Time will salve up grief in the meanest of men; reason in those that will suffer themselves to be ruled thereby, will cure, or at least stay the fits of it sooner: but faith if we stir it up, will give our souls no rest, until it hath brought us to our true rest, that is to God: therefore we should press the heart forward to God present, that Satan make not the rent greater.

Lastly, here we see, that *though the soul be overborne by passion for a time, yet if grace hath once truly seasoned it, it will work itself into freedom again;* grace as oil will be above. The eye when any dust falls into it, is not more tender and unquiet, till it be wrought out again, than a gracious soul is being once troubled: the spirit as a spring will be cleansing of itself more and more; whereas the heart of a carnal man is like a standing pool, whatsoever is cast into it, there it rests: trouble and disquietness in him are in their proper place; it is proper for the sea to rage and cast up dirt; God hath set it down for an eternal rule, that vexation and sin shall be inseparable. Happiness and rest were severed from sin in heaven when the angels fell, and in Paradise when Adam fell, and will remain for ever separated, until the breach be made up by faith in Christ. Gen. iii.

CHAPTER XVI.

OF TRUST IN GOD: GROUNDS OF IT; ESPECIALLY HIS PROVIDENCE.

BUT to come nearer to the unfolding of this trusting in God, which David useth here as a remedy against all distempers: Howsoever confidence and trust be an affection of nature, yet by the Spirit's sanctifying and carrying it to the *right object*, it becomes a grace of wonderful use. In the things of this life usually he that hopes most is the most unwise man; he being most deceived that hopes most, because he trusts in that which is uncertain, and therefore deceitful hope is counted but the dream of a waking man. But in religion it is far otherwise; here, hope is the main supporting grace of the soul, springing from faith in the promises of God.

Trust and hope are often taken in the same sense, though a distinction betwixt them hath sometimes its use: faith looks to the word promising, hope to the thing promised in the word; faith looks to the authority of the promiser, hope (especially) to the goodness of the promise; faith looks upon things as present, hope as to come hereafter. God as the first truth is that which faith relies on, but God as the chief good is that which hope rests on: trust or confidence is nothing else, but the strength of hope; if the thing hoped for be deferred, then of necessity it enforces waiting, and waiting is nothing else but hope and trust lengthened.

Howsoever there may be use of these and such like distinctions, yet usually they are taken promiscuously, especially in the Old Testament. The nature and use of faith is set out by terms of *staying, resting, leaning, rolling ourselves upon God*, &c., which come all to one, and therefore we forbear any further curious distinction.

Now seeing trusting in God is a remedy against all distempers, it is necessary that we should bring the

object and the act (God and the soul) together; for
effecting of which it is good to know something concerning God and something concerning trust. God
is only the fit object of trust, he hath all the properties of that which should be trusted on; a man can
be in no condition wherein God is at a loss and cannot help him; if comforts be wanting, he can create
comforts, not only out of nothing but out of discomforts;
he made the whale that swallowed up Jonas a means
to bring him to the shore. *Jonah* i. 17. The sea was
a wall to the Israelites on both sides: the devouring
flames were a great refreshing to *the three children
in the fiery furnace*, Dan. iii.; that trouble which we
think will swallow us up, may be a means to bring us
to our haven; *so mighty is God in power, and so excellent in working.* Isaiah xxviii. 29. God then, and
God only is a fit foundation for the soul to build itself
upon, for the firmer the foundation is, the stronger
will the building be, therefore those that will build
high must dig deep: the higher the tree riseth, the
deeper the root spreadeth and fasteneth itself below.
So it is in faith, if the foundation thereof be not firm,
the soul cannot build itself strongly upon it; faith
hath a double principle to build on, either a principle
of being, or a principle of knowing; the principle of
being is God himself, the principle of knowing is God's
word, whereby God cometh forth (*out of that hidden
light which none can attain unto*) and discovereth
his meaning towards us for our good.

This then must, 1. be supposed for a ground, *that
there is a God*, and that God is, that is, hath a full
and eternal being and giveth a being, and an order of
being, to all things else; some things have only a
being, some things life and being, some things sense,
&c. and some things have a more *excellent being*, in-
cluding all the former, as the being of creatures indued
with reason; if God had not a being, nothing else
could be: in things subordinate one to another, take
away the first, and you take away all the rest: therefore this proposition (God is) is the first truth of all,
and if this were not, nothing else should be: as we

10

see if the heavenly bodies do not move, there is no motion here below.

2. In the divine nature or being, there is a subsisting of three persons, every one to set out unto us, as fitted for us to *trust in;* the *Father* as a *Creator,* the *Son* as a *Redeemer,* the *Holy Ghost* as a *Comforter,* and all this in reference to us: God in the first person hath decreed the great work of our salvation, and all things tending to the accomplishment of it: God in the *second person* hath exactly and fully answered that decree and plot, in the work of our redemption; God in the *third person* discovers and applies all unto us, and fits us for communion with the Father and the Son from whom he proceeds.

3. GOD cannot be comfortably thought upon out of Christ our Mediator, in whom he was *reconciling the world to himself,* 1 Cor. v. 19, as being a friend both to God and us, and therefore fit to bring God and the soul together, being a middle person in the Trinity; in Christ God's nature becomes lovely to us, and ours to God: otherwise there is an utter enmity betwixt his pure and our impure nature: Christ hath made up the vast gulf between God and us; there is nothing more terrible to think on, than an absolute God out of Christ.

4. Therefore for the better drawing of us to trust in God, we must conceive of him under the sweet relation of a father; God's nature is fatherly now unto us, and therefore lovely.

5. And for further strengthening our faith it is needful to consider what excellence the Scripture giveth unto God, answerable to all our necessities, what sweet names God is pleased to be known unto us by for our comfort, *as a merciful, gracious, long-suffering God,* &c. Exod. xxxiv. 6.

When Moses desired to see the glory of God, God thus manifested himself, in the way of goodness, *I will make all my goodness pass before thee.* Exod. xxxiii. 16.

Whatsoever is good in the creature is first in God as a fountain; and it is in God in a more eminent

manner and fuller measure. All grace and holiness,
all sweetness of affection, all power and wisdom, &c.
as it is in him, so it is from him, and we come to conceive these properties to be in God, 1. by feeling the
comfort and power of them in ourselves; 2. by observing these things in their measure to be in the
best of the creatures, whence we arise to take notice
of what grace and what love, what strength and wisdom, &c. is in God, by the beams of these which
we see in his creature, with adding in our thoughts
fulness peculiar to God, and abstracting imperfection,
incident to the creature; for that is in God in the
highest degree, the sparkles whereof are in us.

6. Therefore is it fit that unto all other eminences
in God, we should strengthen our faith by considering
those glorious singularities, which are altogether in-
communicable to the creature, and which give strength
to his other properties, as that God is not only *gracious* and *loving, powerful, wise,* &c., but that he is
infinitely, eternally, and unchangeably so. All which
are comprised in and drawn from that one name Je-
hovah, as being of himself, and giving a being to all
things else, of nothing; and able when it pleaseth
him to turn all things to nothing again.

7. As God is thus, so he makes it good by answerable actions and dealing towards us, by his continual
providence; the consideration whereof is a great stay
to our faith, for by this providence God makes use of
all his former excellencies for his people's good: for the
more comfortable apprehension of which it is good to
know that God's providence is extended as far as his
creation. Every creature, in every element and place
whatsoever, receiveth a powerful influence from God,
who doth what pleaseth him, both in *Heaven and earth,
in the sea, and all places;* but we must know, God
doth not put things into a frame, and then leave them
to their own motion, as we do clocks, after we have
once set them right, and ships after we have once
built them, commit them to wind and waves; but
as he made all things, and knows all things, so, by a

continued kind of creation, he preserves all things in their being and working, and governs them to their ends; he is the first mover that sets all the wheels of the creature working: one wheel may move another, but all are moved by the first. If God moves not, the clock of the creature stands. If God should not uphold things, they would presently fall (to nothing) from whence they came. If God should not guide things, Satan's malice, and man's weakness would soon bring all to confusion. If God did not rule the great family of the world, all would break and fall to pieces, whereas the wise providence of God keepeth every thing on its right hinges. All things stand in obedience to this providence of God, and nothing can withdraw itself from under it; if the creature withdraw itself from one order of providence, it falls into another; if man (the most unruly and disordered creature of all) withdraw himself from God's gracious government of him to happiness, he will soon fall under God's just government of him to deserved misery; if he shakes off God's sweet yoke, he puts himself under Satan's heavy yoke, who, as God's executioner, hardens him to destruction; and so whilst he rushes against God's will he fulfils it. And whilst he will not willingly do God's will, God's will is done upon him against his will.

The most casual things fall under providence, yea, the most disordered thing in the world, sin, and (of sins the most horrible that ever the sun beheld) *the crucifying of the Lord of life*, was guided by a hand of providence to the greatest good. For that which is casual in regard of a second cause, is not so in regard of the first, whose providence is most clearly seen in casual events that fall out by accident, for in these the effect cannot be ascribed to the next cause; God is said to kill him, who was unwarily slain by the falling of an axe or some instrument of death. Deut. xix. 5.

And though man hath a freedom in working, and of all men, the hearts of *kings* are most free, yet even these are *guided by an overruling power*, Prov. xxi.

1, as the rivers of water are carried in their channels, whither skilful men list to lead them.

For settling of our faith the more, God taketh liberty in using weak means, to great purposes, and setting aside more likely and able means, yea, sometimes he altogether disableth the greatest means, and worketh often by no means at all. It is not for want of power in God, but from abundance and multiplying of his goodness that he useth any means at all! there is nothing that he doth by means, but he is able to do without means.

Nay, God often bringeth his will to pass by crossing the course and stream of means, to show his own sovereignty, and to exercise our dependence; and maketh his very enemies, the accomplishers of his own will, and so, to bring about that which they oppose most. Hence it is that we believe under hope against hope. Psalm cxxxv. 6.

But we must know, God's manner of guiding things is without prejudice of the proper working of the things themselves; he guideth them sweetly according to the instincts he hath put into them; for,

1. He furnishes creatures with a virtue and power to work, and likewise with a manner of working suitable to their own nature, as it is proper for a man when he works, to work with freedom, and other creatures by natural instinct, &c.

2. God maintaineth both the power and manner of working, and perfecteth and accomplisheth the same by acting of it, being nearer to us in all we do, than we are to ourselves. 3. He applies and stirs up our abilities and actions, to this or that particular, as he seeth best. 4. He suspends or removes the hinderances of all actions, and so, powerfully, wisely, and sweetly orders them to his own ends. When any evil is intended, God either puts bars and lets to the execution of it, or else limiteth and boundeth the same, both in regard of time and measure, so that our enemies either shall not do the evil at all, or else not so long a time, or not in such a height of mischief, as their malice would carry them to: *the rod of the*

wicked may light *upon the back of the righteous,*
Psal. cxxv. 3, but it shall *not rest* there; God knows
how to take our enemies off, sometimes by changing,
or stopping their wills, by offering considerations of
some good or ill, danger or profit to them; sometimes
by taking away, and weakening all their strength, or
else by opposing an equal or greater strength against
it.   All the strength our enemies have rests in God:
who if he denies concourse and influence, the arm of
their power (as Jeroboam's, when he stretched it out
against the prophet) shrinks up presently.

God is not only the cause of things and actions,
but the cause likewise of the cessation of them, why
they fall not out at all.   God is the cause why things
are not, as well as why they are; the cause why men
favour us not, or, when they do favour us, want present wisdom and ability to help us, is from God's
withdrawing the concurrence of his light and strength
from them.   If a skilful physician does us no good, it
is because it pleaseth God to hide the right way of
curing at that time from him.   Which should move
us to see God in all that befalls us, who hath sufficient reason, as to do what he doth, so not to do
what he doth not, to hinder, as well as to give way.

The God of spirits hath an influence into the spirits
of men, into the principles and springs of all actions;
otherwise he could not so certainly foretell things to
come.   God had a work in Absalom's heart in that
he refused the best counsel; there is nothing independent of him, who is the mover of all things, and
himself unmoveable.

Nothing so high that is above his providence; nothing so low, that is beneath it; nothing so large, but
· is bounded by it; nothing so confused, but God can
order it; nothing so bad, but he can draw good out of
it; nothing so wisely plotted, but God can disappoint
it, as Ahitophel's counsel; nothing so simply and un-
politically carried, but he can give a prevailing issue
unto it; nothing so freely carried, in regard of the
next cause, but God can make it necessary in regard
of the event; nothing so natural, but he can suspend it

in regard of operation, as heavy bodies from sinking, fire from burning, &c.

It cannot but bring strong security to the soul, to know that in all variety of changes and intercourse good and bad events, God and our God, hath such a disposing hand. Whatsoever befalls us, all serves to bring God's electing love, and our glorification together, God's providence serveth his purpose to save us. All sufferings, all blessings, all ordinances, all graces, all common gifts, nay, our very falls, yea, Satan himself with all his instruments, as over-mastered, and ruled by God, have this injunction upon them to further God's good intendment to us and a prohibition to do us no harm. Augustus taxed the world for civil ends, but God's providence used this as a means for Christ to be born at Bethlehem. Esther vi. 1. Ahasuerus could not sleep, and thereupon calls for the chronicles, the reading of which occasioned the Jews' delivery. God oft disposeth little occasions to great purposes. And by those very ways whereby proud men have gone about to withstand God's counsels, they have fulfilled them, as we see in the story of Joseph and Moses, *in the thing wherein they dealt proudly*, He *was above them*. Exod. x. 11.

CHAPTER XVII.

OF GRACES TO BE EXERCISED IN RESPECT OF DIVINE PROVIDENCE.

WE are under a providence that is above our own; which should be a ground unto us, of exercising those graces that tend to settle the soul in all events. As,

1. Hence to lay our hand upon our mouths, and command the soul an holy silence, not daring to yield to the least rising of our hearts against God. *I was dumb, and opened not my mouth, because thou didst it*, Psalm xxxix. 9, saith David. Thus Aaron when he had lost his two sons, both at once, and that by fire, Lev. x. 1, 2, and by fire from heaven, which carried an evidence of God's great displeasure with

it, yet *held his peace.* In this *silence* and *hope* is *our strength.* Flesh and blood is prone to expostulate with God, and to question his dealing, as we see in Gideon, Jeremy, Asaph, Habakuk, and others, *If the Lord be with us, why then is all this befallen us?* but after some struggling between the flesh and the spirit the conclusion will be, yet howsoever matters go, *God is good to Israel.* Psalm lxxiii. 1. Where a fearful spirit, and a melancholy temper, a weak judgment, and a scrupulous and raw conscience meet in one, there Satan and his, together with men's own hearts, which like sophisters are continually cavilling against themselves, breed much disquiet, and make the life uncomfortable. Such therefore should have a special care as to grow in knowledge, so to stick close to sure and certain grounds, and bring their consciences to the rule. Darkness causeth fears. The more light, the more confidence. When we yield up ourselves to God, we should resolve upon quietness, and if the heart stirs, presently use this check of David, *Why art thou disquieted?*

God's ways seem oft to us full of contradictions, because his course is to bring things to pass by contrary means. There is a mystery not only in God's decree concerning man's eternal estate, but likewise in his providence, as why he should deal unequally with men, otherwise equal. His judgments are a great depth, which we cannot fathom, but they will swallow up our thoughts and understandings. God oft wraps himself in a cloud, and will not be seen till afterward. Where we cannot trace him, we ought with Saint Paul to admire and adore him. When we are in heaven, it will be one part of our happiness, to see the harmony of those things that seem now confused unto us. All God's dealings will appear beautiful in their due seasons, though we for the present see not the contiguity and linking together of one thing with another.

2. Hence likewise proceeds a holy resigning of ourselves to God, *who doth all things according to the counsel of his own will.* His will is a wise will, it

is guided by counsel, a sovereign prevailing will. The only way to have our will is to bring it to God's will. *If we could delight in him, we should have our heart's desire.* Thus David yields up himself to God; *Here I am, let the Lord deal with me as seemeth good unto him.* 2 Sam. xv. 26. And thus Eli, when God foretold by Samuel the ruin of his house, quiets himself, *It is the Lord, let him do what seemeth him good.* 1 Sam. iii. 18. Thus our blessed Saviour stays himself, *Not my will, but thy will be done.* And thus the people of God, when Paul was resolved to go to Jerusalem, submitted, saying, *The will of the Lord be done,* Acts xxi. 14; a speech fit to proceed out of the heart and mouth of a Christian.

We may desire and long after a change of our condition, when we look upon the grievance itself, but yet remember still that it be with reservation, when we look upon the will of God, as, *How long, Lord, holy and true,* &c. Rev. vi. 10. Out of inferior reasons we may with our Saviour desire a removal of the cup; but when we look to the supreme reason of reasons, the will of God, here we must stoop and kiss the rod. *Thus humbling ourselves under his mighty hand,* which by murmuring and fretting we may make more heavy, but not take off, still adding new guilt and pulling on new judgments.

3. The way patiently to suffer God's will, is to inure ourselves first to do it. Passive obedience springs from active. He that endures any thing will endure it quietly, when he knows it is the will of God, and considers that whatever befalls him comes from his good pleasure. Those that have not inured themselves to the yoke of obedience, will never endure the yoke of suffering, they fume and rage, *as a wild boar in a net,* as the prophet speaks. It is worth the considering, to see two men of equal parts under the same cross, how quietly and calmly the one that establisheth his soul on Christ will bear his afflictions, whereas the other rageth as a fool, and is more beaten.

Nothing should displease us that pleaseth God;

neither should any thing be pleasing to us that displeaseth him. This conformity is the ground of comfort. Our own will takes away God, as much as in it lies. *If we acknowledge God in all our ways, he will direct our paths, and lead us in the way that we should go.* Prov. iii. 6. The quarrel betwixt God and us is taken up, when his will and our will are one ; when we have sacrificed ourselves, and our wills unto God; when, as he is highest in himself, so his will hath the highest place in our hearts. We find by experience, that when our wills are so subdued, that we delight to do what God would have us do, and to be what God would have us be, that then sweet peace presently riseth to the soul.

When we can say, Lord, if thou wilt have me poor and disgraced, I am content to be so : if thou wilt have me serve thee in this condition I am in, I will gladly do so. It is enough to me that thou wouldst have it so. I desire to yield readily, humbly, and cheerfully, to thy disposing providence. Thus a godly man says *Amen* to God's *Amen*, and puts his *fiat* and *placet* to God's. As the sea turns all rivers into its own relish, so he turns all to his own spirit, and makes whatsoever befalls him an exercise of some virtue. A heathen could say, that calamities did rule over men, but a wise man hath a spirit overruling all calamities; much more a Christian. For a man to be in this estate is to enjoy heaven *in the world* under heaven ; God's *kingdom comes* where *his will is thus done* and suffered.

None feel more sweet experience of God's providence than those that are most resolute in their obedience. After we have given glory to God in relying upon his wisdom, power, and truth, we shall find him employing these for our direction, assistance, and bringing about of things to our desired issue, yea, above whatever we looked for, or thought of.

In all cases that fall out, or that we can put to ourselves, as in case of extremity, opposition, strange accidents, desertion, and damps of spirit, &c. here we may take sanctuary, that we are in covenant with him who sits at the stern, and rules all, and hath committed the government of all things to his Son, our brother, our Joseph, the second person in heaven. We may be sure no hurt shall befall us, that he can hinder; and what cannot he hinder *that hath the keys of hell and of death?* unto whom we are so near that he carries *our names in his breast, and on his shoulders,* as the high priest did those of the twelve tribes. Though his church seems a widow neglected, yet he will make the world know that she hath a husband who will right her in his good time.

But it may be demanded, What course is to be taken for guidance of our lives in particular actions, wherein doubts may arise what is most agreeable to the will of God?

1. We must not put all carelessly upon a providence but first consider what is our part, and so far as God prevents us with light, and affords us helps and means, we must not be failing in our duty. We should neither outrun, nor be wanting to providence. But in perplexed cases, where the reasons on both sides seem to be equally balanced, see whether part make more for the main end, the glory of God, the service of others, and advancement of our own spiritual good. Some things are so clear and even, that there is not a best between them, but one may be done as well as the other, as when two ways equally tend to one and the same place.

2. We are *not our own,* and therefore must not set up ourselves. We must not consult with flesh and blood either in ourselves or others, for self-love will deprave all our actions, by setting before us corrupt ends. It considers not what is best, but what is safest. By-respects sway the balance the wrong way.

3. When things are clear, and God's will is manifest, further deliberation is dangerous, and for the most part argues a false heart; as we see in Balaam, who though he knew God's mind, yet would be still consulting, till God in judgment gave him up to what his covetous heart led him unto. A man is not fit to deliberate till his heart be purged of false aims; for

else God will give him to the darkness of his own spirit, and he will be always warping, unfit for any bias. Where the aims are good, there God delighteth to reveal his good pleasure. Such a soul is level and suitable to any good counsel that shall be given, and prepared to entertain it. In what measure any lust is favoured, in that measure the soul is darkened. Even wise Solomon, whilst he gave way to his lust, had like to have lost his wisdom.

We must look to our place wherein God hath set us; if we be in subjection to others, their authority ought to sway with us. Neither is it the calling of those that are subjects, to inquire over curiously into the mysteries of government; for that, both in peace and war, breeds much disturbance, and would trouble all designs.

The laws under which we live, are particular determinations of the law of God in some duties of the second table. For example; the law of God says, *Exact no more than what is thy due.* But what in particular is thy due, and what another man's, the laws of men determine, and therefore ought to be a rule unto us so far as they reach; though it be too narrow a rule to be good only so far as man's laws guide unto. Yet law being the joint reason and consent of many men for public good, hath a use for guidance of all actions that fall under the same. Where it conflicts not against God's law, what is agreeable to law, is agreeable to conscience.

The law of God in the due enlargement of it, to the least beginning and occasions, is exceeding broad, and allows of whatsoever stands with the light of reason, or the bonds of humanity, civility, &c., and whatsoever is against these is so far against God's law. So that higher rules be looked to in the first place, there is nothing lovely or praiseworthy among men, but ought to be seriously thought on.

Nature of itself is wild and untamed, and impatient of the yoke; but as beasts that cannot endure the yoke at first, after they are inured awhile unto it bear it willingly, and carry their work more easily by it;

so the yoke of obedience makes the life regular and quiet. The meeting of authority and obedience together maintains the order and peace of the world.

So of that question.

Though blindfold obedience, such as our adversaries would have, be such as will never stand with sound peace of conscience, which always looks to have light to direct it (for else a blind conscience would breed blind fears); yet in such doubtful cases wherein we cannot wind out ourselves, we ought to light our candles at others whom we have cause to think by their place and parts should see further than we. In matters of outward estate, we will have men skilful, of our counsel; and Christians would find more sound peace, if they would advise with their godly and learned pastors and friends. Where there is not a direct word, there is place for the counsel of a prudent man. And it is a happiness for them whose business is much, and parts not large, to have the benefit of those that can give aim, and see further than themselves. The meanest Christian understands his own way, and knows how to do things with better advantage to his soul than a graceless though learned man; yet is still glad of further discovery. In counsel there is peace, the thoughts being thus established.

When we have advised and served God's providence in the use of means, then if it fall out otherwise than we look for, we may confidently conclude, that God would not have it so, otherwise to our grief we may say, it was the fruit of our own rashness.

Where we have cause to think that we have used better means in the search of grounds, and are more free from partial affections than others, there we may use our own advice more safely. Otherwise what we do by consent from others, is more secure and less offensive, as being more countenanced.

In advice with others, it is not sufficient to be generally wise, but experienced and knowing in that we ask, which is an honour to God's gifts where we find them in any kind. When we set about things in passion, we work not as men or Christians, but in a bestial manner. The more passion, the less discretion; because passion hinders the sight of what is to be done. It clouds the soul, and puts it on to action without advisement. Where passions are subdued, and the soul purged and cleared, there is nothing to hinder the impression of God's Spirit; the soul is fitted as a clean glass to receive light from above. And that is the reason why *mortified men are fittest* to advise with in the particular cases incident to a Christian life.

After all advice, extract what is fittest, and what our spirits do most bend unto: for in things that concern ourselves, God affords a light to discern out of what is spoken, what best suiteth us. And every man is to follow most what his own conscience (after information) dictates unto him; because conscience is God's deputy in us, and under God most to be regarded, and whosoever sins against it, in his own construction sins against God. God vouchsafeth every Christian in some degree, the grace of *spiritual prudence*, whereby they are enabled to discern what is fittest to be done in things that fall within their compass.

It is good to observe the particular becks of providence, how things join and meet together: fit occasions and suiting of things are intimations of God's will. Providence hath a language which is well understood by those that have a familiar acquaintance with God's dealing, they see a train of providence, leading one way more than to another.

Take especial heed of not grieving the Spirit, when he offers to be our guide, by studying evasions, and wishing the case were otherwise. This is to be lawgivers to ourselves, thinking that we are wiser than God, the use of discretion is not to direct us about the end, whether we should do well or ill (for a single heart always aims at good); but when we resolve upon doing well, and yet doubt of the manner how to perform it, discretion looks not so much to what is lawful (for that is taken for granted), but what is most expedient. A discreet man looks not to what is best, so much as to what is fittest in such and such respects, by eyeing circumstances, which, if they sort not, do vary the nature of the thing itself.

And because it is not in man to know his own ways, we should look up unto Christ, the great Counsellor of his Church, to vouchsafe the spirit of counsel and direction to us; that may *make our way plain before us*, by suggesting unto us, *this is the way, walk in it*. We owe God this respect, to depend upon him for direction in the particular passages of our lives, in regard that he is our sovereign, and his will is the rule, and we are to be accountable to him as our judge. It is God only that can see through businesses, and all helps and lets that stand about.

After we have rolled ourselves upon God, we should immediately take that course he inclines our hearts unto, without further distracting fear. Otherwise it is a sign we *commit not our way to him*, when we do not quietly trust him, but remain still as thoughtful, as if we did not trust him. After *prayer* and *trust* follows *the peace of God*, Phil. ii. 4, and a heart void of further dividing care. We should therefore presently question our hearts, for questioning his care, and not regard what fear will be ready to suggest, for that is apt to raise conclusions against ourselves, out of self-conceited grounds, whereby we usurp upon God, and wrong ourselves.

It was a good resolution of the three young men in Daniel, *We are not careful to answer thee, O king.* Dan. iii. We know our duty, let God do with us as he pleaseth. If Abraham had hearkened to the voice of nature, he would never have resolved to sacrifice Isaac, but because he cast himself upon God's providing, God in the mount provided a ram instead of his son.

CHAPTER XVIII.

OTHER GROUNDS OF TRUSTING IN GOD: NAMELY, THE PROMISES—AND
TWELVE DIRECTIONS ABOUT THE SAME.

§ I. BUT for the better settling of *our trust in God*,
a further discovery is necessary than of the nature
and providence of God; for though the nature of
God be written in the book of the creatures in so
great letters, as he that runs may read; and though
the providence of God appears in the order and use
of things: yet there is another book whereby to
know the will of God towards us, and our duty towards him: we must therefore have a knowledge of
the promises of God, as well as of his providence, for
though God hath discovered himself most graciously
in Christ unto us, yet had we not a word of promise,
we could not have the boldness to build upon Christ
himself; therefore, from the same grounds, *that there
is a God,* there must be a revealing of the will of God,
for else we can never have any firm *trust in him* further than he offers himself to be trusted; therefore
hath God opened his heart to us in his word, and
reached out so many sweet promises for us to lay hold
on, and stooped so low, by gracious condescending
mixed with authority, as to enter into a covenant
with us to perform all things for our good: for promises are, as it were, the stay of the soul in an imperfect condition, and so is faith in them until all
promises shall end in performance, and faith in sight,
and hope in possession.

Now these promises are, 1. for their *spring* from
whence they proceed, *free engagements of God;* for
if he had not bound himself, who could? and 2. they
are for their value precious; and 3. for their extent
large, even of all things that conduce to happiness;
and 4. for their virtue quickening and strengthening
the soul, as coming from the love of God, and convey-
ing that love unto us by his Spirit in the best fruits
thereof; and 5. for their certainty, they are as sure as

the love of God in Christ is, upon which they are founded, and from which *nothing can separate us,* Rom. viii. 39. For all promises are either Christ himself, *the promised seed,* or else they are of good things made to us in him and for him, and accomplished for his sake; they are all made first to him as *heir of the promise,* as *Angel of the Covenant,* as *head* of his body, and as our elder brother, &c., for promises being the fruits of God's love, and God's love being founded first on Christ, it must needs follow that all the promises are both made, and made good to us in and through him, who is *yesterday and to-day, and for ever the same.* Heb. xiii. 8.

That we should not call God's love into question, he not only gives us his word, but a binding word, his promise; and not only a naked promise, but hath entered into covenant with us, founded upon full satisfaction by the blood of Christ, and unto this covenant *sealed by the blood of the Lord Jesus,* he hath added the seals of sacraments, and unto this he hath added his oath, that there might be no place left of doubting to the distrustful heart of man; there is no way of securing promises amongst men, but God hath taken the same to himself, and all to this end that we might not only know his mind towards us, but be fully persuaded of it, that as verily as he lives, he will make good whatever he hath promised for the comfort of his children. What greater assurance can there be, than for being itself to lay his being to pawn? and for life itself to lay life to pawn, and all to comfort a poor soul?

The boundless and restless desire of man's spirit will never be stayed without some discovery of the chief good, and the way to attain the same: men would have been in darkness about their final condition, and the way to please God, and to pacify and purge their consciences, had not the word of God set down the spring and cause of all evil, together with the cure of it, and directed us how to have communion with God, and to raise ourselves above all the evil which we meet withal betwixt us and happiness, and to make us every way *wise to salvation*. Hence it is that the psalmist prefers the manifestation of God by his word, before the manifestation of him in his most glorious works. *Psalm* xix. 7.

And thus we see the necessity of a double principle for faith to rely on: 1. God, and 2. the word of God revealing his will unto us, and directing us to make use of all his attributes, relations, and providence for our good; and this word hath its strength from him who gives a being and an accomplishment unto it; for words are as the authority of him that uttereth them is; when we look upon a grant in the word of a king, it stays our minds, because we know he is able t make it good; and why should it not satisfy our souls to look upon promises in the word of a God? whose words, as they come from his truth and express his goodness, so they are all made good by his power and wisdom.

By the bare word of God it is that the heavens continue, and the earth (without any other foundation) hangs in the midst of the world, therefore well may the soul stay itself on that, even when it hath nothing else in sight to rely upon; by his word it is that the covenant of day and night, and the preservation of the world from any further *overflowing of waters* continueth; which if it should fail, yet his covenant with his people shall abide firm for ever, though the whole frame of nature were dissolved.

When we have thus gotten a fit foundation for the soul to lay itself upon, our next care must be (by trusting) to build on the same; all our misery is either in having a false foundation, or else in loose building upon a true; therefore having so strong a ground as God's nature, his providence, his promise, &c., to build upon, the only way for establishing our souls is, *by trust*, to rely firmly on him.

Now the reason why trust is so much required, is because 1. it emptieth the soul, and 2. by emptying enlargeth it, and 3. seasoneth and fitteth the soul to join with so gracious an object, and 4. filleth it by carrying it out of itself unto God, who presently, so soon as he is trusted in, conveys himself and his goodness to the soul; and thus we come to have the comfort, and God the glory of all his excellencies. Thus salvation comes to be sure unto us, whilst faith, looking to the promises, and to God freely offering grace therein, resigns up itself to God, making no further question from any unworthiness of its own.

And thus we return to God by cleaving to him, from whom we fell by distrust, living under a new covenant merely of grace, Jer. xxxi. 3; and no grace fitter than that which gives all to Christ, considering the fountain of all our good is (out of ourselves) in him, it being safest for us, who were so ill husbands at the first, that it should be so, therefore it is fit we should have use of such a grace that will carry us out of ourselves to the spring head.

The way then whereby faith quieteth the soul, is by raising it above all discontentments and storms here below, and pitching it upon God, thereby uniting it to him, whence it draws virtue to oppose and bring under whatsoever troubles its peace. For the soul is made for God, and never finds rest till it returns to him again; when God and the soul meet, there will follow contentment; God, simply considered, is not all our happiness, but God as trusted in; and Christ as we are made *one with him*, Matt. ix. 20; the soul cannot so much as *touch the hem of Christ's garment*, but it shall find *virtue coming from him* to sanctify and settle it; God in Christ is full of all that is good; when the soul is emptied, enlarged, and opened by faith to receive goodness offered, there must needs follow sweet satisfaction.

§ II. For the better strengthening of our trust it is not sufficient that we trust in God and his truth revealed, but we must do it by light and strength from him; many believe in the truth by human arguments, but no arguments will convince the soul but such as are fetched from the inward nature, and powerful work of truth itself; no man can know God, but by God; none can know the sun, but by its own light; none can know the truth of God (so as to build upon it) but by the truth itself and the Spirit revealing it by its own light to the soul; that soul which hath felt the power of truth in casting it down, and raising it up again, will easily be brought to rest upon it; it is neither education, nor the authority of others that professes the same truth, or that we have been so taught by men of great parts, &c., will settle the heart; until we find an inward power and authority in the truth itself shining in our hearts by its own beams; hence comes unsettledness in time of troubles, because we have not a *spiritual discerning* of spiritual things.   Supernatural truths must have a supernatural power to apprehend them, therefore God createth a spiritual eye and hand of the soul, which is faith.

In those that are truly converted, all *saving truths* are transcribed out of the Scripture into their hearts, *they are taught of God,* Isa. liv. 13; so as they find all truths both concerning the sinful estate, and the gracious and happy estate of man in themselves; they carry a divinity in them and about them, so as from a saving feeling they can speak of conversion, of sin, of grace, and the comforts of the Spirit, &c., and from this acquaintance are ready to yield and give up themselves to truth revealed and to God speaking by it.   Trust is never sound but upon a spiritual conviction of the truth and goodness we rely upon, for the effecting of which the Spirit of God must likewise subdue the rebellion and malice of our will, that so it may be suitable and level to divine things, and relish them as they are; we must apprehend the love of God and the fruits of it as better than life itself, and then choosing and cleaving to the same will soon follow; for as there is a fitness in divine truths to all the necessities of the soul, so the soul must be fitted by them to savour and apply them to itself; and then from a harmony between the soul and that which it applies itself unto, there will follow not only peace in the soul, but joy and delight surpassing any contentment in the world besides.

As there is that in God to satisfy the whole soul, so trust carries the whole soul to God; this makes trust not so easy a matter, because there must be an exercise of every faculty of the soul, or else our trust is imperfect and lame, there must be a knowledge of him whom we trust, and why we trust and love, &c. Only *they that know God will trust in him;* not that knowledge alone is sufficient, but because the sweetness of God's love is let into the soul thereby, which draweth the whole soul to him; we are bidden to *trust perfectly in God;* therefore seeing we have a God so full of perfection to trust in, we should labour to trust perfectly in him.

And it is good for the exercise of trust to put cases to ourselves of things that probably may fall out, and then return to our souls to search what strength we have if such things should come to pass; thus David puts cases; perfect faith dares put the hardest cases to its soul, and then set God against all that may befall it. Psalm iii. 6; xlvi. 3; xxvii. 3.

Again, labour to fit the promise to every condition thou art in; there is no condition but hath a promise suitable; therefore no condition but wherein God may be trusted, because his truth and goodness is always the same; and in the promise, look both to the good promised, and to the faithfulness and love of the promiser; it is not good to look upon the difficulty of the thing we have a promise against, but who promiseth it, and for whose sake, and so see all good things in Christ made over to us.

We should labour likewise for a single heart to trust in God only; there is no readier way to fall than to trust equally to two stays, whereof one is rotten, and the other sound; therefore as in point of doctrine we are to rely upon Christ only, and to make the Scriptures our rule only; so in life and conversation, whatever we may make use of, yet we should enjoy and rely upon God only; for either God is trusted alone, or not at all; those that trust to other things with God, trust not him but upon pretence to carry their double minds with less check.

Again, labour that thy soul may answer all the relations wherein it stands to God, by cleaving to him, 1. as a *Father* by trusting on his care, 2. as a *Teacher* by following his direction, 3. as a *Creator* by dependence on him, 4. as a *Husband* by inseparable affection of love to him, 5. as a *Lord* by obedience, &c. And then we may with comfort expect whatsoever good these relations can yield? all which God regarding more our wants and weaknesses, than his own greatness, hath taken upon him. Shall these relations yield comfort from the creature, and not from God himself, in whom they are in their highest perfection? shall God make other fathers and husbands faithful, and not be faithful himself? all our comfort depends upon labouring to make these relations good to our souls.

And as we must wholly and only trust in God, so likewise we must trust him in all conditions and times, for all things that we stand in need of, until that time comes wherein we shall stand in need of nothing: for as the same care of God moved him to save us, and to preserve us in the world till we be put in possession of salvation; so the same faith relies upon God for heaven and all necessary provision till we come thither; it is the office of faith to quiet our souls in all the necessities of this life, and we have continual use of trusting while we are here: for even when we have things, yet God still keeps the blessing of them in his own hands, to hold us in a continual dependence upon him: God trains us up this way, by exercising our trust in lesser matters, to fit us for greater; thus it pleaseth God to keep us in a depending condition until he see his own time; but so good is God that as he intends to give us what we wait for, so will he give us the grace and spirit of faith, to sustain our souls in waiting till we enjoy the same. The unruliness of a natural spirit is never discovered more than when God defers, therefore we should labour the more not to withdraw our attendance from God.

Further, we must know that the condition of a Christian in this life, is not to see what he trusts God for: *he lives by faith, and not by sight:* and yet that there is such a virtue in faith, which makes evi-

dent and present, things to come and unseen: because
God where he gives an eye of faith, gives also a glass
of the word to see things in, and by seeing of them in
the truth and power of him that promiseth, they become present, not only to the understanding to apprehend them, but to the will to rest upon them, and
to the affections to joy in them: it is the nature of
faith to work, when it seeth nothing, and oftentimes
best of all then, because God shows himself more
clearly in his power, wisdom and goodness, at such
times; and so his glory shines most, and faith hath
nothing else to look upon then, whereupon it gathers
all the forces of the soul together, to fasten upon God.

It should therefore be the chief care of a Christian
to strengthen his faith, that so it may answer God's
manner of dealing with him in the worst times; for
God usually (1. that he might perfectly mortify our
confidence in the creature, and 2. that he might the
more endear his favours and make them fresh and
new unto us, and 3. that the glory of deliverance may
be entirely his, without the creatures sharing with
him, and 4. that our faith and obedience may be tried
to the uttermost, and discovered,) suffers his children
to fall into great extremities before he will reach forth
his hand to help them, as in Job's case, &c.   Therefore Christians should much labour their hearts to
trust in God in the deepest extremities that may befall
them, even when no light of comfort appears either
from within or without, yea then (especially) when all
other comforts fail; despair is oft the ground of hope,
Isa. l. 10, when the darkness of the night is thickest,
then the morning begins to dawn; that which (to a
man unacquainted with God's dealings) is a ground
of utter despair, the same (to a man acquainted with
the ways of God) is a rise of exceeding comfort; for
infinite power and goodness can never be at a loss,
neither can faith which looks to that, ever be at a
stand, whence it is that both God and faith work best
alone; in a hopeless estate a Christian will see some
door of hope opened, 1. because God shows himself
nearest to us, when we stand most in need of him;

Help, Lord, for vain is the help of man: God is never more seen than in the mount; He *knows our souls best,* and our souls know him best *in adversity;* Pslam xxxi. 7; then he is most *wonderful in his saints.* 2. Because our prayers then are (strong cries) fervent and frequent; God is sure to hear of us at such a time, which pleaseth him well, as delighting to hear the voice of his beloved.

For our better encouragement in these sad times, and to help our trust in God the more, we should often call to mind the former experiences, which either ourselves or others have had of God's goodness, and make use of the same for our spiritual good; *Our fathers trusted in thee,* saith the head of the church, *and were not confounded;* God's truth and goodness is unchangeable, *he never leaves those that trust in him;* so likewise in our own experiences, we should take notice of God's dealings with us in sundry kinds; how many ways he hath refreshed us, and how good we have found him in our worst times; after we have once tried him and his truth, we may safely trust him; God will stand upon his credit, he never failed any yet, and he will not begin to break with us; if his nature and his word, and his former dealing hath been sure and square, why should our hearts be wavering? *Thy word,* saith the Psalmist, *is very pure* (or tried,) *therefore thy servant loveth it;* the word of God is *as silver tried in the furnace, purified seven times;* it is good therefore to observe and lay up God's dealings; experience is nothing else but a multiplied remembrance of former blessings, which will help to multiply our faith; tried truth and tried faith unto it, sweetly agree and answer one another; it were a course much tending to the quickening of the faith of Christians, if they would communicate one to another their mutual experiences; this hath formerly been the custom of God's people, *Come and hear all ye that fear God, and I will declare what he hath done for my soul;* and David urgeth this as a reason to God for deliverance, that then *the righteous would compass him about,* as rejoicing in

the experience of God's goodness to him; the want
of this makes us upon any new trial to call God's care
and love into question, as if he had never formerly
been good unto us; whereas every experiment of
God's love should refresh our faith upon any fresh
onset; God is so good to his children even in this
world, that he trains them up by daily renewed experiences of his fatherly care; for besides those many
promises of good things to come, he gives us some
evidence and taste of what we believe here; that by
that which we fell we might be strengthend in that
we look for, that so in both (1. sense of what we feel,
and 2. certainty of what we look for) we might have
full support.

But yet we must trust God, as he will be trusted,
(namely, in doing good;) or else we do not trust him
but tempt him. Our commanding of our souls to
trust in God, is but an echo of what God commands
us first; and therefore in the same manner he commands us, we should command ourselves. As God
commands us to trust him in doing good, so should
we *commit our souls to him in well doing,* and trust
him when we are about his own works, and not in
the works of darkness; we may safely expect God in
his ways of mercy, when we are in his ways of obedience; for religion as it is a doctrine of what is to be believed, so it is a doctrine according to godliness; and
the *mysteries of faith are mysteries of godliness,* because they cannot be believed, but they will enforce
a godly conversation; where any true impression of
them is, there is holiness always bred in that soul;
therefore a study of holiness must go jointly together,
with a study of trusting in God; faith looks not only
to promises, but to directions to duty, and breeds in
the soul a liking of whatsoever pleaseth God; there is
a mutual strengthening in things that are good, trusting stirs to duty, and duty strengthens trusting by in-
creasing our liberty and boldness with God.

Again, we must maintain in our souls, a *high esteem* of the grace of *faith;* the very trial whereof is
more precious than gold, 1 Pet. i. 7; what then is the

grace of faith itself, and the promises which it layeth hold on? certainly they transcend in worth whatever may draw us from God; whence it is that the soul sets a high price upon them, and on faith that believes them; it is impossible that any thing in the world should come betwixt the heart and those things, if once we truly lay hold on them, to undermine faith or the comfort we have by it; the heart is never drawn to any sinful vanity, or frighted with any terror or trouble, till faith first loseth the sight and estimation of divine things, and forgets the necessity and excellency of them. Our Saviour, Christ, when he would stir up a desire of *faith*, in his disciples, Luke xvii. 6, showed them the power and excellency of the same; great things stir up faith, and keep it above, and faith keeps the soul that nothing else can take place of abode in it; when the *great things of God* are brought into the heart by faith, what is there in the whole world that can out-bid them? assurance of these things, upon spiritual grounds, overrules both sense and reason, or whatever else prevails with carnal hearts.

CHAPTER XIX.

FAITH TO BE PRIZED, AND OTHER THINGS UNDERVALUED, AT LEAST NOT TO BE TRUSTED TO AS THE CHIEF.

THAT faith may take the better place in the soul and the soul in God, the heart must continually be taught of what little worth all things else are, as reputation, riches, and pleasures, &c.; and to see their nothingness in the word of God, and inexperience of ourselves and others, that so our heart being weaned from these things, may open itself to God, and embrace things of a higher nature; otherwise baser things will be nearer thy soul than faith, and keep possession against it, so that faith will not be suffered to set up a throne in the heart; there must be an unloosing of the heart, as well as a fastening of it, and God helps us in both:

for, besides the word discovering the vanity of all things else out of God, the main scope of God's dealing with his children in any danger or affliction whatsoever, is to embitter all other things but himself unto them: indeed it is the power of God properly which makes the heart to trust, but yet the Spirit of God useth this way to bring all things else out of request with us in comparison of those inestimable good things, which the soul is created, redeemed, and sanctified for; God is very jealous of our trust, and can endure no idol of jealousy to be set up in our hearts. Therefore it behoves us to take notice, not only of the deceitfulness of things, but of the deceitfulness of our hearts in the use of them; our hearts naturally hang loose from God, and are soon ready to join with the creature; now the more we observe our hearts in this, the more we take them off, and labour to set them where they should be placed; for the more we know these things, the less we shall trust them.

But may we not trust in riches, and friends, and other outward helps at all?

Yes, so far as they are subordinate to God, our chief stay, with reservation and submission to the Lord: only so far, and so long as it shall please him to use them for our good. Because God ordinarily conveys his help and goodness to us by some creature; we must trust in God to bless every mercy we enjoy, and to make all helps serviceable to his love towards us. In a word, we must trust and use them in and under God, and so as if all were taken away, yet to think God (being all-sufficient) can do without them, whatsoever he doth by them for our good. Faith preserves the chastity of the soul, and cleaving to God is a spiritual debt which it oweth to him, whereas cleaving to the creature is spiritual adultery.

It is an error in the foundation to substitute false objects either in religion, or in Christian conversation; for 1. in religion trusting in false objects, as saints, and works, &c., breeds false worship, and false worship breeds idolatry, and so God's jealousy and hatred. 2. In Christian conversation false objects of trust breed false comforts, and true fears; for in what measure we trust in any thing that is uncertain, in the same measure will our grief be when it fails us; the more men rely upon deceitful crutches, the greater is their fall; God can neither endure false objects, nor a *double object*, as hath been showed, for a man to rely upon any thing equally in the same rank with himself; for the propounding of a double object, argues a double heart, and a double heart is always unsettled, James i. 8, for it will regard God no longer than it can enjoy that which it joins together with him; therefore it is said, *you cannot serve two masters*, Luke xvi. 13, not subordinate one to another; whence it was that our Saviour told those worldly men which followed him: *that they could not believe in him, because they sought honour one of another*, John v. 44; and in case of competition, if their honour and reputation should come into question, they would be sure to be false to Christ, and rather part with him than their own credit and esteem in the world.

David here, by charging his soul to trust in God, saw there was nothing else that could bring true rest and quiet unto him; for whatsoever is besides God, is but a creature; and whatever is in the creature is but borrowed, and at God's disposing; and changeable, or else it were not a creature; David saw his error soon, for the ground of his disquiet was trusting something else besides God, therefore when he began to say, *My hill is strong, I shall not be moved*, &c. Psalm xxx. 6; then presently *his soul was troubled*. Out of God there is nothing fit for the soul to stay itself upon; for

1. Outward things are not fitted to the spiritual nature of the soul; they are dead things and cannot touch it being a lively spirit, unless by way of taint.

2. They are beneath the worth of the soul, and therefore debase the soul, and draw it lower than itself. As a noble woman, by matching with a mean person, much injures herself, especially when higher matches are offered. Earthly things are not given for stays wholly to rest on, but for comforts in our

way to Heaven; they are no more fit for the soul, than that which hath many angles is fit to fill up that which is round, which it cannot do, because of the unevenness and void places that will remain; outward things are never so well fitted for the soul, but that the soul will presently see some voidness and emptiness in them, and in itself in cleaving to them; for that which shall be a fit object for the soul, must be 1. for the nature of it spiritual, as the soul itself is; 2. constant; 3. full and satisfying; 4. of equal continuance with it; and 5. always yielding fresh contents: we cast away flowers, after once we have had the sweetness of them, because there is not still a fresh supply of sweetness. Whatever comfort is in the creature, the soul will spend quickly, and look still for more; whereas the comfort we have in God is *undefiled and fadeth not away;* how can we trust to that for comfort, which by very trusting proves uncomfortable to us? outward things are only so far forth good, as we do not trust in them; thorns may be touched, but not rested on, for then they will pierce; we must not set our hearts upon things which are never evil to us, but when we *set our hearts upon them.* Psalm lxii. 10.

By trusting any thing but God, we make it 1. an idol; 2. a curse, and not a blessing; 3. it will prove a lying vanity, not yielding that good which we look for; and 4. a vexation, bringing that evil upon us we look not for.

Of all men Solomon was the fittest to judge of this, because 1. he had a large heart able to comprehend the variety of things; and 2. being a mighty king, had advantages of procuring all outward things that might give him satisfaction; and 3. he had a desire answerable, to search out and extract whatever good the creature could yield; and yet upon the trial of all, he passeth this verdict upon all, that they are but *vanity,* Eccles. i. 2; whilst he laboured to find that which he sought for in them, he had like to have lost himself; and seeking too much to strengthen himself by foreign combination, he weakened himself the more thereby, until he came to know where the *whole of man* consists, *Eccles.* xii. 13. So that now we need not try further conclusions after the peremptory sentence of so wise a man.

But our nature is still apt to think there is some secret good in the forbidden fruit, and to buy wisdom dearly when we might have it at a cheaper rate, even from former universal experience.

It is a matter both to be wondered at and pitied, that the soul having God in Christ set before it, alluring it unto him, that he might raise it, enlarge it, and fill it, and so make it above all other things, should yet debase and make itself narrower and weaker, by leaning to things meaner than itself.

The kingdom, sovereignty, and large command of man, continueth while he rests upon God, in whom he reigns, in some sort, over all things under him; but so soon as he removes from God to any thing else, he becomes weak and narrow and slavish presently; for,

The soul is as that which it relies upon; if on vanity, itself becomes vain; for that which contents the soul must satisfy all the wants and desires of it which no particular thing can do, and the soul is more sensible of a little thing that it wants, than of all other things which it enjoys.

But see the insufficiency of all other things (out of God) to support the soul, in their several degrees. First, all outward things can make a man no happier than outward things can do, they cannot reach beyond their proper sphere: but our greatest grievances are spiritual. And as for inward things, whether gifts or graces, they cannot be a sufficient stay for the mind; for 1. gifts as policy and wisdom, &c., they are at the best very defective, especially when we trust in them; for wisdom makes men often to rebel, and thereupon God delighteth to blast their projects: none miscarry oftener than men of the greatest parts; as none are oftener drowned than those that are most skilful in swimming, because it makes them confident.

And for grace, though it be the beginning of a new creature in us, yet it is but a creature, and therefore not to be trusted in, nay, by trusting in it we imbase it, and make it more imperfect: so far as there is truth of grace, it breeds distrust of ourselves, and carries the soul out of itself to the fountain of strength.

And for any works that proceed from grace, by trusting thereunto they prove like the reed of Egypt, which not only deceives us, but hurts us with the splinters: good works are good, but confidence in them is hurtful; and there is more of our own in them (for the most part) to humble us, than of God's Spirit to embolden us so far as to trust in them. Alas, they have nothing from us but weakness and defilement, and therefore since the fall, God would have the object of our trust to be (out of ourselves) in him; and to that purpose he useth all means to take us out of ourselves, and from the creature, that he only might be our trust.

Yea, we must not trust itself, but God whom it relies on, who is therefore called our trust. All the glorious things that are spoken of trust are only made good by God in Christ, who, as trusted, doth all for us.

God hath prescribed trust as the way to carry our souls to himself, in whom we should only rely, and not in our imperfect trust, which hath its ebbing and flowing; neither will trust in God himself for the present suffice us for future strength and grace, as if trusting in God to-day would suffice to strengthen us for to-morrow; but we must renew our trust for fresh supply, upon every fresh occasion. So that we see God alone must be the object of our trust.

There is still left in man's nature a desire of pleasure, profit, and of whatever the creature presents as good, but the desire of gracious good is altogether lost, the soul being wholly infected with a contrary taste. Man hath a nature capable of excellency, and desirous of it, and the Spirit of God in and by the word reveals where true excellency is to be had; but corrupt nature leaving God, seeketh it elsewhere, and so crosseth its own desires, till the Spirit of God discovers where these things are to be had, and so nature is brought to its right frame again, by turning the stream into the right current; grace and sinful nature have the same general object of comfort; only *sinful nature seeks it in broken cisterns, and grace in the fountain;* the beginning of our true happiness is from the discovery of true and false objects, so as the soul may clearly see what is best and safest, and then steadfastly rely upon it.

It were a happy way to make the soul better acquainted with trusting in God, to labour to subdue at the first all unruly inclinations of the soul to earthly things, and to take advantage of the first tenderness of the soul, to weed out that which is ill, and to plant knowledge and love of the best things in it; otherwise where affections to any thing below get much strength in the soul, it will by little and little be so overgrown, that there will be no place left in it, either for (object or act) God or trust; God cannot come to take his place in the heart by trust, but where the powers of the soul are brought under to regard him and those great things he brings with him, above all things else in the world besides.

In these glorious times wherein so great a light shineth, whereby so great things are discovered, what a shame is it to be so narrow hearted as to fix upon present things; our aims and affections should be suitable to the things themselves set before us; our hearts should be more and more enlarged, as things are more and more revealed to us; we see in the things of this life, as wisdom and experience increaseth, so our aims and desires increase likewise; a young beginner thinks it a great matter if he have a little to begin withal, but as he grows in trading, and seeth further ways of getting, his thoughts and desires are raised higher: children think as children, but riper age puts away childishness, when their understandings are enlarged to see what they did not see before; we should never rest till our hearts, according to the measure of revelation of those excellent things which God hath for us, have answerable apprehension of the same. Oh, if we had but faith to answer those glorious truths which God hath revealed, what manner of lives should we lead!

CHAPTER XX.

OF THE METHOD OF TRUSTING IN GOD; AND THE TRIAL OF THAT TRUST.

LASTLY, to add no more, our trusting in God should follow God's order in promising. The first promise is of forgiveness of sin to repentant believers; next, 2. of healing and sanctifying grace; then, 3. the inheritance of the kingdom of heaven to them that are sanctified; and then the promises of all things needful in our way to the kingdom, &c. Now answerably the soul being enlightened to see 'its danger, should look first to God's mercy in Christ pardoning sin, because sin only divides betwixt God and the soul; next to the promises of grace for the leading of a Christian life, for true faith desires healing mercy as well as pardoning mercy, and then to heaven and all things that may bring us thither.

By all this we see that it is not so easy a matter as the world takes it, to bring God and the soul together by trusting on him; it must be effected by the mighty power of God, raising up the soul to himself, to lay hold upon the glorious power, goodness, and other excellencies that are in him: God is not only the object, but the working cause of our trust; for such is our proneness to live by sense, and natural reason, and such is the strangeness and height of divine things, such our inclination to a self-sufficiency and contentment in the creature, and so hard a matter is it to take off the soul from false bottoms, by reason of our unacquaintance with God and his ways; besides, such guilt still remains upon our souls for our rebellion and unkindness towards God, that it makes us afraid to entertain serious thoughts of him; and so great is the distance betwixt his infinite majesty, (be-

12

fore whom the very angels do cover their faces) and us, by reason of the unspiritualness of our nature, being opposite to his most absolute purity, that we cannot be brought to any familiarity with the Lord, so as to come into his holy presence with confidence to rely upon him, or any comfort to have communion with him, till our hearts be sanctified and lifted up by divine vigour infused into them.

Though there be some inclination by reason of the remainder of the image of God in us, to an outward moral obedience of the law, yet, alas, we have not only no seeds of evangelical truths and of faith to believe them, but an utter contrariety in our natures, as corrupted, either to do this, or any other good. When our conscience is once awaked, we meditate nothing but fears and terrors, and dare not so much as think of an angry God, but rather how we may escape and fly from him. Therefore, together with a deep consideration of the grounds we have of trusting God, it is necessary we should think of the indisposition of our hearts unto it, especially when there is greatest need thereof, that so our hearts may be forced to put out that petition of the disciples to God: *Lord increase our faith, Lord, help us against our unbelieving hearts,* &c. By prayer and holy thoughts stirred up in the use of the means, we shall feel divine strength infused and conveyed into our souls to trust.

The more care we ought to have to maintain our trust in God, because, besides the hardness of it, it is a radical and fundamental grace; it is as it were the mother root and great vein whence the exercise of all graces have their beginning and strength. The decay of a plant, though it appears first from the withering of the twigs and branches, yet it arises chiefly from a decay in the root; so the decay of grace may appear to the view, first in our company, carriage, and speeches, &c.; but the primitive and original ground of the same is weakness of faith in the heart; therefore it should be our wisdom, especially, to look to the feeding of the root; we must, 1. look that our princi-

ples and foundation be good, and, 2. build strongly
upon them, and, 3. repair our building every day as
continual breeches shall be made upon us, either by
corruptions and temptations from within or without;
and we shall find that the main breaches of our lives
arise either from false principles or doubts, or mind-
lessness of those that are true; all sin is a turning of
the soul from God to some other seeming good, but
this proceeds from a former turning of the soul from
God by distrust. As faith is the first return of the
soul to God, so the first degree of departing from God
is by infidelity, and from thence comes a departure by
other sins, by which, as sin is of a winding nature, our
unbelief more increaseth, and so the rent and breach
betwixt our souls and God is made greater still, which
is that Satan would have, till at length by departing
further and further from him, we come to have that
peremptory sentence of *everlasting departure* pronounced against us; so that our departure from God
now is a degree to separation for ever from him.
Therefore it is Satan's main care to come between
God and the soul, that so unloosing us from God, we
might more easily be drawn to other things; and if
he draws us to other things, it is but only to unloose
our hearts from God the more; for he well knows
whilst our souls cleave close to God, there is no prevailing against us by any created policy or power.

It was the cursed policy of Balaam to advise Balak
to draw the people from God (by fornication), that so
God might be drawn from them: the sin of their base
affections crept into the very spirits of their mind,
and drew them from God to idolatry; bodily adultery
makes way for spiritual; an unbelieving heart is an
ill heart, and a treacherous heart, because it makes us
to *depart from God, the living God,* &c. Heb. iii. 12.
Therefore we should especially take heed of it as we
love our lives, yea, our best life, which ariseth from
the union of our souls with God.

None so opposed as a Christian, and in a Christian
nothing so opposed as his faith, because it opposeth
whatsoever opposes God, both within and without

us: it captivates and brings under whatsoever rises up against God in the heart, and sets itself against whatsoever makes head against the soul.

And because mistake is very dangerous, and we are prone to conceive that to trust in God is an easy matter, therefore it is needful that we should have a right conceit of this trust, what it is, and how it may be discerned, lest we trust to an untrusty trust, and to an unsteady stay.

We may, by what hath been said before, partly discern the nature of it, to be nothing else but an exercise of faith, whereby looking to God in Christ through the promises, we take off our souls from all other supports, and lay them upon God for deliverance and upholding in all ill, present or future, felt or feared, and the obtaining of all good, which God sees expedient for us.

Now that we may discern the truth of our trust in God the better, we must know, that true trust is *willing to be tried* and searched, and can say to God as David, *Now, Lord, what wait I for, my hope is in thee*, Psalm xxxix. 7; and as it is willing to come to trial, so it is able to endure trial, and to hold out in opposition, as appears in David; if faith had a promise, it will rely and rest upon it, say flesh and blood what it can to the contrary; true faith is as large as the promise, and will take God's part against whatsoever opposes it.

And as faith singles not out one part of divine truth to believe and rejects another, so it relies upon God for every good thing, one as well as another; the ground whereof is this, the same love of God that intends us heaven, intends us a supply of all necessaries that may bring us thither.

A child that believes his father will make him heir, doubts not but he will provide him food and nourishment, and give him breeding suitable to his future condition; it is a vain pretence to believe that God will give us heaven, and yet leave us to shift for ourselves in the way.

Where trust is rightly planted, it gives boldness to

the soul in going to God, for it is grounded upon the
discovery of God's love first to us, and seeth a warrant from him for whatsoever it trusts him for; though
the things themselves be never so great, yet they are
no greater than God is willing to bestow; again, trust
is bold because it is grounded upon the worthiness of
a mediator, who hath made way to God's favour for
us, and appears now in heaven to maintain it towards
us.

Yet this boldness is with humility, which carries
the soul out of itself; and that boldness which the soul
by trust hath with God, is from God himself; it hath
nothing to allege from itself but its own emptiness
and God's fulness, its own sinfulness and God's mercy,
its own humble obedience and God's command; hence
it is that the true believer's heart is not lifted up, nor
swells with self-confidence; as trust comes in, that
goes out; trust is never planted, and grows but in an
humble and low soul; trust is a holy motion of the
soul to God, and motion arises from want; those, and
those only, seek out abroad that want succour at
home; plants move not from place to place, because
they find nourishment where they stand; but living
creatures seek abroad for their food, and for that end
have a power of moving from place to place; and
this is the reason why trust is expressed by going to
God.

Hereupon trust is a dependent grace, answerable
to our dependent condition; it looks upon all things,
it hath or desires to have, as coming from God and
his free grace and power; it desireth not only wisdom
but to be wise in his wisdom, to see in his light, to be
strong in his strength, the thing itself contents not this
grace of trust, but God's blessing and love in the thing,
it cares not for any thing further than it can have it
with God's favour and good liking.

Hence it is that trust is an obsequious and an observing grace, stirring up the soul to a desire of pleasing God in all things, and to a fear of displeasing
him: he that pretends to trust the Lord in a course
of offending, may trust to this that God will meet him

in another way than he looks for: he that is a tenant at courtesy will not offend his Lord : hence it is that the apostle enforceth that exhortation to *work out our salvation with fear and trembling*, because it is God that worketh the will and the deed, and according to *his good pleasure, not ours :* therefore faith is an effectual working grace, it works in Heaven with God, it works within us, commanding all the powers of the soul, it works without us, conquering whatsoever is in the world on the right hand to draw us from God, or on the left hand to discourage us; it works against hell and the powers of darkness; and all by virtue of trusting, as it draweth strength from God; it stirs up all other graces and keeps them in exercise, and thereupon the acts of other graces are attributed to faith, as Heb. xi. It breeds a holy jealousy over ourselves, lest we give God just cause to stop the influence of his grace towards us, so to let us see that we stand not by our own strength: those that take liberty in things they either know or doubt will displease God, show they want the fear of God, and this want of fear shows their want of dependency, and therefore want of trust; dependency is always very respective, it studieth contentment and care to comply; this was it made *Enoch walk with God, and study how to please him*, Heb. xi. 5; when we know nothing can do us good or hurt but God, it draws our chief care to approve ourselves to him. Obedience of faith and obedience of life will go together; and therefore he that commits his soul to God to save, will commit his soul to God to sanctify and guide in a way of well pleasing: not only the tame, but the most savage creatures, will be at the beck of those that feed them, though they are ready to fall violently upon others; disobedience, therefore, is against the principles of nature.

This dependency is either in the use of means, or else when means fail us; true dependency is exactly careful of all means. When God hath set down a course of means, we must not expect that God should alter his ordinary course of providence for us; deserved disappointment is the fruit of this presumptuous confidence; the more we depend on a wise physician, the more we shall observe his directions, and be careful to use what he prescribes; yet we must use the means as means, and not set them in God's room, for that is the way to blast our hopes; the way to have any thing *taken away and not blest,* is to *set our heart too much upon it.* Too much grief in parting with any thing, shows too much trust in the enjoying of it; and therefore he that uses the means in faith, will always join prayer unto God, from whom, as *every good thing comes,* so likewise doth the blessing and success thereof; where much endeavour is and little seeking to God, it shows there is little trust; the widow that trusted in God, continued likewise *in prayers day and night.*

The best discovery of our not relying too much on means, is, when all means fail, if we can still rely upon God, as being still where he was, and hath ways of his own for helping us, either immediately from himself, or by setting to work other means, and those, perhaps, very unlikely, such as we think not of. God hath ways of his own. Abraham never honoured God more, than when he trusted in God for a son against the course of nature, and when he had a son, was ready to sacrifice him, upon confidence that God would raise him from the dead again. This was the ground upon which Daniel, with such great authority, reproved Balthasar that he had not a care to glorify God, in whose hand *his breath was, and all his ways.* The greatest honour we can do unto God, is when we see nothing, but rather all contrary to that we look for, then to shut our eyes to inferior things below, and look altogether upon his all-sufficiency; God can convey himself more comfortably to us when he pleaseth, without means than by means. True trust, as it sets God highest in the soul, so in danger and wants it hath present recourse to him, as the conies to the rocks.

And because God's times and seasons are the best, it is an evidence of true trust when we can wait God's leisure, and not make haste, and so run before God; for else the more haste the worse speed; God seldom makes any promise to his children, but he exerciseth their trust in waiting long before, as David for a kingdom, Abraham for a son, the whole world for Christ's coming, &c.

One main evidence of true trust in God is here in the text: we see here it hath a quieting and stilling virtue, for it stays the soul upon the fulness of God's love, joined with his ability to supply our wants and relieve our necessities, though faith doth not, at the first especially, so stay the soul, as to take away all suspicious fears of the contrary: there be so many things in trouble that press upon the soul, as hinder the joining of God and it together, yet the prevailing of our unbelief is taken away, the reign of it is broken. If the touch of Christ in his abasement on earth drew virtue from him, certain it is that faith cannot touch Christ in heaven, but it will draw a quieting and sanctified virtue from him, which will in some measure stop the issues of an unquiet spirit; the needle in the compass will stand north, though with some trembling.

A ship that lies at anchor may be something tossed, but yet it still remains so fastened, that it cannot be carried away by wind or weather; the soul, after it hath cast anchor upon God, may, as we see here in David, be disquieted awhile, but this unsettling tends to a deeper settling; the more we believe, the more we are established; faith is an establishing grace, *by faith we stand,* and stand fast, and are able to withstand whatsoever opposeth us. For what can stand against God, upon whose truth and power faith relies? the devil fears us not, but him whom we fly unto for succour; it is the ground we stand on secures us, not ourselves.

As it is our happiness, so it must be our endeavour to bring the soul close to God, that nothing get between, for then the soul hath no sure footing. When we step from God, Satan steps in by some temptation or other presently. It requires a great deal of self-denial, to bring a soul either swelling with carnal confidence, or sinking by fear and distrust, to lie level upon God, and cleave fast to him: square will lie fast upon square: but our hearts are so full of unevenness, that God hath much ado to square our hearts fit for him, notwithstanding the soul hath no rest without this.

The use of trust is best known in the worst times, for naturally in sickness we trust to the physician, in want to our wit and shifts, in danger to policy and the arm of flesh, in plenty to our present supply, &c., but when we have nothing in view, then indeed should God be God unto us. In times of distress, when he shows himself in the ways of his mercy and goodness, then we should especially magnify his name, which will move him to discover his excellencies the more, the more we take notice of them. And therefore David strengthens himself in these words, that he hoped for better times, wherein God would show himself more gracious to him, because he resolved to praise him.

This trusting joints the soul again, and sets it in its own trust resting-place, and sets God in his own place in the soul, that is, the highest; and the creature in its place, which is to be under God, as in its own nature, so in our own hearts. This is to ascribe *honour due unto God*, Psalm xxix. 2, the only way to bring peace into the soul: thus, if we can bring our hope and trust to the God of hope and trust, we shall stand impregnable in all assaults, as will best appear in these particulars.

CHAPTER XXI.

OF QUIETING THE SPIRIT IN TROUBLES FOR SIN, AND OBJECTIONS ANSWERED.

To begin with troubles of the spirit, which indeed are the spirit of troubles, as disabling that which should uphold a man in all his troubles. A spirit set in tune, and assisted by a higher spirit, will stand out against ordinary assaults, but when God (the God of the spirits of all flesh) shall seem contrary to our spirits, whence then shall we find relief?

Here all is spiritual, God a spirit, the soul a spirit, the terrors spiritual, the devil who joins with these a spirit; yea, that which the soul fears for the time to come, is spiritual, and not only spiritual, but eternal, unless it pleaseth God at length to break out of the thick cloud, wherewith he covers himself, and shine upon the soul, as in his own time he will.

In this estate, comforts themselves are uncomfortable to the soul; it quarrels with every thing, the better things it hears of, the more it is vexed. Oh what is this to me, what have I to do with these comforts? the more happiness may be had, the more is my grief; as for comforts from God's inferior blessings, as friends, children, estate, &c., the soul is ready to misconstrue God's end in all, as not intending any good to him thereby.

In this condition God does not appear in his own shape to the soul, but in the shape of an enemy; and when God seems against us, who shall stand for us? our blessed Saviour in his agony had the angels to comfort him; but had he been a mere man, and not assisted by the godhead, it was not the comfort (no, not) of angels that could have upheld him, in the sense of his Father's withdrawing his countenance from him. Alas, then, what will become of us in such a case, if we be not supported by a spirit of power and the power of an almighty Spirit?

If all the temptations of the whole world and hell itself were mustered together, they were nothing to this, whereby the great God sets himself contrary to his poor creature. None can conceive so, but those that have felt it. If the hiding of his face will so trouble the soul, what will his frown and angry look do? needs must the soul be in a woful plight, when as God seems not only to be absent from it, but an enemy to it. When a man sees no comfort from above, and looks inward and sees less; when he looks about him, and sees nothing but evidences of God's displeasure; beneath him, and sees nothing but desperation; clouds without, and clouds within, nothing but clouds in his condition; here he had need of faith to break through all, and see sun through the thickest cloud.

Upon this, the distressed soul is in danger to be set upon a temptation, called the temptation of blasphemy, that is, to entertain bitter thoughts against God, and especially against the grace and goodness of God, wherein he desires to make himself most known to his creature. In those that have wilfully resisted divine truths made known unto them, and after taste, despised them, a persuasion that God hath forsaken them, set on strongly by Satan, hath a worse effect, it stirs up a hellish hatred against God, carrying them to a revengeful desire of opposing whatsoever is God's, though not always openly (for then they should lose the advantage of doing hurt) yet secretly and subtly, and under pretence of the contrary. To this degree of blasphemy God's children never fall, yet they may feel the venom of corruption stirring in their hearts, against God and his ways, which he takes with them; and this adds greatly to the depth of their affliction, when afterward they think with themselves what hellish stuff they carry in their souls. This is not so much discerned in the temptation, but after the fit is somewhat remitted.

In this kind of desertion, seconded with this kind of temptation, the way is to call home the soul, and to check it, and charge it to trust in God, even though he shows himself an enemy, for it is but a show, he doth but put on a mask with a purpose to reveal himself the more graciously afterward; his manner is to work by contraries. In this condition God lets in some few beams of light, whereby the soul casts a longing look upon God, even when he seems to forsake it; it will, with Jonas in the belly of hell, look back to the holy temple of God, Jonah ii. 4, it will steal a look unto Christ. Nothing more comfortable in this condition, than to fly to him, that by experience knew what this kind of forsaking meant, for this very end that he might be the fitter to succour us in the like distress.

Learn, therefore, to appeal from God to God, oppose his gracious nature, his sweet promises to such as are *in darkness, and see no light,* Isa. l. 10, inviting them to trust in him, though there appear to the eye of sense and reason nothing but darkness: here make use of that sweet relation of God in Christ, becoming a Father to us: *Doubtless thou art our Father,* Isa. lxiii. 16: flesh would make a doubt of it, and thou seemest to hide thy face from us, yet doubtless thou art our Father, and hast in former time showed thyself to be so, we will not leave thee till we have a blessing from thee, till we have a kinder look from thee: this wrestling will prevail at length, and we shall have such a sight of him, as shall be an encouragement for the time to come, when *we shall be able to comfort others, with those comforts whereby we have been refreshed ourselves.* 2 Cor. i. 4. With the saint's case remember the saint's course, which is to trust in God. So Christ the Head of the Church commits himself to that God, whose favour for the present he felt not; so Job resolves upon trust, though God should kill him.

But these holy persons were not troubled with the guilt of any particular sin, but I feel the just displeasure of God kindled against me for many and great offences.

True it is, that sin is not so sweet in the committing, as it is heavy and bitter in the reckoning. When Adam had once offended God, Paradise itself was not Paradise to him. The presence of God, which was most comfortable before, was now his greatest terror, had not God out of his free, infinite and preventing mercy come betwixt him and hell, by the promise of the blessed seed. This seed was made sin to satisfy for sin; sin passive in himself to satisfy for sin active in us. 1 Cor. v. 21.

When God once charges sin upon the soul, alas, who shall take it off? when the great God shall frown, the smiles of the creature cannot refresh us.

Sin makes us afraid of that which should be our greatest comfort; it puts a sting into every other evil, upon the seizing of any evil, either of body, soul, or condition, the guilty soul is imbittered and enraged; for from that which it feels, it fore-speaks to itself worse to come. It interprets all that befalls as the messengers of an angry God, sent in displeasure to take revenge upon it. This weakeneth the courage, wasteth the spirits, and blasteth the beauty even of God's dearest ones. Psalm xxxviii. There is not the stoutest man breathing, but if God sets his conscience against him, it will pull him down, and lay him flat, and fill him with such inward terrors, as he shall be more afraid of himself, than of all the world beside. This were a doleful case, if God had not provided in Christ a remedy for this great evil of evils, and if the holy Spirit were not above the conscience, able as well to pacify it by the sense of God's love in Christ, as to convince it of sin, and the just desert thereby.

But my sins are not the sins of an ordinary man, my spots are not as the spots of the rest of God's children.

Conceive of God's mercy as no ordinary mercy, and Christ's obedience as no ordinary obedience. There is something in the very greatness of sin, that may encourage us to go to God, for the greater our sins are, the greater the glory of his powerful mercy pardoning, and his powerful grace in healing will appear. The great God delights to show his greatness in the greatest things; even men glory, when they are put upon that, which may set forth their worth in any kind. God *delighteth in mercy*, Mic. vii. 18, it pleaseth him (nothing so well) as being his chief name, which then we take in vain, when we are not moved by it to come unto him.

That which Satan would use as an argument to drive us from God, we should use as a strong plea with him. Lord, the greater my sins are, the greater will be the glory of thy pardoning mercy. David after his heinous sins, cries not for *mercy*, but for *abundance of mercy, according to the multitude of thy mercies, do away mine offences,* Psalm li: his mercy is not only above his own works, but above ours too.   If we could sin more than he could pardon, then we might have some reason to despair.   Despair is a high point of atheism, it takes away God and Christ both at once.   Judas, in betraying our Saviour, was an occasion of his death as man, but in despairing he did what lay in him to take away his life as God.

When, therefore, conscience joining with Satan sets out the sin in its colours, labour thou by faith to set out God in his colours, infinite in mercy and loving kindness.   Here lies the art of a Christian ; it is divine rhetoric thus to persuade and set down the soul.   Thy sins are great, but Adam's was greater, who being so newly advanced above all the creatures, and taken into so near an acquaintance with God, and having ability to persist in that condition if he would, yet willingly overthrew himself and all his whole posterity, by yielding to a temptation, which though high (as being promised to be like unto God,) yet such as he should and might have resisted ; no sin we can commit, can be a sin of so tainting and spreading a nature, yet as he fell by distrust, so he was recovered by trusting, and so must we by relying on a second Adam, whose obedience and righteousness *from thence reigns.* Rom. v. 17, to the taking away not only of that one sin of Adam, and ours in him, but of all, and not only to the pardon of all sin, but to a right of everlasting life. The Lord thinks himself disparaged, when we have no higher thoughts of his mercy, than of our sins, when we bring God down to our model, when as *the heavens are not so much higher than the earth, than his thoughts of love and goodness are above the thoughts of our unworthiness.* Isa. lv. 9.   It is a kind of taking away the Almighty, to limit his boundless mercy in Christ, within the narrow scantling of our apprehension ; yet infidelity doth this, which should stir up in us a loathing of it above all other sins.   But this is Satan's fetch, when once he hath brought us into sins against the law, then to bring us into sins of a higher nature, and deeper danger, even against the blessed

Gospel, that so there may be no remedy, but that mercy itself might condemn us.

All the aggravations, that conscience and Satan helping it, are able to raise sin unto, cannot rise to that degree of infiniteness, that God's mercy in Christ is of. If there be a spring of sin in us, there is a spring of mercy in him, and a fountain opened daily to wash ourselves in. If we sin oft, let us do as Paul, who prayed oft *against the prick of the flesh.* Zac. xiii. 1. If it be a devil of long continuance, yet fasting and prayer will drive him out at length.

Nothing keeps the soul more down than sins of long continuance, because corruption of nature hath gotten such strength in them, as nature is added to nature, and custom doth so determine and sway the soul one way, that men think it impossible to recover themselves, they see one link of sin draw on another, all making a chain to fasten them to destruction, they think of necessity they must be damned, because custom hath bred a necessity of sinning in them, and conceive of the promise of mercy, as only made to such as turn from their sinful courses, in which they see themselves so hardened, that they cannot repent.

Certain it is, the condition is most lamentable, that yielding unto sin brings men unto. Men are careful to prevent dangerous sickness of the body, and the danger of law concerning their estates; but seldom consider into what a miserable plight their sins, which they so willingly give themselves up unto, will bring them. If they do not perish in their sins, yet their yielding will bring them into such a doleful condition, that they would give the whole world, if they were possessors of it, to have their spirits at freedom from this bondage and fear.

To such as bless themselves in an ill way upon hope of mercy, we dare not speak a word of comfort, because God doth not, but threatens, his wrath shall burn to hell against them. Yet because while life continues there may be as a space, so a place, and grace for repentance, these must be dealt withal in such a manner, as they may be stayed and stopped in their dangerous courses, there must be a stop before a turn.

And when their consciences are thoroughly awaked with sense of their danger, let them seriously consider whither sin, and Satan by sin, is carrying of them, and lay to heart the justice of God, standing before them as an angel with a drawn sword, ready to fall upon them if they post on still.

Yet to keep them from utter sinking, let them consider withal, the unlimited mercy of God, as not limited to any person, or any sin, so not to any time; there is no prescription of time can bind God, his mercy hath no certain date that will expire, so as those that fly unto it, shall have no benefit. Invincible mercy will never be conquered, and endless goodness never admits of bounds or end.

What kind of people were those that followed Christ? were they not such as had lived long in their sinful courses? he did not only raise them that were newly dead, but Lazarus that had laid *four days in the grave.* They thought Christ's power in raising the dead had reached to a short time only, but he would let them know, that he could as well raise those that had been long as lately dead. If Christ be the physician, it is no matter of how long continuance the disease be. He is good at all kinds of diseases, and will not endure the reproach of disability to cure any. Some diseases are the reproaches of other physicians, as being above their skill to help, but no conceit more dangerous when we are to deal with Christ.

" The blessed martyr Bilney was much offended when he heard an eloquent preacher inveighing against sin, saying thus, Behold thou hast laid rotten in thy own lusts, by the space of sixty years, even as a beast in his own dung, and wilt thou presume in one year to go forward towards heaven, and that in thine old age, as much as thou wentest backward from heaven to hell in sixty years? is not this a goodly argument? saith Bilney; is this preaching of repentance in the name of Jesus? it is as if Christ had died in vain for such a man, and that he must make satisfaction for himself. If I had heard, saith he, such preaching of repentance in times past, I had utterly despaired of mercy;" we must never think the door of hope to be shut against us, if we have a purpose to turn unto God. As there is nothing more injurious to Christ, so nothing more foolish and groundless than to distrust, it being the chief scope of God in his word to draw our trust to him in Christ, in whom is always open a breast of mercy for humbled sinners to fly unto.

But thus far the consideration. of our long time spent in the devil's service should prevail with us, as to take more shame to ourselves, so to resolve more strongly for God and his ways, and to account it more than sufficient that we have spent already so much precious time to so ill purposes; and the less time we have, to make the more haste to work for God, and bring all the honour we can to religion in so little a space. Oh how doth it grieve those that have felt the gracious power of Christ in converting their souls, that ever they should spend the strength of their parts in the work of his and their enemy! and might they live longer, it is their full purpose for ever to renounce their former ways. There is bred in them an eternal desire of pleasing God, as in the wicked there is an eternal desire of offending him, which eternity of desires God looks to in both of them, and rewards them accordingly, though he cuts off the thread of their lives.

But God in wisdom will have the conversions of such as have gone on in a course of sinning (especially after light revealed) to be rare and difficult. Births in those that are ancienter, are with greater danger than in the younger sort. God will take a course, that his grace shall not be turned into wantonness. He oft holds such upon the rack of a troubled conscience, that they and others may fear to buy the pleasure of sin at such a rate. Indeed where sin abounds, there grace superabounds, but then it is where sin that abounded in the life abounds in the conscience in grief and detestation of it, as the great-

13

est evil. Christ groaned at the raising of Lazarus, which he did not at others, because that although to an Almighty power all things are alike easy, yet he will show that there be degrees of difficulties in the things themselves, and make it appear to us that it is so. Therefore those that have enjoyed long the sweet of sin, may expect the bitterest sorrow and repentance for sin.

Yet never give place to thoughts of despair, as coming from him that would overturn the end of the Gospel, which lays open the riches of God's mercy in Christ, which riches none set out more than those that have been *the greatest of sinners,* as we see in Paul. We cannot exalt God more than by taking notice, and making use of that great design of infinite wisdom in reconciling justice and mercy together, so as now he is not only merciful, but *just in pardoning sins.* Rom. iii. 26. Our Saviour, as he came towards the latter age of the world, when all things seemed desperate; so he comes to some men in the latter part of their days. The mercy showed to Zacchæus, and the good thief was personal, but the comfort intended by Christ was public, therefore *still trust in God.*

In this case we must go to God, with whom all things are possible, to put forth his almighty power, not only in the pardoning, but in subduing our iniquities. He that can make a *camel go through a needle's eye,* can make a high conceited man lowly, a rich man humble. Therefore never question his power, much less his willingness, when he is not only ready to receive us when we return, but persuades and entreats us to come in unto him, yea, after backsliding and false dealing with him, wherein he allows no mercy to be showed by man, yet he will take liberty to show mercy himself. Jer. iii. 2.

But I have often relapsed and fallen into the same sin again and again.

If Christ will have us pardon our brother seventy-seven times, can we think that he will enjoin us more, than he will be ready to do himself, when in case of showing mercy he would have us think his thoughts to be far above ours? Adam lost all by once sinning. Isa. lv. 1, but we are under a better covenant, a covenant of mercy, and are encouraged by the Son to go to the Father every day for the sins of that day.

Where the work of grace is begun, sin loses strength by every new fall; for hence issues deeper humility, stronger hatred, fresh indignation against ourselves, more experience of the deceitfulness of our hearts, renewed resolutions until sin be brought under. That should not drive us from God, which God would have us make use of to fly the rather to him, since there is a throne of grace set up in Jesus Christ we may boldly make use of, and let us be ashamed to sin, and not be ashamed to glorify God's mercy in begging pardon for sin. Nothing will make us more ashamed to sin, than thoughts of so free and large mercy. It will grieve an ingenuous spirit to offend so good a God. Ah that there should be such a heart in me, as to tire the patience of God, and dam up his goodness, as much as in me lies! but this is our comfort, that the plea of mercy from a broken spirit to a gracious Father, will ever hold good. When we are at the lowest in this world, yet there are these three grounds of comfort still remaining. 1. That we are not yet in the place of the damned, whose estate is unalterable. 2. That whilst we live there is time and space for recovering of ourselves. 3. That there is grace offered, if we will not shut our hearts against it.

O, but every one hath his time, my good hour may be past.

That is counsel to thee, it is not past if thou canst raise up thy heart to God, and embrace his goodness. Show by thy yielding unto mercy, that thy time of mercy is not yet out, rather than by concluding uncomfortably, willingly betray thyself to thy greatest enemy, enforcing that upon thyself, which God labours to draw thee from. As in the sin against the Holy Ghost, fear shows that we have not committed it: so in this, a tender heart fearing lest our time be past, shows plainly that it is not past.

Look upon examples, when the prodigal in his

forlorn condition was going to his father, his father stayed not for him, but *meets him* in the way. Luke xv., he did not only go, but ran to meet him. God is more willing to entertain us, than we are to cast ourselves upon him: as there is *a fountain opened for sin, and for uncleanness,* so it is a living fountain of living water, that runs for ever, and can never be drawn dry.

Here remember, that I build not a shelter for the presumptuous, but only open a harbour for the truly humbled soul, to put himself into.

CHAPTER XXII.

OF SORROW FOR SIN, AND HATRED FOR SIN, WHEN RIGHT AND SUFFICIENT. HELPS THERETO.

AH! *there's my misery. If I could be humbled for sin, I might hope for mercy, but I never yet knew what a broken heart meant, this soul of mine was never as yet sensible of the grief and smart of sin, then how can I expect any comfort?*

It is one of Satan's policies to hold us in a dead and barren condition, by following us with conceits, that we have not sorrowed in proportion to our offences. True it is, we should labour that our sorrow might in some measure answer to the heinousness of our sins: but we must know sorrow is not required for itself in that degree as faith is: if we could trust in God without much sorrow for our sins, then it would not be required, for God delights not in our sorrow as sorrow, God in mercy both requires it and works it, as thereby making us capable vessels of mercy, fit to acknowledge, value, and walk worthy of Christ; he requires it as it is a means to imbitter sin, and the delightful pleasures thereof unto us, and by that means bring us to a right judgment of ourselves, and the creature, with which sin commits spiritual adultery, that so we may recover our taste before lost. And then, when with the prodigal we return unto ourselves, having lost ourselves before, we are fit to judge of the baseness of sin, and. of the worth of mercy; and so upon grounds of right reason, be willing to alter our condition, and embrace mercy upon any terms it shall please Christ to enjoin.

Secondly, if we could grieve and cast down ourselves beneath the earth as low as the nethermost pit, yet this would be no satisfaction to God for sin; of itself, it is rather an entrance, and beginning of hell.

Thirdly, we must search what is the cause of this want of grief which we complain of; whether it be not a secret cleaving to the creature, and too much contentment in it, which oft stealeth away the heart from God, and brings in such contentment as is subject to fail and deceive us, whereupon from discontentment we grieve, which grief, being carnal, hinders grief of a better kind.

Usually the causes of our want of grief for sin are these.   First, a want of serious consideration, and dwelling long enough upon the cause of grief, which springs either from an unsettledness of nature, or distractions from things without.   Moveable dispositions are not long affected with any thing.   One main use of crosses, is to take the soul from that it is dangerously set upon, and to fix our running spirits.   For though grief for crosses hinders spiritual grief, yet worldly delights hinder more.   That grief is less distant from true grief, and therefore nearer to be turned into it.

And in case we could call off our minds from other things, and set them on grief for our sins, yet it is only God's Spirit that can work our hearts to this grief and for this end, perhaps God holds us off from it, to teach us, that he is the teacher of the heart to grieve.   And thereupon it is our duty to wait, till he reveal ourselves so far to ourselves, as to stir up this affection in us.

Another cause may be a kind of doubleness of heart, whereby we would bring two things together that cannot suit.   We would grieve for sin so far as we think it an evidence of a good condition: but then because it is an irksome task, and because it cannot

be wrought without severing our hearts from those
sweet delights it is set upon; hence we are loath God
should take that course to work grief, which crosseth
our disposition.   The soul must therefore by self-
denial be brought to such a degree of sincerity and
simplicity, as to be willing to give God leave to work
this sorrow, not to be sorrowed for, 2 Cor. xvii. 10,
by what way he himself pleaseth.   But here we must
remember again, that this self-denial is not of ourselves, but of God, who only can take us out of ourselves, and if our hearts were brought to a stooping
herein to his work, it would stop many a cross, and
continue many a blessing which God is forced to take
from us, that he may work that grief in us which he
seeth would not otherwise be kindly wrought.

God giveth some larger spirits, and so their sorrows
become larger.   Some from quickness of apprehension, and the ready passages betwixt the brain and
the heart, are quickly moved: where the apprehension is deeper, and the passages slower, there sorrow
is long in working, and long in removing.   The
deepest waters have the stillest motion.   Iron takes
fire more slowly than stubble, but then it holds it
longer.

Again, *God that searcheth and knows our hearts*
better than ourselves, *knows when and in what measure it is fit to grieve;* he sees it is fitter for some
dispositions to go on in a constant grief.   We must
give that honour to the wisdom of the great physician
of souls, to know best how to mingle and minister his
potions.   And we must not be so unkind to take it ill
at God's hands, when he out of gentleness and for-
bearance, ministers not to us that churlish physic he
doth to others, but cheerfully embrace any potion
that he thinks fit to give us.

Some holy men have desired to see their sin in the
most ugly colours, and God hath heard them in their
requests.   But yet his hand was so heavy upon them,
that they went always mourning to their very graves;
and thought it fitter to leave it to God's wisdom to
mingle the potion of sorrow, than to be their own

choosers. For a conclusion then of this point, if we grieve that we cannot grieve, and so far as it is sin, make it our grief: then put it amongst the rest of our sins, which we beg pardon of, and help against, and let it not hinder us from going to Christ, but drive us to him. For herein lies the danger of this temptation, that those who complain in this kind, think it would be presumption to go to Christ: when as he especially calleth *the weary and heavy laden sinner to come unto him,* and therefore such as are sensible that they are not sensible enough of their sin, must know *though want of feeling be quite opposite to the life of grace, yet sensibleness of the want of feeling shows some degree of the life of grace.* The safest way in this case is from that life and light that God hath wrought in our souls, to see and feel this want of feeling, to cast ourselves and this our indisposition upon the pardoning and healing mercy of God in Christ.

We speak only of those that are so far displeased with themselves for their ill temper, as they do not favour themselves in it, but are willing to yield to God's way in redressing it, and do not cross the Spirit, moving them thus with David to check themselves, and to trust in God. Otherwise, an unfeeling and careless state of spirit will breed a secret shame of going to God, for removing of that we are not hearty in labouring against so far as our conscience tells us we are enabled.

The most constant state the soul can be in, in regard of sin, is, upon judgment to condemn it upon right grounds, and to resolve against it. Whereupon repentence is called *an after wisdom and change of the mind.* And this disposition is in God's children at all times. And for affections, love of that which is good, and hatred of that which is evil; these likewise have a settled continuance in the soul. But grief and sorrow rise and fall as fresh occasions are offered, and are more lively stirred up upon some lively representation to the soul of some hurt we receive by sin, and wrong we do to God in it. The reason hereof is, because till the soul be separated from the body, these affections have more communion with the body, and therefore they carry more outward expressions than dislike or abomination in the mind doth. We are to judge of ourselves more by that which is constant, than by that which is ebbing and flowing.

But what is the reason that the affections do not always follow the judgment, and the choice or refusal of the will?

1. Our soul being a finite substance, is carried with strength but one way at one time.

2. Sometimes God calls us to joy as well as to grief; and then no wonder if grief be somewhat to seek.

3. Sometimes when God calleth to grief, and the judgment and will goeth along with God, yet the heart is not always ready, because, it may be, it hath run out so far that it cannot presently be called in again.

4. Or, the spirits, which are the instruments of the soul, may be so wasted that they cannot hold out to feel a strong grief; in which case, the conscience must rest in settled judgment and hatred of ill; which is the surest and never failing character of a good soul.

5. *Ofttimes God in mercy takes us off from grief and sorrow, by refreshing occasions:* because sorrow and grief are affections very much afflicting both of body and soul.

When is godly sorrow in that degree wherein the soul may stay itself from uncomfortable thoughts about its condition?

1. *When we find strength against that sin which formerly we fell into, and ability to walk in a contrary way;* for this answers God's end in grief, one of which is a prevention from falling for the time to come. For God hath that affection in him which he puts into parents, which is by smart to prevent their children's boldness of offending for the time to come.

2. *When that which is wanting in grief is made up in fear.* Here there is no great cause of com-

plaint of the want of grief, for *this holy affection is the awe-band of the soul*, whereby it is kept from starting from God and his ways.

3. When after grief we find inward peace; for true grief being God's work in us, he knows best how to measure it. Therefore, whatsoever frame God brings my soul into, I am to rest in his goodness, and not except against his dealing. That peace and joy which riseth from grief in the use of means, and makes the soul more humble and thankful to God, and less censorious and more pitiful to others, is no illusion nor false light.

The main end of grief and sorrow is to make us value the grace and mercy of God in Christ, above all the contentments which sin feeds on. Which, where it is found, we may know that grief for sin, hath enough possessed the soul before. The sufficiency of things is to be judged by an answerableness to their use and ends: God makes sin bitter, that Christ may be sweet: *that measure of grief and sorrow is sufficient, which brings us, and holds us to Christ.*

Hatred, being the strongest, deepest, and steadiest affection of the soul against that which is evil; grief for sin is then right, when it springs from hatred, and increaseth further hatred against it.

Now the soul may be known to hate sin, when it seeks the utter abolishing of it; for hatred is an implacable and irreconcileable affection.

True hatred is carried against the whole kind of sin, without respect of any wrong done to us, but only out of a mere antipathy, and contrariety of disposition to it. As the lamb hateth the whole kind of wolves, and man hateth the whole kind of serpents. A toad does us no harm, but yet we hate it.

That which is hateful to us, the nearer it is the more we shun and abhor it, as venomous serpents, and hurtful creatures, because the nearness of the object affects us more deeply. Therefore, if our grief spring from true hatred of sin, it will make no new league with it, but grieve for all sin, especially for our own particular sins, as being contrary to the work of God's grace in us, then is grief an affection of the new creature, and every way of the right breed.

But for fuller satisfaction in this case, we must know *there is sometimes grief for sin in us, when we think there is none*: it wants but stirring up by some quickening word; the remembrance of God's favours and our unkindness, or the awaking of our consciences by some cross, will raise up this affection feelingly in us. As in the affection of love many think that they have no love to God at all: yet let God be dishonoured in his name, truth, or children, and their love will soon stir and appear in just anger.

In want of grief for sin, we must remember, 1. *That we must have this affection from God, before we can bring it unto God.*

And, therefore, in the second place, our chief care should be not to harden our hearts against the motions of the Spirit, stirring us to seasonable grief, for that may cause a judicial hardness from God. God oft inflicteth some spiritual judgment as a correction upon men, for not yielding to his Spirit at the first, they feel a hardness of heart growing upon them; this made the Church complain, *Why hast thou hardened our hearts from thy fear?* Which if Christians did well consider, they would more carefully entertain such impressions of sorrow, as the Spirit in the use of the means, and observation of God's dealing towards themselves or others, shall work in them, than they do. It is a saying of Austin, *Let a man grieve for his sin, and joy for his grief*, though we can neither love, nor grieve, nor joy of ourselves, as we should, yet our hearts tell us, we are often guilty of giving a check to the spirits of stirring these affections in us, which is a main cause of the many sharp afflictions we endure in this life, though God's love in the main matter of salvation be most firm unto us.

We must not think to have all this grief at first, and at once, for oftentimes it is deeper after a sight and feeling of God's love than it was before. God is a free agent, and knows every man's several mould, and

the several services he is to use them in, and oft takes
liberty afterwards to humble men more (when he hath
enabled them better to bear it) than in their first entrance into religion: grief before springs commonly
from self-love, and fear of danger. Let no man suspect his estate because God spares him in the beginning. For Christians many times meet with greater
trial after their conversion than ever they thought
on. *When men take little fines, they mean to take
the greater rent.* God will have his children first or
last to feel what sin is; and how much they are beholden to him for Christ.

*This grief doth not always arise from poring on
sin, but by oft considering of the infinite goodness
of God in Christ,* and thereby reflecting on our own
unworthiness, not only in regard of sin past, but likewise of the sin that hangeth upon us, and issues daily
from us. The more holy a man is, the more he sees
the holiness of God's nature, with whom he desires
to have communion, the more he is grieved that there
should be any thing found in him, displeasing to so
pure a Majesty.

And as all our grief comes not at first, so God will
not have it come all at once, but to be a stream always
running, fed with a spring, yet within the banks, though
sometimes deeper, sometimes shallower. Grief for sin
is like a constant stream; grief for other things is like
a torrent, or swelling waters, which are soon up, soon
down; what it wants in greatness is made up in continuance.

Again, *if we watch not our nature, there will be
a spice of popery* (which is a natural religion) *in this
great desire of more grief:* as if we had that, then
we had something to satisfy God withal, and so our
minds will run too much upon works. This grief must
not only be wrought by God revealing our sin, and his
mercy unto us in Christ; but when it is wrought, we
must altogether rest (in a sense of our own emptiness)
upon the full satisfaction and worthiness of Christ our
Saviour.

All this that hath been said tends not to the abating

of our desire to have a tender and bleeding heart for sin; but that in the pursuit of this desire, we be not cast down so as to question our estates, if we feel not that measure of grief which we desire and endeavour after, or to refuse our portion of joy which God offers us in Christ. Considering grief is no further good than it makes way for joy: which caused our Saviour to join them together: *blessed are the mourners, for they shall be comforted.* Being thus disposed, we may commit our souls to God in peace, notwithstanding Satan's troubling of us in the hour of temptation.

CHAPTER XXIII.

OTHER SPIRITUAL CAUSES OF THE SOUL'S TROUBLE DISCOVERED AND REMOVED: AND OBJECTIONS ANSWERED.

ANOTHER thing that disquiets and casts down the soul very much, is that inward conflict betwixt grace and corruption: this makes us most work, and puts us to most disquietment. It is the trouble of troubles to have two inhabitants so near in one soul, and these to strive one against another, in every action, and at all times in every part and power in us: the one carrying us upward, higher and higher still, till we come to God: the other pulling us lower and lower, further from him. *This cannot but breed a great disquiet, when a Christian shall be put on to that which he would not, and hindered from that which he would do, or troubled in the performance of it.* Rom. vii. The more light there is to discern, and life of grace to be sensible hereof; and the more love of Christ, and desire from love to be like him, the more irksome will this be: no wonder then that the apostle cried out, *O wretched man that I am,* &c. Rom. vii.

Here is a special use of trust, in the free mercy of God in justification, considering all is stained that comes from us, it is one main end of God's leaving us in this conflicting condition, that we may live and die by faith in the perfect righteousness of Christ, whereby we glorify God more, than if we had perfect

righteousness of our own. Hereby likewise we are
driven to make use of all the promises of grace, and
to trust in God for the performance of them, in
strengthening his own party in us, and not only to
trust in God for particular graces, but for his Spirit
which is the spring of all graces, which we have
through and from Christ: who will help us in this
fight until he hath made us like himself. We are
under the government of grace, sin is deposed from
the rule it had, and shall never recover the right it
had again; *it is left in us for matter of exercise, and
ground of triumph.*

Oh (say some) *I shall never hold out, as good give
over at first as at last. I find such strong inclinations to sin in me, and such weakness to resist temptation, that I fear I shall but shame the cause; I
shall one day perish by the hand of Satan, strengthening my corruption.*

Why art thou thus troubled? *Trust in God,* grace
will be above nature, God above the devil, the Spirit
above the flesh. Be strong in the Lord, the battle
is his, and the victory ours beforehand. If we fought
in our own cause and strength, and with our weapons, it were something: but as we fight in the power of God, so are *we kept by that mighty power
through faith unto salvation.* It lies upon the faithfulness of Christ, to put us into that possession of
glory which he hath purchased for us: therefore
charge the soul to make use of the promises, and
rely upon God for perfecting the good work that he
hath begun in thee.

Corruptions be strong, but stronger is he that is in
us, than that corruption that is in us. When we
are weak in our own sense, then are we strong in
him, who perfecteth strength in our weakness felt and
acknowledged. Our corruptions are God's enemies
as well as ours, and therefore in trusting to him, and
fighting against them, we may be sure he will take
our part against them.

*But I have great impediments, and many dis-
couragements in my Christian course.*

What if our impediments be mountains, faith is able to remove them; *who art thou, O mountain?* Zac. iv. 7, saith the prophet. What a world of impediments were there betwixt Egypt and the land of Canaan, betwixt the return out of Babylon and Jerusalem? yet faith removed all, by looking to God's power and truth in his promise. The looking too much to the Anakims and giants, and too little to God's omnipotency, shut the Israelites out of Canaan, and put God to his oath, that they should *never enter into his rest,* Psalm xxv., and it will exclude our souls from happiness at length, if looking too much upon these Anakims within us and without us, we basely despair and give over the field, considering all our enemies are not only conquered for us by our head, but shall be conquered in us, so that in strength of assistance we fight against them. God gave the Israelites' enemies into their hands; but yet they must fight it out, and what coward will not fight when he is sure of help and victory?

But I carry continually about me a corrupt heart, if that were once changed, I could have some comfort.

A new heart is God's creature, and he hath promised to *create it in us.* A creating power cannot only bring something out of nothing, but contrary out of contrary. Where we are sure of God's truth, let us never question that power to which all things are possible. If our hearts were as ill, as God is powerful and good, there were some ground of discouragement. In what measure we give up our hearts to God, in that measure we are sure to receive them better. That grace which enlargeth the heart to desire good, is therefore given, that God may increase it, being both a part and a pledge of further grace. There is a promise of pouring clean water upon us, which faith must sue out. Christ hath taken upon him to purge his spouse, and make her fit for himself. Eph. v.

But I have many wants and defects to be supplied.

It pleaseth him, that in Christ *all fulness shall dwell,* from whose fulness grace sufficient is dispensed to us answerable to the measure of our faith, whereby we fetch it from the fountain. The more we trust, the more we have. When we look therefore to our own want, we should look withal to Christ's fulness, and his nearness to us, and take advantage from our misery to rest upon his all-sufficiency, whose fulness, is ours, as himself is. Our fulness with our life is hid in Christ, and distilled into us, in such measure as his wisdom thinketh fit, and as showeth him to be a free agent, and yet so as the blame for want of grace lieth upon us, seeing he is beforehand with us in his offers of grace, and our own consciences will tell us, that our feelings are more from cherishing of some lusts, than from unwillingness in him to supply us with grace.

But God is of pure eyes and cannot endure such services as I perform.

Though God be of pure eyes, yet he looks upon us in *him who is blameless and without spot,* who by virtue of his sweet-smelling sacrifice, appears for us in heaven, and mingles his odours with our services, and in him will God be known to us by the name of a kind Father, not only in pardoning our defects, but accepting our endeavours. We offer our services to God, not in our own name, but in the name of our high priest, who takes them from us, and presents them to his Father, as stirred up by his Spirit, and perfumed by his obedience. Jonas's prayer was mingled with a great deal of passion and imperfection, yet God could discern something of his own in it, and pity and pardon the rest.

CHAPTER XXIV.

OF OUTWARD TROUBLES DISQUIETING THE SPIRIT: AND COMFORTS IN THEM.

As for the outward evils that we meet withal in this life, they are either *such,* 1. *As deprive us of the com-*

forts our nature is supported with; or else, 2. they
bring such misery upon our nature or condition
that hinders our well-being in this world.

For the first, trust in God, and take out of his all-
sufficiency whatsoever we want.   Sure we are by his
promise, that we shall want nothing that is good.
What he takes away one way, he can give another;
what he takes away in one hand he can give another;
what he withholds one way, he can supply in a better.
Whatsoever comfort we have in goods, friends, health,
or any other blessings it is all conveyed by him; who
still remains, though these be taken from us.   And
we have him bound in many promises for all that is
needful for us.   We may sue him upon his own
bond; can we think that he who will give us a kingdom, will fail us in necessary provision to bring us
thither, who himself is our portion?

As for those miseries which our weak nature is
subject to, they are all under Christ; they come and
go at his command; they are his messengers, sent
for our good, and called back again when they have
done what they came for.   Therefore look not so
much upon them, as to him for strength and comfort
in them, mitigation of them and grace to profit by
them.

To strengthen our faith the more in God, he calleth
himself a buckler for defence from ill, and an *exceed-*
ing great reward for a supply of all good.   A sun
for the one, and a shield for the other.   Trust him
then with health, wealth, good name, all that thou
hast.   It is not in man to take away that from us
which God will give us, and keep for us.   It is not
in man's power to make others conceive what they
please of us.

Among crosses, this is that which disquieteth not
the mind least, to be deceived in matter of trust,
when as if we had not trusted, we had not been deceived.   The very fear of being disappointed, made
David in his haste think *all men were liars.* Psalm
cxvi.   But as it is a sharp cross, so nothing will drive
us nearer unto God, who never faileth his.

Friends often prove as the *reed of Egypt, as a broken staff, and as a deceitful brook,* Job vi. 15, that fails the weary passenger in summer-time, when there is most need of refreshing; and it is the unhappiness of men, otherwise happy in the world, that during their prosperous condition, they know not who be their friends, for when their condition declines, it plainly appears, that many were friends of their estates, and not of their persons: but when men will know us least, God will know us most; he knows our souls in adversity, and knows them so as to support and comfort them, and that from the spring-head of comfort, whereby the sweetest comforts are fetched. What God conveyed before by friends, that he doth now instil immediately from himself. The immediate comforts are the strongest comforts. Our Saviour Christ told his disciples, that they would *leave him alone; yet,* saith he, *I am not alone, but the Father is with me.* At Paul's first appealing *all forsook him, but the Lord stood by him.* He wants no company that hath Christ for his companion. *I looked for some to take pity,* saith David, *but there was none.* This unfaithfulness of man is a foil to set out God's truth, who is never nearer than when trouble is nearest; there is not so much as a shadow of change in him or his love.

It is just with God when we lay too much weight of confidence upon any creature, to let us have the greater fall; man may fail us and yet be a good man, but God cannot fail us and be God, because he is truth itself. Shall God be so true to us, and shall not we be true to him and his truth?

The like may be said in the departure of our friends. Our life is oft too much in the life of others, which God takes unkindly: how many friends have we in him alone? who rather than we shall want friends, can make our enemies our friends. A true believer is to Christ as his mother, brother, and sister, because he carries that affection to them, as if they were mother, brother, and sister, to him indeed. As Christ makes us all to him, so should we make him all in all

14

to ourselves. If all comforts in the world were dead, we have them still in the living Lord.

Sicknesses are harbingers of death, and in the apprehension of many they be the greatest troubles, and tame great spirits, that nothing else could tame; herein we are more to deal with God than with men, which is one comfort sickness yieldeth above other troubles. It is better to be troubled with the distempers of our own bodies, than with the distempers of other men's souls; in which we have not only to deal with men, but with the devil himself, that ruleth in the humours of men.

The example of Asa teaches us in this case not to lay too much trust upon the physician, but with Hezekiah first look up to God, and then use the means. If God will give us a *quietus est*, and take us off from business by sickness, then we have a time of serving God by patient subjection to his will. If he means to use our service any further, he will restore our health and strength to do that work he sets us about. Health is at his command, and sickness stays at his rebuke. In the mean time, the time of sickness is a time of purging from that defilement we gathered in our health, till we come purer out; which should move us the rather willingly to abide God's time. Blessed is that sickness that proves the health of the soul. We are best, for the most part, when we are weakest. Then it appears what good proficients we have been in time of health.

Carnal men are oft led along by false hopes suggested by others, and cherished by themselves, that they shall live still, and do well, till death comes and cuts off their vain confidence and their life 'both at once, before ever they are acquainted what it is to trust in God aright, in the use of means. We should labour to learn of St. Paul in desperate cases, *to receive the sentence of death*, and not to trust in ourselves, but in God *that raiseth the dead*. He that raiseth our dead bodies out of the grave, can raise our diseased bodies out of the bed of sickness, if he hath a pleasure to serve himself by us.

In all kind of troubles, it is not the ingredients that God puts into the cup so much afflicts us, as the ingredients of our distempered passions mingled with them. The sting and core of them all is sin: when that is not only pardoned, but in some measure healed, and the proud flesh eaten out, then a healthy soul will bear any thing. After repentance, that trouble that before was a correction, becomes now a trial and exercise of grace. *Strike, Lord*, saith Luther, *I bear any thing willingly, because my sins are forgiven.* We should not be cast down so much about outward troubles, as about sin, that both procures them and envenoms them. We see by experience, when conscience is once set at liberty, how cheerfully men will go under any burthen; therefore labour to keep out sin, and then let come what will come.

It is the foolish wisdom of the world to prevent trouble by sin, which is the way indeed to pull the greatest trouble upon us. For sin dividing betwixt God and us, moveth him to leave the soul to entangle itself in its own ways. When the conscience is clear, then there is nothing between God and us to hinder our trust. Outward troubles rather drives us nearer unto God, and stand with his love. But sin defileth the soul, and sets it further from God. It is well doing that enables us to commit our souls cheerfully unto him. Whatsoever our outward condition be, *if our hearts condemn us not*, we may have *boldness with God.* In any trouble our care should be not to avoid the trouble: but sinful miscarriage in and about the trouble, and so trust God. It is a heavy condition to be under the burthen of trouble, and under the burthen of a guilty conscience both at once. When men will *walk in the light of their own fire*, and *the sparks which they have kindled themselves*, it is just with God that *they should lie down in sorrow.*

Whatsoever injuries we suffer from those that are ill affected to us, let us commit our cause to the *God of vengeance*, and not meddle with his prerogative. He will revenge our cause better than we can, and more perhaps than we desire. The wronged side is the safer side. If, instead of meditating revenge, we can so overcome ourselves as to pray for our enemies, and deserve well of them, we shall both sweeten our own spirits, and prevent a sharp temptation which we are prone unto, and have an undoubted argument that we are sons of that Father that doth good to his enemies, and members of that Saviour that prayed for his persecutors. And withal by *heaping coals* upon our enemies, shall melt them either to conversion or to confusion.

But our greatest trial of trust is in our last encounter with death, wherein we shall find not only a deprivation of all comforts in this life, but a confluence of all ill at once, but we must know, God will be the God of his unto death, and not only unto death, but in death. We may trust God the Father with our bodies and souls which he hath created; and God the Son, with the bodies and souls which he hath redeemed; and the holy Spirit, with those bodies and souls that he hath sanctified. We are not disquieted when we put off our clothes and go to bed, because we trust God's ordinary providence to raise us up again. And why should we be disquieted when we put off our bodies, and sleep our last sleep, considering we are more sure to rise out of our graves, than out of our beds? Nay, we are raised up already in Christ, our head: *who is the resurrection and the life*, in whom we may triumph over death, that triumpheth over the greatest monarchs as a disarmed and conquered enemy. Death is the death of itself, and not of us. If we would have faith ready to die by, we must exercise it well in living by it, and then it will no more fail us than the good things we lay hold on by it, until it hath brought us into heaven, where that office of it is laid aside: here is the prerogative of a true Christian above a hypocrite and a worldling, when as their trust, and the thing they trust in, fails them, then a true believer's trust stands him in greatest stead.

In regard of our *state after death*, a Christian need

not be disquieted, for the angels are ready to do their office in carrying the soul to paradise, those mansions *prepared for him.* His Saviour will be his judge, and the head will not condemn the members: then he is to receive the fruit and end of his faith, the reward of his hope; which is so great and so sure, that our trusting in God for that, strengtheneth the heart to trust him for all other things in our passage; so that the refreshing of our faith in these great things, refreshes its dependence upon God for all things here below. And how strong helps have we to uphold our faith in those great things which we are not able to conceive of, till we come to possess them? Is not our husband there? and hath he not taken possession for us? Doth he not keep our place for us? Is not our flesh there in him? and his spirit below with us? have we not some first-fruits and earnest of it beforehand? Is not Christ now fitting and preparing of us daily, for what he hath prepared and keeps for us? Whither tends all we meet with in in this world, that comes betwixt us and heaven, as desertions, inward conflicts, outward troubles, and death at last, but to fit us for a better condition hereafter, and by faith therein to stir up a strong desire after it? *Comfort one another with these things,* saith the apostle, 1 Thes. iv. 18; these be the things will comfort the soul.

CHAPTER XXV.

OF THE DEFECTS OF GIFTS, DISQUIETING THE SOUL—AS ALSO THE AFFLIC-
TIONS OF THE CHURCH.

AMONG other things, there is nothing more disquiets a Christian, that is called to the fellowship of Christ and his Church here, and to glory hereafter, than that he sees himself unfurnished with those gifts that are fit for the calling of a saint; as likewise for that particular standing and place wherein God hath set him in this world, by being a member of a body politic.

For our Christian calling, we must know that

Christianity is a matter rather of grace than of gifts, of obedience than of parts. Gifts may come from a more common work of the Spirit, they are common to castaways, and are more for others than for ourselves. Grace comes from a peculiar favour of God, and especially for our own good. In the same duty, where there is required gifts and grace, as in prayer, one may perform it with evidence of greater grace, than another of greater parts. Moses, a man not of the best speech, was chosen before Aaron, to speak to God, Exod. vii. 11; and to strive with him by prayer, whilst Israel fought with Amalek with the sword. It is a business more of the heart than of the tongue, more of groans than of words, which groans and sighs, the Spirit will always stir up even in the worst condition. Yet for parts there is no member, but it is fitted with some abilities, to do service in the body, and by faith may grow up to a greater measure. For God calls none to that high condition, but whom in some measure he fits to be a useful member, and endows with a public spirit.

But that is the measure which Christ thinks fit; who will make up that in the body which is wanting in any particular member. God will increase the measure of our gifts, as occasion shall be offered to draw them forth; for there is not the greatest but may have use both of the parts and graces of the meanest in the church. And here the soul may by a spirit of faith go to God in this manner: Lord, the estate of Christianity unto which thy love in Christ hath called and advanced me, is a high condition; and there is need of a great measure of grace to uphold the credit and comfort of it. Whom thou callest unto it, thou dost in some measure furnish to walk worthy of it. Let this be an evidence to my soul of the truth of thy call, that I am enabled by the Spirit for those duties that are required; in confidence of which assistance, I will set upon the work: *thou hast promised to give wisdom to them that ask it, and to upbraid none with their unworthiness. Nay, thou hast promised the Spirit of all grace to those that beg it,*

James i. 5; it is that which I need, and it is no more than thou hast promised.

Only it must be remembered, that we do not walk above our parts and graces, the issue whereof will be discouragement in ourselves, and disgrace from others.

The like may be said for our particular calling, wherein we are to express the graces of our Christian calling, and *serve one another in love*, Gal. v. 13, as members of the state as well as of the church; therefore every one must have, 1. a calling; 2. a lawful; 3. a useful calling; 4. a calling fitted for his parts, that he may be even for his business; 5. a lawful entrance, and calling thereunto; 6. and a lawful demeanour in the same. Though the orb and sphere we walk in be little, yet we must keep within the bounds of it, because for our carriage in that, we must give a strict account, and there is no calling so mean but a man shall find enough to give a good account for. Our care must be to know our work, and then to do it, and so to do it as if it were unto God; with conscience of moderate diligence for over-doing and over-working any thing, comes either from ostentation or distrust in God: and negligence is so far from getting any blessing, that it brings us under a *curse for doing God's work negligently*. Jer. xlviii. 10. For we must think our callings to be services of God, who hath appointed us our standing therein.

That which belongs to us in our calling is care of discharging our duty; that which God takes upon him is assistance and good success in it. Let us do our work, and leave God to do his own. Diligence and trust in him is only ours, the rest of the burthen is his. In a family the father's and the master's care is the greatest, the child's care is only to obey, and the servant's to do his work; care of provision and protection doth not trouble them. Most of our disquietness in our calling is, that we trouble ourselves about God's work. Trust God and be doing, and let him alone with the rest. He stands upon his credit so much, that it shall appear we have not trusted him in vain, even when we see no appearance of doing any good. Peter fished all night and catched nothing, yet upon Christ's word he casts in his net again, and caught so many fish as break his net. Luke v. 6. Covetousness, when men will be richer than God would have them, troubles all, *it troubles the house*, the whole family, and the house within us, our precious soul, which should be a quiet house for God's spirit to dwell in, whose seat is a quiet spirit. If men would follow Christ's method, and *seek first the kingdom of heaven*, Matt. vi. 33, all other things would be cast upon them. If thoughts of insufficiency in our places discourage us, remember what God saith to Moses, when he pretended disability to speak, *who hath made man's mouth, have not I the Lord?* Exod. iv. 11. All our sufficiency for every calling is from God.

But you will say, *though by God's blessing my particular condition be comfortable, yet the state of God's people abroad, and the miseries of the times disquiet me.*

We complain of the times, but let us take heed we be not a part of the misery of the times: that they be not the worse for us. Indeed he is a dead member that takes not to heart the ill of the times, yet here is place for that complaint, *help, Lord.* Psalm xii. In these tempests do as the disciples did, cry to Christ to rebuke the tempests and storms. This is the day of Jacob's trouble, let it also be the day of Jacob's trust; let the body do as the head did in the like case, and in time it shall be with the body as it is with the head.

In this case it is good to lay before God all the promises made to his church, with the examples of his presence in it, and deliverance of the same in former times. God is never nearer his church than when trouble is near: when in earth they conclude an utter overthrow, God is in heaven concluding a glorious deliverance: usually after the lowest ebb, follows the highest spring-tide. Christ stands upon Mount Zion. There is a counsel in heaven, that will dash the mould of all contrary counsels on earth;

and which is more, God will work the raising of the
Church, by that very means by which his enemies
seek to ruin it. *Let us stand still and behold the
salvation of the Lord.* God gave too dear a price
for his Church, to suffer it long in the hands of mer-
ciless enemies.

As for the seeming flourishing of the enemies of
God's Church, it is but for a time, and that a short
time, and a measured time. *The wicked plot against
the just,* Psalm xxxvii. 12; they are *plotters and
ploughers of mischief,* Job iv. 8: they are skilful
and industrious in it, but they reap their own ruin.
Their day is a coming, Psalm xxxvii. 12; and *their
pit is in digging,* Psalm xciv. 13; take heed therefore
of *fretting,* Psalm xxxvii. 7; because of the man *that
bringeth wicked devices to pass,* for *the arms of the
wicked shall be broken.** Psalm xxxvii. 17. We
should help our faith by observing God's executing
of judgment in this kind. It cannot but vex the
enemies of the Church, to see at length a disappointing of their projects, but then to see the mould of all
their devices turned upon their own heads, will more
torment them.

In this case, it will much comfort to go into the
sanctuary, for there we shall be able to say, *Yet God
is good to Israel.* Psalm lxxiii. God hath an ark for
his, there is no condition so ill, but there is a balm in
Gilead, comfort in Israel. *The depths of misery are
never beyond the depths of mercy.* God oft for this
very end, strips his Church of all helps below, that it
may only rely upon him: and that it may appear
that the Church is ruled by a higher power than it is
opposed by. And *then is the time when we may expect great deliverances of the Church, when there is
a great faith in the great God.*

From all that hath been said, we see that the only
way to quiet the soul is, to lay a charge upon it to
trust God, and that unquietness and impatience are
symptoms and discoveries of an unbelieving heart.

* Read Psalms x. xxxvii. xciv. cxxix. &c.

CHAPTER XXVI.

To go on [*I shall yet praise him.*]

In these words David expresseth the reasons and grounds of his trust, namely from the interest he had in God by experience and special covenant: wherein in general we may observe, that those who truly trust in God, labour to back their faith with sound arguments; faith is an understanding grace, it knows whom it trusts, and for what, and upon what grounds it trusts: reason of itself cannot find what we should believe, yet when God hath discovered the same, faith tells us there is great reason to believe it; faith useth reason though not as a ground, yet as a sanctified instrument to find out God's grounds, that it may rely upon them. He believes best, that knows best why he should believe; confidence, and love, and other affections of the soul, though they have no reason grafted in them, yet thus far they are reasonable, as that they are in a wise man raised up, guided, and laid down with reason; or else men were neither to be blamed nor praised for ordering their affections aright; whereas not only civil virtue, but grace itself is especially conversant in ruling the affections by sanctified reason.

The soul guides the will and affections otherwise than it doth the outward members of the body. It sways the affections of confidence, love, joy, &c., as a prince doth his wiser subjects, and as counsellors do a well ordered state by ministering reasons to them; but the soul governs the outward members by command, as a master doth a slave, his will is enough. The hand and foot move upon command, without regarding any reason; but we will not trust and rejoice in God without reason, or a show of reason at the least.

Sin itself never wanted a reason, such as it is, but we call it unreasonable, because it hath no good reason for it; for reason being a beam of God, cannot strengthen any work of darkness. God having made man an understanding creature, guides him by a way suitable to such a condition, and that is the reason why God in mercy yields so far to us in his word, as to give us so many reasons of our affiance in him. What is encouragement and comfort, but a demonstration to us of greater reasons to raise us up, than there are to cast us down?

David's reasons here are drawn partly from some promise of deliverance, and partly from God's nature and dealing with him, whom, as he had formerly found a healing and a saving God, so he expects to find him still; and partly from the *covenant of grace,* he is my God.

The chief of his reasons are fetched from God, what he is in himself, and what he is and will be to his children, and what to him in particular; though godly men have reasons for their trust, yet those reasons be divine and spiritual as faith itself is; for as naturally as beams come from the sun, and branches from the root, even so by divine discourse one truth issueth from another. And as the beams and the sun, as the root and branches are all of one nature, so the grounds of comfortable truths, and reasons taken from those grounds, are both of the same divinity and authority, though in time of temptation discourse is oft so troubled, that it cannot see how one truth riseth from another; this is one privilege of heaven, that our knowledge there shall not be so much discoursive, proving one thing by another, as definitive, seeing things in their grounds with a more present view; the soul being then raised and enlarged to a present conceiving of things, and there being no flesh and blood in us to raise objections that must be satisfied with reasoning.

Sometimes in a clearer state of the soul, faith hath not so much use of reasons, but upon near and sweet communion with God, and by reason of some likeness between the soul that hath a divine nature stamped upon it, that soul presently, without any long discourse, runneth to God as it were by a supernatural instinct, as by a natural instinct a child runneth to his father in any distress.   Yea, and from that common light of nature, which discovereth there is a God, even natural men in extremities will run to God, and God as the author of nature will sometimes hear them, as he doth the young ravens, that cry unto him; but comfortably, and with assurance only those have a familiar recourse unto him, that have a sanctified suitable disposition unto God, as being well acquainted with him.

Sometimes again faith is put to it to use reasons to strengthen itself, and therefore the soul studieth arguments to help itself by, either from inward store laid up in the soul, or else it hearkeneth and yields to reason suggested by others ; and there is no gracious heart but hath a frame suitable and agreeable to any holy and comfortable truth that shall be brought and enforced upon it; there is something in his spirit that answers whatever comes from the Spirit of God : though perhaps it never heard of it before, yet it presently claims kindred of it, as coming from the same blessed spring, the Holy Spirit; and therefore a gracious heart sooner takes comfort than another, as being prepared to close with it.

The reasons here brought by David, are not so much arguments to convince his judgment, as motives and inducements to incline his will to trust in God ; for trusting being a holy relying upon God, carrieth especially the will to him ; now the will is led with the goodness of things, as the understanding is led with truth; the heart must be sweetened with consideration of love and mercy in him whom we trust, as well as convinced of his ability to do us good, the cords that draw the heart to trust are the *cords of love*, and the cords of love are especially the love of him to us whom we love ; and therefore the most prevailing reasons that carry the whole heart, are such as are drawn from the sweetness of God, whereby the heart is opened and enlarged to expect all good, and nothing but good from him.

But we must remember that neither reasons from the truth and power of God, nor inducements or allurements from the goodness of God, will further prevail with the soul, than it hath a fresh light and relish brought into it by the Spirit of God, to discern of those reasons, and answer the contrary.

[*I will praise him.*] David here minds praising of God more than his own delivery, because he knew his own delivery was intended on God's part, that he might be glorified. It is an argument of an excellent spirit, when all self-respects are drowned in the glory of God: and there is nothing lost therein; for our best being is in God. A Christian begins with loving God for himself; but he ends in loving himself in and for God: and so his end, and God's end, and the end of all things else concentre and agree in one. We may aim at our own good, so we bring our hearts to refer it to the chief good, as a less circle may well be contained in a greater, so that the lines drawn from both circles, meet in one middle point. It is an excellent ground of sincerity to desire the favour of God, not so much out of self-aims, as that God may have the more free and full praise from us, considering the soul is never more fit for that blessed duty, than when it is in a cheerful plight.

It rejoiced David more that he should have a large heart to serve God, than that he should have enlargement of condition. Holy dispositions think not so much of the time to come, that it will be sweet to them, as that it will further God's praise. True grace raiseth the soul above self-respects, and resteth not till it comes to the chief end wherein its happiness consists.

God is glorified in making us happy, and we (enjoying happiness) must glorify God. Although God condescend so low unto us, as not only to allow us, but to enjoin us to look to our own freedom from misery, and enjoyment of happiness, yet a soul thoroughly seasoned with grace, mounteth higher, and is carried with pure respects to advance God's glory; yea sometimes so far as to forget its own happiness, it respects itself for God, rather than God for itself. A heavenly soul is never satisfied, until it be as near God as is attainable. And the nearer a creature comes to God, the more it is emptied of itself, and all self-aims. Our happiness is more in him, than in ourselves. *We seek ourselves most when we deny ourselves most.* And the more we labour to advance God, the more we advance our own condition in him.

[*I will praise.*] David thinks of his own duty in praising God, more than of God's work in delivering him; let us think of what is our duty, and God will think of what shall be for our comfort; we shall feel God answering what we look for from him, in doing what he expects from us. Can we have so mean thoughts of him, as that we should intend his glory, and he not much more intend our good?

This should be a strong plea unto us in our prayers, to prevail with God, when we engage ourselves upon the revelation of his mercy to us, to yield him all the praises. Lord, as the benefit and comfort shall be mine, so the praises shall be thine.

It is little less than blasphemy to praise God for that which by unlawful shifts we have procured; for besides the hypocrisy of it, in seeming to sacrifice to him, when we sacrifice indeed to our own wits and carnal helps, we make him a patron of those ways which he most abhors; and it is idolatry in the highest degree, to transform God so in our thoughts, as to think he is pleased with that which comes from his greatest enemy, and there is a gross mistake to take God's curse for a blessing; to thrive in an ill way, is a spiritual judgment, extremely hardening in the heart.

It is an argument of David's sincerity here, that he meant not to take any indirect course for delivering himself, because he intended to praise God, which as no guilty conscience can offer, being afraid to look God in the face, so God would abhor such a sacrifice, were it offered to him. St. Paul was stirred up to praise God, but withal he was assured *God would preserve him from every evil work.* 2 Tim. iv. 18.

Sometimes indeed where there is no malicious intention God pardons some breakings out of flesh and blood, endeavouring to help ourselves in danger, so far as not to take advantage of them to desert us in trouble, as in David, who escaped from Achish by counterfeiting, 1 Sam. xxvii. 10 ; and this yields a double ground of thankfulness, partly for God's overlooking our miscarriage, and partly for the deliverance itself. Yet this indulgence of God, will make the soul more ashamed afterwards, for these sinful shifts, therefore it must be no precedent to us. There can neither be grace nor wisdom in setting upon a course, wherein we can neither pray to God for success in, nor bless God when he gives it. In this case God most blesseth where he most crosseth, and most curseth where the deluded heart thinks he blesseth most.

CHAPTER XXVII.

IN OUR WORST CONDITION WE HAVE CAUSE TO PRAISE GOD—STILL AMPLE
CAUSE IN THESE DAYS.

I SHALL *yet praise him.* Or, yet *I will praise God;* that is, however it goeth with me, yet as I have cause, so I have a spirit to praise God ; when we are at the lowest, yet it is a mercy that we are not consumed ; we are never so ill, but it might be worse with us ; whatsoever is less than hell, is undeserved. It is a matter of praise, that yet we have time and opportunity to get into a blessed condition. *The Lord hath afflicted me sore, but he hath not delivered me to death,* saith David. Psalm xviii. 18.

In the worst times there is a presence of God with his children.

1. In moderating the measure of the cross, that it be not above their strength.

2. In moderating the time of it, *The rod of the wicked shall not rest long upon the lot of the righteous.* Psalm cxxv. 3. God limits both measure and time.

3. He is present in mixing some comfort, and so allaying the bitterness of a cross.

4. Yea, and he supports the soul by inward strength : so as though it faint, yet it shall not utterly fail.

5. God is present in sanctifying a cross for good, and at length when he hath perfected his own work in his, he is present for a final deliverance of them. A sound hearted Christian hath always a God to go to, a promise to go to, former experience to go to, besides some present experiences of God's goodness which he enjoys ; for the present he is a child of God, a member of Christ, an heir of heaven : he dwells in the love of God in the cross, as well as out of it, he may be cast out of his happy condition in the world, but never out of God's favour.

If God's children have cause to praise God in their worst condition, what difference is there betwixt their best estate and their worst?

Howsoever God's children have continual occasion to praise God, yet there be some more especial seasons of praising God than others, there be days of *God's own making*, of purpose to rejoice in, wherein we may say, *This is the day which the Lord hath made, let us rejoice therein.* Psal. xviii. 24. And this I think is chiefly intended here. David comforts himself with this, that however it was now with him, yet God would deal so graciously with him hereafter, that he should have cause to bless his name.

Though in evil times we have cause to praise God, yet so we are, and such are our spirits, for the most part, that affliction straightens our hearts. Therefore the apostle thought it the fittest duty in affliction to pray. *Is any afflicted? let him pray,* saith James ; *Is any joyful? let him sing Psalms,* James v. 13 ; showing that the day of rejoicing is the fittest day of praising God. Every work of a Christian is beautiful in its own time, the graces of Christianity have their several offices at several seasons ; in trouble, prayer is in its season : in the evil day call upon me, saith God; in better times praises should appear and show themselves. When God manifests his goodness to his, he gives them grace with it, to manifest their thankfulness to him. Praising of God is then most comely though never out of season, when God seems to call for it, by renewing the sense of his mercies in some fresh favour towards us. If a bird will sing in winter, much more in the spring; if the heart be prepared in the winter time of adversity to praise God, how ready will it be when it is warmed with the glorious sunshine of his favour?

Our life is nothing but as it were a web woven with interminglings of wants and favours, crosses and blessings, standings and fallings, combat and victory, therefore there should be a perpetual intercourse of praying and praising in our hearts. There is always a ground of communion with God in one of these kinds, till we come to that condition wherein all wants shall be supplied, where indeed is only matter of praise. Yet praising God in this life hath this prerogative, that here we praise him *in the midst of his enemies.* In heaven all will be in concert with us. God esteems it an honour in the midst of devils, and wicked men, whose life is nothing but a dishonour of him, to have those that will make his name as it is in itself so, great in the world.

David comforts himself in this, that he should praise God: which shows he had inured himself well before to this holy exercise, in which he found such comfort, that he could not but joy in the forethoughts of that time, wherein he should have fresh occasion of his former acquaintance with God. Thoughts of this nature enter not into a heart that is strange to God.

It is a special art in time of misery, to think of matter of joy, if not for the present, yet for the time to come; for joy disposeth to praise, and praise again stirs up joy; these mutually breed one another, even as the seed brings forth the tree, and the tree brings forth the seed. It is wisdom therefore to set faith on work, to take as much comfort as we can, from future promises, that we may have comfort and strength for

15

the present, before we have the full possession of them. It is the nature of faith to antedate blessings, by making them that are to be performed hereafter, as present now, because we have them in the promise. If God had not allowed us to take many things in trust for the time to come, both for his glory and our good, he would never have left such rich promises to us. For faith doth not only give glory to God, for the present (in a present believing of his truth, and relying upon him) but as it looks forward, it sees an everlasting ground of praising God, and is stirred up to praise him now, for that future matter of praise which it is sure to have hereafter. The very hopes of future good, made David praise God for the present. If the happy condition we look for were present, we would embrace it with present praises. Now *faith is the evidence of things not seen*, Heb. xi. 1; and gives a being to that which is not; whereupon a true believing soul cannot but be a praising soul. For this end God reveals beforehand what we shall have, that beforehand we should praise him, as if we possessed it. For that is a great honour to his truth, when we esteem of what he speaks, as done, and what he promiseth, as already performed. Had we not a perpetual confidence in the perpetuity of his love to us, how is it possible we should praise him?

But we want those grounds for the time to come which David had, he had particular promises which we want.

Though we want urim and thummim, and the prophets to foretell us what the times to come shall be, yet we have the canon of Scripture enlarged, we live under a more glorious manifestation of Christ, and under a more plentiful shedding of the Spirit, whereby that want is abundantly supplied; we have general promises for the time to come, that *God will never fail nor forsake us*, Deut. xxxi. 6; *that he will be with us in fire and in water, that he will give an issue to the temptation, and that the issue of all things shall be for our good, that we shall reap the quiet fruit of righteousness,* Heb. xii. 11; *and no good thing will he withhold from them that lead a godly life,* &c., Psalm lxxxiv. 11. If we had a spirit of faith to apply these generals, we should see much of God's goodness in particular.

Besides general promises, we have some particular ones for the time to come; of the confusion of Antichrist, of the conversion of the Jews, and fulness of the Gentiles, &c., which though we perhaps shall never live to see, yet we are members of that body, which hereafter shall see the same, which should stir up our hearts to praise God, as if we did enjoy the present fulfilling of them ourselves, for faith can present them to the soul, as if they were now present.

Some that have a more near communion with God, may have a particular faith of some particular deliverances, whereupon they may ground particular prayer. " Luther, praying for a sick friend, who was very comfortable, and useful to him, had a particular answer for his recovery, whereupon he was so confident, that he sent word to his friend, that he should certainly recover. Latimer prayed with great zeal for three things. 1. That Queen Elizabeth might come to the crown. 2. That he might seal the truth with his heart's blood. 3. And that the gospel might be restored *once again, once again,* which he expressed with great vehemency of spirit, all which three, God heard him in. But the privileges of a few must not be made a general rule for all. Privileges go not out of the persons, but rest there. Yet if men would maintain a nearer communion with God, there is no doubt but he would reveal himself in a more familiar manner to them, in many particulars than usually he doth. Those particular promises in Psalm xci. and other places, are made good to such as have a particular faith, and to all others, with those limitations annexed to promises of that nature, so far forth as God seeth it will conduce to their good and his own glory, so far forth as they depend upon him in the use of means; and is not this sufficient to stay a gracious heart?

But not to insist upon particular promises and revelations (the performance whereof we enjoy here in this present life) we have rich and precious promises of final and full deliverance from all evil, and perfect enjoying of all good in that life which is to come; yet not so to come, but that we have the earnest and first fruits of it here; all is not kept for heaven; we may say with David, *Oh how great is thy goodness, which thou hast laid up for them that fear thee,* Psalm xxxi. 19; and (not only so, but) how great is that goodness which thou hast wrought in them that trust in thee, even *before the sons of men!* God treasures not up all his goodness for the time to come, but lays much of it out daily before such as have eyes to behold it.

Now God's main end in revealing such glorious promises of the life to come is, that they might be a ground of comfort to us, and of praise to him even in this life; and indeed what can be grievous in this world to him that hath heaven in his eye? What made our blessed Saviour *endure the cross and despise shame,* Heb. xii. 2, but the joy *of glory to come set before him?*

The duty that David brought his heart to before he had a full enjoyment of what he looked for, was patient waiting, it being God's use to put a long date oftentimes to the performances of his promises; David, after he had the *promise of a kingdom,* was put off a long time ere he was invested with it; Abraham was an old man before he enjoyed his son of the promise; Joseph stayed a long time before he was exalted; our blessed Saviour himself was thirty-four years old before he was exalted up into glory.

God defers, but his deferring is no empty space, wherein no good is done, but there is in that space a fitting for promises. Whilst the seed lieth hid in the earth, time is not lost, for winter fits for spring, yea, the harder the winter, the more hopeful the spring; yet were it a mere empty space, we should hold out, because of the great things to come; but being only a preparing time, we should pass it with the less discouragement. Let this support us in all the thwartings of our desire; it is a folly to think, that we should have physic and health both at once; we must endure the working of God's physic; when the sick humour is carried away and purged, then we shall enjoy desired health. God promiseth forgiveness of sin, but thou findest the burthen of it daily on thee. Cheer up thyself, when the morning is darkest, then comes day; after a weary week comes a sabbath, and after a fight victory will appear. God's time is best, therefore resolve upon waiting his leisure. For the better demeaning of ourselves herein, we must know we must so wait, that we provoke not in the mean time his patience on whom we depend, by putting forth our hand to any evil, which indeed is a crossing of our hopes. Therefore waiting upon God is always joined with doing good. There is an influence in the thing hoped for, in the spirit of him that truly hopes, stirring him up to a suitable conformity, by purging himself of whatsoever will not stand with the holiness of that condition. Waiting implies all graces, as patience, perseverance, long-suffering in holding out, notwithstanding the tediousness of time deferred; courage, and breaking through all difficulties that stand between. For what is waiting indeed, but a continuing in a gracious inoffensive course, till the accomplishment of our desires!

Whence we may discern a main difference betwixt a Christian and a carnal man, who is short-spirited, and all for the present; he will have his good here, whereas a saint of God continues still waiting, though all things seem contrary to what he expects. The presence of things to come is such to faith, as it makes it *despise the pleasure of sin for a season.* What evidence of goodness is it for a man to be good only upon the apprehension of something that contents him? Here is the glory of faith, that it can upon God's bare promise, cross itself in things pleasing to nature, and raise up the soul to a disposition some ways answerable to that blessed estate which, though yet it enjoys not, yet it is undoubtedly persuaded of, and looks for. What can encourage us more to wait, than this, that the good we wait for is greater than we are able to conceive, yea, greater than we can desire or hope for?

This was no presumptuous resolution of David's own strength, but it issued from his present truth of heart, so far as he knew the same; together with an humble dependence upon God, both for deliverance, and a heart to praise him for it; because God's benefits are usually entire, and are sweetened with such a sense of his love, as causeth a thankful heart, which to a true Christian, is a greater blessing than the deliverance itself, as making the soul better. David doth acknowledge with humble admiration, that a heart enlarged comes from God, *Who am I*, saith he, *and who are my people.*

He mentioneth here praising God, instead of deliverance, because a heart enlarged to praise God is indeed the greatest part of the deliverance: for by it the soul is delivered out of its own straits and discontent.

CHAPTER XXVIII.

DIVERS QUALITIES OF THE PRAISE DUE TO GOD—WITH HELPS THEREIN— AND NOTES OF GOD'S HEARING OUR PRAYERS.

THOUGH this be God's due and our duty, and itself a delightful thing, yet it is not so easy a matter to praise God, as many imagine; music is sweet, but the setting of the strings in tune is unpleasing; our souls will not be long in tune, and it is harsh to us to go about the setting them in order; like curious clocks, a little thing will hinder the motion; especially passion, which disturbs not only the frame of grace in us, but the very frame of nature, putting man out of the power and possession of himself; and therefore David here, when he had thoughts of praising God, was fain to take up the quarrel betwixt him and his soul first; praising sets all the parts and graces of the soul to work; and therefore the soul had need gather itself and its strength together to this duty.

It requires especially self-denial, from a conscience of our own wants, weaknesses, and unworthiness; it requires a giving up of ourselves, and all ours to be at God's disposal; the very ground and the fruit which it yields are both God's; and they never gave themselves truly up to God, that are not ready to give all they have to him whensoever he calls for it; thankfulness is a sacrifice, and in sacrifices there must be killing before offering, otherwise the sacrifice will be as the offering up some unclean creature; thanksgiving is an incense, and there must be fire to burn that incense; thanksgiving requires not only affections, but the heat of affections; there must be some assurance of the benefit we praise God for; and it is no easy matter to maintain assurance of our interest in the best things.

Yet in this case if we feel not sense of assurance, it is good we should praise God for what we have; we cannot deny but God offers himself in mercy to us, and that he intends our good thereby, for so we ought to construe his merciful dealing towards us, and not have him in jealousy without ground; if we bring our hearts to be willing to praise God, for that we cannot but acknowledge comes from him, he will be ready in his time to show himself more clearly to us; we taste of his goodness many ways, and it is accompanied with much patience, and these in their natures lead us not only to repentance, but likewise to thankful acknowledgment; and we ought to follow that which God leads us unto, though he hath not yet acquainted us with his secrets.

It is good in this case to help the soul with a firm resolution, and to back resolution with a vow not only in general that we will praise, but particularly of something within our own power, provided it prove no snare to us. For by this means the heart is perfectly gained, and the thing is as good as done in regard of God's acceptance and our comfort; because strong resolutions discover sincerity without any hypocritical reservation and hollowness. Always so much sincerity as a man hath, so much will his inward peace be. Resolution as a strong stream bears down all before it; little good is done in religion without this, and with it all is as good as done.

So soon as we set upon this work, we shall feel our spirits to rise higher and higher as the waters in the sanctuary, as the soul grows more and more heated; see how David riseth by degrees. *Be glad in 'the Lord*, and then, *rejoice, ye righteous*, and then, *shout for joy all ye that are upright in heart*, the Spirit of God will delight to carry us along in this duty, until it leaves our spirits in heaven, praising God with the saints and glorious angels there: *To him that hath* and useth *it shall be given:* he that knoweth God aright, will honour him by trusting of him; he that honours him by trusting him, will honour him by praying; and he that honours him by prayer, shall honour him by praises; he that honours him by praises here, shall perfect his praises in heaven; and this will quit the labour of setting and keeping the soul in tune; this trading with God is the richest trade in the world; when we return praises to him, he returns new favours to us, and so an everlasting ever-increasing intercourse betwixt God and the soul is maintained; David here resolved to praise God, because he had assurance of such a deliverance as would yield him a ground of praising him.

Praising of God may well be called incense, because as it is sweet in itself, and sweet to God, so it sweetens all that comes from us. Love and joy are sweet in themselves, though those whom we love and joy in, should not know of our affection, nor return the like; but we cannot love and joy in God but he will delight in us; when we neglect the praising of God, we lose both the comfort of God's love, and our own too; it is a spiritual judgment to want or lose the sight or sense of God's favours, for it is a sign of want of spiritual life, or at least liveliness; it shows we are not yet in the state of those whom God hath chosen, to set forth the riches of his glory upon.

When we consider that if we answer not kindness and favour showed unto us by men, we are esteemed unworthy of respect, as having sinned against the bond of human society and love, we cannot but much more take shame to ourselves, when we consider the disproportion of our carriage, and unkind behaviour towards God; when instead of being temples of his praise, we become graves of his benefits; what a vanity is this in our nature, to stand upon exactness of justice, in answering petty courtesies of men, and yet to pass by the substantial favours of God, without scarce taking notice of them? The best breeding is to acknowledge greatest respects where they are most due, and to think, that if unkindness and rudeness be a sin in civility, it is much more in religion; the greatest danger of unthankfulness is in the greatest matter of all; if we arrogate any spiritual strength to ourselves in spiritual actions, we commit either sacrilege in robbing God of his due, or mockery, by praising him for that which we hold to be of ourselves; if injustice be to be condemned in man, much more in denying God his due, religion being the first due. It takes much from thankfulness, when we have common conceits of peculiar favours; praise is not comely in the mouth of fools, God loves no *blind sacrifice.*

We should therefore have wisdom and judgment, not only to know upon what grounds to be thankful, but in what order, by discerning what be the best and first favours whence the rest proceed, and which add a worthiness to all the rest; it is good to see blessings, as they issue from grace and mercy. It much commends any blessing, to see the love and favour of God in it, which is more to be valued than the blessing itself, as it much commends any thing that comes from us, when we put a respect of thankfulness, and love to God upon it; and if we observe, we shall find the unkindness of others to us is but a correction of our unkindness to God.

In praising God, it is not good to delay, but take advantage of the freshness of the blessing; what we add to delay, we take from thankfulness; and withal, lose the prime and first-fruits of our affections: it is a wise redeeming of time, to observe the best *seasons of thankfulness;* a cheerful heart will best close with a cheerful duty; and therefore it is not good to waste so fit a temper in frivolous things, but after some con tentment given to nature, let God have the fruit of his own planting, otherwise it is even no better than the refreshing of him that standeth by a good fire, and crieth, *Ah, ah, I am warm.*

David doth not say, *I will thank God,* but *I shall praise him;* though he intends *that.*   Thanks is then best when it tends to praising, and there ends: for thanks alone show respect to our own good only, praises, to God's glory; and in particular to the glory of such excellencies whence the benefit comes; and from thence the soul is enlarged to think highly of all God's excellencies.

Hannah, upon particular thanks for hearing her about a child, takes occasion to set out God's other excellencies, and riseth higher and higher, from one to many, from the present time to that which was to come, from particular favours to herself, she stirs up others to praise God for his mercy to them; so David, *Deliver me, O God, and my tongue shall sing of thy praises;* he propounds this as an engagement to the Lord to help him, because it should tend to the enlargement of his glory; he was resolved to improve God's favour this way.

The Spirit of God works like new wine, enlarging the spirit from one degree of praising God to another; and because it foresees the eternity of God's love, as far as it can, it endeavours an eternity of God's praise; a gracious heart upon taste of favour showed to itself, is presently warmed to spread the praise of God to others, and the more it sees the fruit of trusting God, and his truth in performing promise, the more it still honours that trusting, as knowing that it lies upon God's honour, to honour those that honour him.

Blessing will procure blessing; the soul hath never such freedom from sin, as when it is in a thankful frame; for thankfulness issues from a heart truly humbled and emptied of itself, truly loving and rejoicing in God; and upon any sin the spirit is grieved and straitened, and the lips sealed up in such a heart; for the conscience upon any sin looks upon it not only as disobedience against God's will and authority, but as unthankfulness to his goodness, and this melteth a godly heart most of all: when Nathan told David God had done this, and this for him, and was ready to do more, he could not hold in the confession of his sin, but relented, and gave in presently.

We ought not only to give thanks, but to be thankful, to meditate and study the praises of God. Our whole life should be nothing else but a continual blessing of his holy name, endeavouring to bring in all we have, and to lay it out for God and his people, to see where he hath any receivers: our goodness is nothing to God: we need bring no water to the fountain, nor light to the sun. Thankfulness is full of invention, it deviseth liberal things, though it be our duty to be good stewards of our talents, yet thankfulness adds a lustre, and a more gracious acceptance, as having more of that which God calls for.

Our praising God should not be as sparks out of a flint, but as water out of a spring, natural, ready, free, as God's love to us is; mercy pleases him, so should praise please us: it is our happiness when the best part in us is exercised about the best and highest work; it was a good speech of him that said, If God had made me a nightingale, I would have sung as a nightingale, but now God hath made me a man, I will sing forth the *praises of God* which is the work of a saint only: *all thy works bless thee, and thy saints praise thee:* all things are either blessings in their nature, or so blessed, as they are made blessings to us by the overruling coming of him, who maketh all things serviceable to his, even the worst things in this sense are made spiritual to God's people against their own nature; how great is that goodness which makes even the worst things good?

Little favours come from no small love, but even from the same love that God intends the greatest things to us, and are pledges of it; the godly are more thankful for the least favours, than worldly men for the greatest: the affection of the giver enhances the gift.

O then let us labour to improve both what we have and what we are to his glory: it discovers that we love God, not only with all our understanding, heart, and affections, but when with all our might and power, so far as we have advantage by any part, relation, or calling whatsoever, we endeavour to do him service, we cannot have a greater honour in the world, than to be honoured of God, to be abundant in this kind.

Our time here is short, and we shall all ere long be called to a reckoning, therefore let us study real praises. God's blessing of us is in deed, and so should ours be of him. Thanks in words is good, but in deeds is better; leaves are good, but fruit is better; and of fruit, that which costs us most. True praise requires our whole man, the judgment to esteem, the memory to treasure up, the will to resolve, the affections to delight, the tongue to speak of, and the life to express the rich favours of God: what can we think of? what can we call to mind? What can we resolve upon? what can we speak? What can we express in our whole course better than the praises of him, *of whom, and through whom, and to whom* we and *all things are?*

Our whole life should speak nothing but thankfulness; every condition and place we are in should be a witness of our thankfulness; this will make the times and places we live in the better for us; when we ourselves are monuments of God's mercy, it is fit we should be patterns of his praises, and leave monuments to others: we should think life is given us, to do something better than live in; we live not to live;

our life is not the end of itself, but the praise of the giver: God hath joined his glory and our happiness together; it is fit that we should refer all that is good to his glory, that hath joined his glory to our best good, in being glorified in our salvation.

David concludes, that he *should certainly praise God*, because he had prayed unto him. Prayers be the seeds of praises: I have sown, therefore I will reap; what we receive as a fruit of our prayers, is more sweet than what we have by a general providence.

But how do we know that God hears our prayers?

1. If we regard them ourselves, and expect an issue; prayer is a sure adventure, we may well look for a return.

2. It is a sign that God hath heard our prayers, when he stirs up thankfulness aforehand upon assurance; thankfulness cannot be without either the grace of God, by which we are thankful, or some taste of the things we are thankful for. God often accepts the prayer, when he doth not grant the thing, and will give us thereby occasion of thanksgiving for his wise care, in changing one blessing for another fitter for us. God regards my prayers, when by prayer my heart is wrought to that frame which he requires, that is an humble subjection to him, from an acknowledgment of my wants, and his fulness, There is nothing stirred up in our hearts by the Spirit, no, not so much as a gracious desire, but God will answer it, if we have a spirit to wait.

3. We may know God hath accepted our prayer, when he makes the way easy and plain after prayer by a gracious providence, when the course of things begin to change, and we meet with comforts instead of former crosses, and find our hearts quieted and encouraged against what we most feared.

4. Likewise earnestness in prayer is a sign God hears our prayers, as fire kindled from heaven showeth God accepts the sacrifice; the ground of prevailing by our prayer, is, that they are put up in a gracious

name, and for persons in favour, and dictated by God's
own Spirit; they work in the strength of the blessed
Trinity, not their own, giving God the glory of all his
excellencies.

It is God's direction *to call upon him in trouble,*
and it is his promise to deliver; and then both his direction and promise that we shall glorify him: when
troubles stir up prayer, God's answer to them will
stir up praises.   David when he saith, *I shall praise
God,* presupposes God would deliver him, that he
might have ground of praising his name.   And he
knew God would deliver him, because from faith he
had prayed for deliverance, so he knew it was the order of God's dealing, to revive after drooping, and refresh after fainting.   God knows otherwise that our
spirits would fail before him.

A thankful disposition is a special help in an afflicted condition, for thankfulness springs from love,
and *love rejoiceth in suffering.*   Thankfulness raises
the soul higher than itself, it is trading with God,
whereby as we by him, so he gains by us.   Therefore the saints used this as a motive to God, that he
would grant their desires, because *the living praise
him,* and not the dead.   If God expect praise from
us, sure he will put us into a condition of praise.

Unthankfulness is a sin detestable both to God and
men, and the less punishment it receives from human
laws, the more it is punished inwardly by secret shame,
and outwardly by public hatred, if once it prove no-
torious.   When God's arrests come forth for denying
him his tribute, he chiefly eyes an unthankful heart,
and hates all sin the worse, as there is more unthankfulness in it: the neglect of kindness is taken most unkindly.   Why should we load God with injuries, that
loadeth us with his blessings? who would requite
good with evil?   Such men's mercies will prove at
last so many indictments against them.

I beseech you therefore labour to be men of praises.
If in any duty we may expect assistance, we may in
this, that altogether concerns God's glory; the more
we praise God, the more we shall praise him.   When

God by grace enlarges the will, he intends to give the deed. God's children wherein their wills are conformable to God's will, are sure to have them fulfilled. In a fruitful ground, a man will sow his best seed. God intends his own glory in every mercy, and he that *praises him, glorifies him.* When our wills therefore carry us to that which God wills above all, we may well expect he will satisfy our desires. The living God is a living fountain never drawn dry, he hath never done so much for us, but he can and will do more. If there be no end of our praises, there shall be no end of his goodness, no way of thriving like to this. By this means we are sure never to be very miserable; how can he be dejected, that by a sweet communion with God sets himself in heaven? nay, maketh his heart a kind of heaven, *a temple, a holy of holies,* wherein incense is offered unto God? It is the sweetest branch of our priestly office, to offer up these daily sacrifices; it is not only the beginning, but a further entrance of our heaven upon earth, and shall be one day our whole employment for ever.

Praise is a just and due tribute for all God's blessings; for what else especially do the best favours of God call for at our hands? How do all creatures praise God, but by our mouths? It is a debt always owing, and always paying; and the more we pay the more we shall owe; upon the due discharge of this debt, the soul will find much peace. A thankful heart to God for his blessings, is the greatest blessing of all. Were it not for a few gracious souls, what honour should God have of the rest of the unthankful world? which should stir us up the more to be trumpets of God's praises in the midst of his enemies, because this, in some sort, hath a prerogative above our praising God in heaven; for their God hath no enemies to dishonour him.

This is a duty that none can except against, because it is especially a work of the heart. All cannot show their thankfulness in giving or doing great matters, but all may express the willingness of their hearts. *All within us may praise his holy name,*

Psalm ciii. ; though we have little or nothing *without us;* and that within us is the thing God chiefly requires. Our heart is the altar on which we offer this incense ; God looks not to quantity, but to proportion ; he accepts a mite where there is no more to be had.

But how shall we be enabled to this great duty?

Enter into a deep consideration of God's favours, past, present, and to come; think of the greatness and suitableness of them to our condition, the seasonableness and necessity of them every way unto us. Consider how miserable our life were without them, even without common favours; but as for spiritual favours, that make both our natural and civil condition comfortable, our very life were death, our light were darkness without these. In all favours think not of them so much, as God's mercy and love in Christ, which sweetens them. Think of the freeness of this love, and the smallness of thy own deserts. How many blessings doth God bestow upon us, above our deserts, yea, above our desires, nay, above our very thoughts? He had thoughts of love to us when we had no thoughts ourselves. What had we been if God had not been good unto us? How many blessings hath God bestowed upon us, that we never prayed for? and yet we are not so ready to praise God, as to pray unto him; this more desire of what we want than esteeming of what we have, shows too much prevailing of self-love. But,

Secondly, comparing also ourselves with others, will add a great lustre to God's favour, considering we are all hewed out of one rock, and differ nothing from the meanest, but in God's free love. Who are we that God should single us out for the glory of his rich mercy.

Considering, likewise, *that the blessings of God to us are such as if none but we had them, and God cares for us, as if he had none else to care for in the world besides.* These things well pondered, should set the greater price upon God's blessings; what are we in nature and grace but God's blessings; what is in us, about us, above us? What we see, taste we, enjoy we, but blessings: all we have or hope to have, are but dead favours to use, unless we put life into them by a spirit of thankfulness. And shall we be as dead as the earth, as the stones we tread on? Shall we live as if we were resolved God should have no praise by us? Shall we make ourselves God, ascribing all to ourselves? Nay, shall we, as many do, fight against God with his own favours, and turn God's blessings against himself? Shall we abuse peace to security? Plenty to ease, promises to presumption, gifts to pride? How can we please the devil better than thus doing? Oh! the wonderful patience of God, to continue life to those whose life is nothing else but a warring against him the giver of life.

As God hath thoughts of love to us, so should our thoughts be of praises to him, and of doing good in our places to others for his sake. Think with thyself, is there any I may honour God by relieving, comforting, counselling? Is there any of Jonathan's race? 2 Sam. ix. 1. Is there any of Christ's dear ones? I will do good to them, that they together with me, and for me, may praise God, Psalm cxviii. 1. As David here checks himself for the failing and disquietness of his spirit, and as a cure thereof, thinks of praising God: so let us, in the like case, stir up our souls as he did, and say, *Praise the Lord, O my soul, and all that is within me, set forth his holy name*, Psalm ciii. 1. We never use our spirits to better purpose, than when by that light we have from God, we stir them up to look back again to him.

By this it will appear to what good purposes we had a being here in the world, and were brought into communion with Christ by the gospel. The carriage of all things to the right end, shows whose we are, and whither we tend. It abundantly appears by God's revealing of himself many ways to us, as by promises, sacraments, sabbaths, &c., that he intended to raise up our hearts to this heavenly duty. The whole gracious dispensation of God in Christ tends to this, that our carriage should be nothing else, but an expression of thankfulness to him; that by a free,

16

cheerful, and gracious disposition, we might show we are the people of God's free grace, set at liberty from the spirit of bondage, *to serve him without fear,* Luke i. 74, with a voluntary childlike service, *all the days of our lives.*

CHAPTER XXIX.

OF GOD'S MANIFOLD SALVATION FOR HIS PEOPLE, AND WHY OPEN, OR EX-
PRESSED IN THE COUNTENANCE.

I PROCEED.

He is the salvation of my countenance.

As David strengthens his trust in God, by reason fetched from the future goodness of God, apprehended by faith; so he strengthens that reason with another reason fetched from God, whom he apprehends here as *the salvation of his countenance.* We need reason against reason, and reason upon reason, to steel and strengthen the soul against the onset of contrary reasons.

He is the salvation of my countenance: that is, he will so save as I shall see, and my enemies shall see it; and upon seeing, my countenance shall be cheered and lifted up; God's saving kindness shall be read in my countenance, so that all who look on me, shall say, God hath spoken peace to my soul, as well as brought peace to my condition.

He saith not salvation, but salvations; because as our life is subject to many miseries, in soul, body, and estate, public and private, &c., so God hath many salvations: if we have a thousand troubles, he hath a thousand ways of help; as he hath more blessings than one, so he hath more salvations than one. He saves our souls from sin, our bodies from danger, and our estates from trouble. *He is the Redeemer of his people;* and not only so, but with him is *plenteous redemption* of all persons, of all parts both of body and soul, from all ill, both of sin and misery, for all times, both, now and hereafter. He is an everlasting salvation.

David doth not say, God will save me; but God is

salvation itself, and nothing but salvation. Our sins only stop the current of his mercy, but it being above all our sins, will soon scatter that cloud, remove that stop, and then we shall see and feel nothing but salvation from the Lord. *All his ways are mercy and peace* to a repentant soul that casts itself upon him.

Christ himself is nothing else but salvation clothed in our flesh. So old Simeon conceived of him, when he had him in his arms, and was willing thereupon to yield up his spirit to God, having seen Christ, the salvation of God: when we embrace Christ in the arms of our faith, we embrace nothing but salvation. He makes up that sweet name given him by his Father, and brought from heaven by an angel to the full, Luke ii. 14: a name in the faith of which, it is impossible for any believing soul to sink.

The devil in trouble presents God to us as a revenging destroyer, and unbelief presents him under a false vizard; but the skill of faith is, to present him as a Saviour clothed with salvation. We should not so much look what destruction the devil and his threaten, as what salvation God promiseth. Psalm lxviii. 20. To God belong *the issues of death;* and of all other troubles, which are lesser deaths. Cannot he that hath vouchsafed an issue in Christ from eternal death, vouchsafe an issue from all temporal evils? If he will raise our bodies, cannot he raise our conditions? He that brought us into trouble can easily make a way out of it when he pleaseth. This should be a ground of resolute and absolute obedience, even in our greatest extremities, considering God will either deliver us (from death, or by death, and) at length out of death.

So then, when we are in any danger, we see whither to go for salvation, even to him that is nothing else but salvation; but then we must trust in him, as David doth, and conceive of him as salvation, that we may trust in him. If we will not trust in salvation, what will we trust in? and if salvation itself cannot save us, what can? out of salvation there is nothing but destruction, which those that seek it any where out of God, are sure to meet with. How pitiful then is their case, who go to a destroyer for salvation? that seek for help from hell?

Here also we see to whom to return praise in all our deliverances, even to the God of our salvation. The virgin Mary was stirred up to magnify the Lord, but why? *Her spirit rejoiced in God her Saviour.* Luke i. Whosoever is the instrument of any good, yet salvation is of the Lord; whatsoever brings it, he sends it. Hence in their holy feasts for any deliverance, the cup they drank of was called *the cup of salvation:* and therefore David when he summons his thoughts, *what to render unto God,* he resolves upon this, to take *the cup of salvation.* But always remember this, that when we think of God as salvation, we must think of him as he is in Christ to his. For, so every thing in God is saving, even his most terrible attributes of justice and power: out of Christ, the sweetest things in God are terrible. Salvation itself will not save out of Christ, who is the only way of salvation, called the way, the truth, and the life.

David addeth, *He is the salvation of my countenance;* that is, he will first speak salvation to my soul, and say, *I am thy salvation:* and when the heart is cheered, which is as it were *the sun of this little world,* the beams of joy that will shine in the countenance. *True joy begins at the centre, and so passeth to the circumference the outward man.* The countenance is as the glass of the soul, wherein you may see the naked face of the soul, according as the several affections thereof stand. In the countenance of an understanding creature, you may see more than a bare countenance. The spirit of one man may see the countenance of another's inner man in his outward countenance; which hath a speech of its own, and declares what the heart saith, and how it is affected.

But how comes God to be the salvation of our countenance?

I answer: God only graciously shines in the face of Jesus Christ, which we with the eye of faith beholding, receive those beams of his grace, and reflect them back again; God shineth upon us first, and we shine in that *light of his countenance* upon us. *The joy of salvation*, especially of spiritual and eternal salvation, is the only true joy: all other salvations end at last in destruction, and are no further comfortable than they issue from God's saving love.

God will have the body partake with the soul; as in matter of grief, so in matter of joy, the lantern shines in the light of the candle within.

Again, *God brings forth the joy of the heart into the countenance, for the further spreading and multiplying of joy to others.*

Next unto the sight of the sweet countenance of God, is the beholding of the cheerful countenance of a Christian friend, rejoicing from true grounds. Whence it is that the joy of one becomes the joy of many, and the joys of many meet in one; by which means, as many lights together make the greater light, so many lightsome spirits make the greater light of spirit: and God receiveth the more praise, which makes him so much to delight in the prosperity of his children. Hence it is, that in any deliverance of God's people, *the righteous do compass them about,* Psalm cxlii. 7, to know *what God hath done for their souls;* and keep a spiritual feast with them in partaking of their joy. And the godly have cause to joy in the deliverance of other Christians, because they suffered in their afflictions, and it may be in their sins the cause of them, which made them somewhat ashamed. Whence it is, that David's great desire was, that *those who feared God might not be ashamed because of him,* Psalm lxix. 6: insinuating that those who fear God's name are ashamed of the falls of God's people. Now when God delivers them, this reproach is removed, and those that had part in their sorrow have part in their joy.

Again, God will have salvation so open, that it shall appear in the countenance of his people, the more to daunt and vex the enemies. Cainish hypocrites hang down their heads, when God lifts up the countenance of their brethren; when the countenance of God's children clears up, then their enemies' hearts and looks are cloudy. *Jerusalem's joy is Babylon's sorrow.* It is with the church and her enemies as it is with a balance, the scales whereof when one is up the other is down. Whilst God's people are under a cloud, carnal people insult over them, as if they were men deserted of God. Whereupon they hang down their heads, and the rather, because they think that by reason of their sins, Christ and his religion will suffer with them. Hence David's care was, that the miseries of God's people *should not be told in Gath.* 2 Sam. i. 20. The chief reason why the enemies of the Church gnash their teeth at the sight of God's gracious dealing, is, that they take the rising of the Church to be a presage of their ruin. A lesson which Haman's wife had learned. Esther vi. 13.

This is a comfort to us in these times of Jacob's trouble and Zion's sorrow: the captivity of the Church shall return, *as rivers in the south.* Psalm cxxvi. 1. Therefore the Church may say, *Rejoice not over me, O my enemy, though I am fallen, I shall rise again.* Mic. vii. 8. Though Christ's spouse be now as black as the pots, yet she shall be as white as the dove. If there were not great dangers, where were the glory of God's great deliverance? The Church at length will be as *a cup of trembling,* and as *a burthensome stone.* Zec. xii. 2. The blood of the saints cry, their enemies' violence cries, the prayers of the Church cry for deliverance and vengeance upon the enemies of the Church; and, as that *importunate widow,* Luke xi. 5, will at length prevail. Shall the importunity of one poor woman prevail with an unrighteous judge, and shall not the prayers of many that cry unto the righteous God take effect? If there were armies of prayers, as there are armies of men, we should see the stream of things turned another way. A few Moses in the mount would do more good than many soldiers in the valley. If we would lift up our hearts and hands to God, he would lift up our countenance. But, alas, we either pray not, or cross our own prayers for want of love to the truth of God and his people.

It is we that keep Antichrist and his faction alive, to plague the unthankful world. The strength he hath is not from his own cause, but from our want of zeal; we hinder those hallelujahs by private brabbles, coldness and indifferency in religion. The Church begins at this time a little to lift up her head again: now is the time to follow God with prayers, that he would perfect his own work, and plead his own cause; that he would be revenged not only of ours, but his enemies: that he would wholly free his Church from that miserable bondage. These beginnings give our faith some hold to be encouraged to go to God for the fulfilling of his gracious promise, that the Church may rejoice in the *salvation of the Lord.* God doth but look for some to seek unto him: Christ doth but stay until he is awaked by our prayers. But it is to be feared that God hath not yet perfected his work in Zion. The Church is not fully prepared for a full and glorious deliverance. If God had once his ends in the humiliation of the Church for sins past, with resolution of reformation for the time to come, then this age perhaps might *see the salvation of the Lord,* which the generations to come shall be witness of: *we should see Zion in her perfect beauty.* The generations of those that came out of Egypt saw and enjoyed the pleasant land which their progenitors were shut out of: who by reason of their murmuring and looking back to Egypt, and forgetfulness of the wonders which God had done for and before them, perished in the wilderness.

There is little cause therefore of envying the present flourishing of the enemies of the Church, and of joining and colluding with them: for it will prove the wisest resolution to resolve to fall and rise with the Church of Christ, considering the enemies themselves shall say, God hath done great things for them: kings shall lay their crowns at *Christ's feet,* and *bring all their glory to the Church.* Rev. xxi. 24.

And for every Christian, this may be a comfort, that though their light for a time may be eclipsed, yet it shall break forth. David at this time was ac-

counted an enemy of the state, and had a world of
false imputations laid upon him, which he was very
sensible of; yet, we see here, he knew at length God
would be *the salvation of his countenance.*

But some, as Gideon, *may object, if God intend to
be so gracious, why is it thus with us?*

The answer is, salvation is God's own work, humbling and casting down is his strange work, whereby
he comes to his own work. For, when he intends to
save, he will seem to destroy first: and when he will
justify, he will condemn first: whom he will revive,
he will kill first. Grace and goodness countenanced
by God, have a native inbred majesty in them, which
maketh the face to shine, and borroweth not its lustre
from without, which God at length will have to appear in its own likeness, howsoever malice may cast
a veil thereon, and disguise it for a time: and though
wickedness, as it is base born, and a child of darkness,
may shelter itself under authority awhile, yet it shall
hide itself and run into corners. The comfort of comforts is, that at that great day, the day of all days, that
day *of the revelation of the righteous judgment of
God,* Dan. xii.; the righteous shall then shine as the
sun in the firmament, then Christ will come to be glorious in his saints, and will be the *salvation of the
countenance* of all his. Then all the works of darkness shall be driven out of countenance, and adjudged
to the place from whence they came. In the mean
time let us, with David, support ourselves with the
hopes of these times.

CHAPTER XXX.

OF GOD, OUR GOD, AND OF PARTICULAR APPLICATION.

My God. These words imply a special interest that
the holy man had in God, as his God, being the ground
of all which was said before; both of the duty of trusting, and of praising, and of the salvation that he expected from God. He is my God, therefore be not

disquieted, but trust him. He is my God, therefore he will give me matter to praise him, and will be *the salvation of my countenance;* God hath some special ones in the world, to whom he doth as it were pass over himself, and whose God he is by virtue of a more special covenant; whence we have these excellent expressions, *I will be your God, and you shall be my people,* Jer. xxxi. 33; *I will be your Father, and you shall be my sons and daughters.* 2 Cor. vi. 18.   Since the fall we having lost our communion with God the chief good, our happiness stands in recovering again fellowship with him.   For this end we were created, and for this redeemed, and for effecting of this, the word and sacraments are sanctified to us, yea, and for this end God himself, out of the bowels of his compassion, vouchsafed to enter into a gracious covenant with us, founded upon Jesus Christ, and his satisfaction to divine justice ; so that by faith we become one with him, and receive him as offered of his Father to *be all in all to us.*

Hence it is, that Christ hath his name *Emanuel, God with us.* Not only because he is God and man too, both natures meeting in one person, but because being God in our nature, he hath undertook this office to bring God and us together.   The main end of Christ's coming and suffering was to reconcile, and to gather together in one ; and, as Peter expresseth it, *to bring man again to God.* 1 Pet. iii. 18. *Emanuel* is the bond of this happy agreement, and appears for ever in heaven to make it good.   As the comfort hereof is great, so the foundation of it is sure and everlasting.   God will be our God, so long as he is Christ's God; and because he is Christ's God. John xx. 10.   Thus the father of the faithful, and all other holy men before Christ, apprehended God to be their God in the Messias to come.   Christ was the ground of their interest.   He was *yesterday* to them as well as *to-day* to us. Heb. xiii.   Hence it is that God is called the *portion,* Psalm lxxiii. 26, of his people, and they his *jewels,* Mal. iii. 25; he is their only *rock* and *strong tower,* Psalm lxxi., and they his peculiar ones,

Well may we wonder that the great God should stoop so low, to enter into such a covenant of grace and peace, founded upon such a mediator, with such utter enemies, base creatures, sinful dust and ashes as we are. This is the wonderment of angels, a torment of devils, and glory of our nature and persons; and will be matter of admiration, and praising God unto us for all eternity.

As God offereth himself to be ours in Christ, (else durst we lay no claim to him) so there must be in us an appropriating grace of faith, to lay hold of this offer. David saith here, My God. But by what spirit? by a spirit of faith, which looking to God's offer, maketh it his own whatsoever it lays hold of. God offereth himself in covenant, and faith catcheth hold thereon presently. With a gracious offer of God there goeth a gracious touch of his Spirit to the soul, giving it sight and strength, whereby, being aided by the same Spirit, it layeth hold on God showing himself in love. God saith to the soul, *I am thy salvation,* and the soul saith again, *Thou art my God. Faith is nothing else but a spiritual echo, returning that voice back again which God first speaks to the soul.* For what acquaintance could the soul claim with so glorious a majesty, if he should not first condescend so low, as to speak peace, and whisper secretly to the soul, that he is our loving God and Father, and we his peculiar ones in Christ, that our sins are all pardoned, his justice fully satisfied, and our persons freely accepted in his dear Son?

But to come more particularly to the words, *My God.* The words are pregnant; in the womb of them, all that is graciously and comfortably good is contained; they are the spring-head of all particular blessings. All particular relations and titles that it pleaseth God to take upon him, have their strength from hence, that God is our God. More cannot be said, and less will not serve the turn. Whatsoever else we have, if we have not God, it will prove but an empty cistern at last; he is our proper element, every thing desires to live in its own element, fishes in the sea, birds in the air: in this they are best preserved.

There is a greater strength in this *My God* than in any other title, it is more than if he had said *My King,* or *My Lord;* these are words of sovereignty and wisdom; but this implies not only infinite power, sovereignty, and wisdom, but likewise infinite bounty and provident care; so that when we are said to be God's people, the meaning is, that we are not only such over whom God hath a power and command, but such as toward whom he shows a loving and peculiar respect.

In the words is implied, 1. A propriety and interest in God. 2. An improvement of the same for the quieting of the soul.

David here lays a particular claim, by a particular faith unto God. The reason is, 1. The virtue of faith is as to lay hold, so to appropriate to itself, and make its own whatever it lays hold on, and it doth no more in this, than God gives it leave by his gracious promises to do.

2. As God offers, so faith receives, but God offers himself in particular to the believing soul by his Spirit, therefore our faith must be particular. That which the sacraments seal, is a peculiar interest in Christ. This is that which hath always upheld the saints of God, and that which is ever joined with the life of Christ in us. *The life that I live,* saith Paul, *is by the faith of the Son of God, who loved me, and gave himself for me.* Gal. ii. 20. The spirit of faith is a spirit of application.

This is implied in all the articles of our faith; we believe God to be our Father, and Christ to be *born for us,* that he *died* for us, and *rose again* for our good, and now sits at the right hand of God making requests for us in particular.

3. This is that which distinguisheth the faith of a true Christian from all hypocrites and cast-aways whatsoever. Were it not for this word of possession (*mine*) the devil might say the *Creed* to as good purpose as we; he believes there is a God, and a Christ: but that which torments him is this, he can say (*my*) to never an article of faith.

4. A general apprehension of God's goodness and

mercy may stand with desperation. Take away *my* from *God*, and take away God himself in regard of comfort; what comfort was it for Adam, when he was shut out of Paradise, to look upon it after he had lost it? The more excellencies are in God, the more our grief if we have not our part in them: the very life-blood of the gospel lies in a special application of particular mercy to ourselves. All relations that God and Christ have taken upon them, imply a necessity of application; what if God be a rock of salvation, if we do not rest upon him? What if he be a foundation, and we do not build on him? What if he offers himself as a husband, if we will not accept of him, what avails it us? How can we rejoice in the salvation of our souls, unless we can in particular say, *I rejoice in God my Saviour.*

5. Without particular application, we can neither entertain the love of God, nor return love again, by which means we lose all the comfort God intends us in his word, which of purpose was written for our solace and refreshment; take away particular faith, and we let out all the spirits of cheerful and thankful obedience.

This possessive particle (*my*) hath place in all the golden chain of our salvation. The first spring of all God's claim to us as his is in his election of us; we were by grace his before we were; those that are his from that eternal love, he gives to Christ; this is hid in the breast of God, till he calls us out of the rest of the world into communion with Christ. In answering of which call, by faith, we become one with Christ, and so one with him. Afterwards in justification we feel God experimentally to be reconciled unto us, whence arises joy and inward peace. And then upon further sanctification God delights in us as his, bearing his own image, and we from a likeness to God delight in him as ours in his Christ, and so this mutual interest betwixt God and us continues until at last God becomes *all in all* unto us.

But how can a man that is not yet in the state of grace say with any comfort, My God?

Whilst a man *regards iniquity in his heart* without any remorse or dislike of the same, if he saith, My God, his heart will give his tongue the lie, however in an outward profession and opinion of others, he may bear himself as if God were his, upon false grounds. For there can be no more in a conclusion, than it hath from the principle and premises out of which it is drawn. The principle here is, that God is the God of all that trust in him. Now if we can make it good, that we truly trust in God, we may safely conclude of comfort from him; for the more certain clearing of which, try yourselves by the signs of trust delivered.

It is no easy matter to say in truth of heart, My God, the flesh will still labour for supremacy, God should be *all in all* unto us, but this will not be till these bodies of flesh, together with the body of sin, be laid aside. He that says, God is my God, and doth not yield up himself unto God, raiseth a building without a foundation, layeth a claim without a title, and claimeth a title without an evidence, reckoning upon a bargain, without consent of the party with whom he would contract.

But if a man shall out of the sight and sense of sin, thirst after mercy in Christ, and call upon God for pardon, then God, who is a God *hearing prayer,* Psalm lxv. 2, and delighteth to be known by the name of merciful, will be ready to close and meet with the desire of such a soul, so far as to give it leave to rely upon him for mercy, and that without presumption, until he further discovers himself graciously unto it; upon sense of which grace the soul may be encouraged to lay a further claim unto God, having further acquaintance with him. Hence are those exhortations so oft in the Prophets, to *turn unto the Lord our God,* Zac. i. 3, because upon our first resolution to turn unto God, we shall find him always ready to answer those desires, that he stirs up by his own spirit in us.

We are not therefore to stay our turning unto God, till we feel him saying to our hearts, *I am thy God;*

but when he prevents us by his grace, enabling us to desire grace, let us follow the work begun in the strength of what grace we have, and then God will further manifest himself in mercy to us.

Yet God, before we can make any thing towards him, letteth into our hearts some few beams of mercy, thereby drawing us unto him, and reaching us out a hint to lay hold upon.

And as sin causeth a distance betwixt God and us, so the guilt of sin in the conscience, causeth further strangeness, insomuch that we dare not look up to heaven, till God open a little crevice to let in a little light of comfort at least into our souls, whereby we are by little and little drawn nearer to him. But this light at the first is so little, that in regard of the greater sense of sin, and a larger desire of grace, the soul reckons the same as no light at all, in comparison of what it desires and seeks after. Yet the comfort is, that this dawning light will at length clear up to a perfect day.

Thus we see how this claim of God to be our God, is still in growth until full assurance, and that there is a great distance betwixt the first act of faith in cleaving to God, offering himself in Christ to be ours, and between the last fruit of faith the clear and comfortable feeling, that God is our God indeed. We first by faith apply ourselves to God, and then apply God to us, to be ours; the first is the conflicting exercise of faith, the last is the triumph of faith; therefore faith properly is not assurance. And to comfort us the more, the promises are specially made to the act of faith, fuller assurance is the reward of faith.

If God hath not chosen me in Christ to be his, what ground have I to trust in him? I may cast away myself upon a vain confidence.

We have no ground at first to trouble ourselves about God's election. Secret things belong to God; God's revealed will is, *that all that believe in Christ shall not perish.* John iii. 15. It is my duty therefore, knowing this, to believe, by doing whereof, I put that question (*whether God be mine or no?*) out of all question: for all that believe in Christ are Christ's, and all that are Christ's are God's. It is not my duty to look to God's secret counsel, but to his open offer, invitation, and command, and thereupon to adventure my soul. And this adventure of faith will bring at length a rich return unto us. In war men will adventure their lives, because they think some will escape, and why not they? In traffic beyond the seas many adventure great estates, because some grow rich by a good return, though many miscarry. The husbandman adventures his seed, though sometime the year proves so bad, that he never sees it more: and shall we not make a spiritual adventure in casting ourselves upon God, when we have so good a warrant as his command, and so good an encouragement as his promise, that he will not fail those that rely on him? God bids us *draw near to him*, and he will *draw near to us*. Whilst we in God's own ways draw near to him, and labour to entertain good thoughts of him, he will delight to show himself favourable unto us. Whilst we are striving against an unbelieving heart, he will come in and help us, and so fresh light will come in.

Pretend not thy unworthiness and inability, to keep thee off from God, for this is the way to keep thee so still; if any thing help us, it must be God; and if ever he help us, it must be by casting ourselves upon him: for then he will reach out himself unto us in the promise of mercy to pardon our sin, and in the promise of grace to sanctify our natures. It was a good resolution of the lepers, *If we enter into the city, the famine is there, and we shall die*, say they; *if we sit still, we shall die also: let us therefore fall into the host of Assyrians, if they save us, we shall live; if they kill us, we shall but die.* So we should reason: if we sit still under the load of our sin, we shall die; if we put ourselves into the hands of Christ, if he save us, we shall live; if he save us not, we shall but die. Nay, surely, he will not suffer us to die. Did ever Christ thrust any back from him, that put themselves upon him? unless it were by that means to draw them the nearer unto him, as we see in the *woman of Canaan*. His denial was but to increase her importunity. We should therefore do as she did, gather all arguments to help our faith. Suppose *I am a dog*, saith she, yet I am one of the family, and therefore have a right *to the crumbs that fall*. So, Lord, I have been a sinner, yet I am thy creature; and not only so, but such a creature as thou hast set over the rest of the works of thy hands; and not only so, but one whom thou hast admitted into thy Church by baptism, whereby thou wouldst bind me to give myself unto thee beforehand; and more than this, thou hast brought me under the means, and therein hast showed thy will concerning my turning towards thee. Thou hast not only offered me conditions of peace, but wooed me by thy ministers to give up myself unto thee, as thine in thy Christ. Therefore I dare not suspect thy good meaning towards me, or question thy intendment, but resolve to take thy counsel, and put myself upon thy mercy. I cannot think, if thou hadst meant to cast me away, and not to own me for thine, thou wouldst ever have kindled these desires in me. But it is not this state I rest in, my purpose is to wait upon thee, until thou dost manifest thyself further unto me. It is not common favours that will content me, though I be unworthy of these, because I hear of choice blessings towards thy chosen people, that thou enterest into a peculiar covenant withal, *sure mercies*, Isa. lv. 3, and such as accompany salvation. These be the favours I wait for at thy hand. *O visit me with the salvation of thy chosen.* Psalm cvi. 4, 5. O remember me with the favour of thy people, that I may see *the good of thy chosen*. Whilst the soul is thus exercised, more sweetness falls upon the will and affections, whereby they are drawn still nearer unto God. The soul is in a getting and thriving condition; for God delights to show himself gracious to those that strive to be well persuaded of him, concerning his readiness to show mercy to all that look towards him in Christ. In worldly things how do we cherish hopes upon little grounds? if there shineth never so little hope of gain or preferment, we make after it: why then should we forsake our own mercy, which God offers to be our own, if we will embrace it, having such certain grounds for our hope to rest on?

It was the policy of the servants of Benhadad to watch if any word of comfort fell from the King of Israel, when he named Benhadad his brother, they catched presently at that, and cheered themselves. Faith hath a catching quality at whatsoever is near to lay hold on. Like the branches of the vine, it windeth about that which is next, and stays itself upon it, spreading further and further still. If nature taught Benhadad's servants to lay hold upon any word of comfort that fell from the mouth of a cruel king, shall not grace teach God's children to lie in wait for a token that he will show for good to them? How should we stretch forth the arms of our *faith to him, that stretcheth out his arms all the day long to a rebellious people?* Isa. lxv. 2. God will never shut his bosom against those, that in an humble obedience fly unto him: we cannot conceive too graciously of God. Can we have a fairer offer, than for God in Christ to make over himself unto us? which is more than if he should make over a thousand worlds; therefore our chief care should be first by faith to make this good, and then to make it useful unto us, by living upon it as our chiefest portion, which we shall do; 1. By proving God to be our God in particular; 2. By improving of it in all the passages of our lives.

CHAPTER XXXI.

MEANS OF PROVING AND EVIDENCING TO OUR SOULS THAT GOD IS OUR GOD.

Now we prove it to our souls, that God is ours, when we take him at his offer, when we bring nothing but a sense of our own emptiness with us, and a good conceit of his faithfulness and ability to do us good, when we answer God in the particular passages of salvation, which we cannot do, till he begins unto us. Therefore if we be God's, it is a certain sign that God is ours. If we choose him, we may conclude he hath chosen us first. If we love him, we may know that *he hath loved us first.* 1 John iv. 19. If we apprehend him, it is because he hath apprehended us first. Whatsoever affection we show to God, it is a reflection of his first to us. If cold and dark bodies have light and heat in them, it is because the sun hath shined upon them first. Mary answers not Rabboni till Christ said Mary to her. If we say to God, I am thine, it is because he hath first said unto us, Thou art mine; after which, the voice of the faithful soul is, *I am my beloved's and my beloved is mine.* We may know God's mind to us in heaven, by the return of our hearts upwards again to him: only as the reflected beams are weaker than the direct, so our affections in their return to God, are far weaker than his love falling upon us. God will be to us whatsoever we make him by our faith to be; when by grace we answer his condition of trusting, then he becomes ours to use for our good.

2. We may know God to be *our God* when we pitch and plant all our happiness in him, when the desires of our souls are towards him, and we place all our contentment in him. As this word (*my*) is a term of appropriation springing from a special faith, so it is a word of love and peculiar affection, showing that the soul doth repose and rest itself quietly and securely upon God. Thus David proves God to be his God, by *early seeking of him,* by *thirsting,* and *longing after his presence,* and that upon good reason, *because God's loving kindness was better to him than life;* this he knew would *satisfy his soul as with marrow and fatness.* So St. Paul proved Christ to be his Lord, by *accounting all else as dung and dross in comparison of him.*

Then we make God our God, and set a crown of majesty upon his head, when we set up a throne for him in our hearts, where self-love before had set up

the creature above him; when the heart is so unloosed
from the world, that it is ready to part with any thing
for God's sake, giving him now the supremacy in our
hearts, and bringing down every high thought, in captivity to him; making him our trust, our love, our
joy, our delight, our fear, our all; and whatsoever we
esteem or affect else, to esteem and affect it under
him, in him, and for him; when we cleave to him
above all, depending upon him as our chief good,
and contenting ourselves in him, as all-sufficient to
give our souls fit and full satisfaction. When we resign up ourselves to his gracious government, to do
and suffer what he will, offering ourselves and all
our spiritual services as sacrifices to him; when faith'
brings God into the soul as ours, we not only love
him, but love him dearly, making it appear, that we
are at good terms with God, we are at a point for
other things. How many are there that will adventure the loss of the love of God for a thing of nothing,
and redeem the favour of men with the loss of God's?
certain it is whatsoever we esteem, or affect most, that
whatsoever it be in itself, yet we make it our god.
The best of us all may take shame to ourselves herein
in that we do not give God his due place in us, but
set up some idol or other in our hearts above him.

When the soul can without hypocrisy say, *My God*,
it engageth us to universal and unlimited obedience,
we shall be ambitious of doing that which may be acceptable and well pleasing to him; and therefore this
is prefixed as a ground before the Commandments,
enforcing obedience? *I am the Lord thy God*, therefore *thou shalt have no other gods before me*, Exod.
xx, whomsoever else we obey, it must be *in the Lord*,
because we see a beam of God's authority in them;
and it is no prejudice to any inferior authority, to
prefer God's authority above it, in case of difference
one from the other.

When we know we are a peculiar people, we cannot but be zealous of good works. *If I be a Father,
where is mine honour?* special relations are special
enforcements to duty.

4. The Spirit of God, which knows the deep things of God, and the depths of our hearts, doth reveal this mutual interest betwixt God and those that are his, it being a principal work of the Spirit to seal this unto the soul, by discovering such a clear and particular light in the use of means, as swayeth the soul to yield up itself wholly to God. When we truly trust, we may say with St. Paul, *I know* whom *I have trusted;* he knew both that he trusted, and whom he trusted. The Spirit of God that reveals God to be ours, and stirs up faith in him, both reveals this trust to our souls, and the interest we have in God thereby. *The Lord is my portion saith my soul;* but God said so to it first. If instinct of nature teaches dams to know their young ones, and their young ones them, in the midst of those that are alike : shall not the Spirit of God much more teach the soul to know its own father? as none knows what is in man, but the spirit of man, so none knows what love God bears to those that are his, but the Spirit of God in his : all the light in the world cannot discover the sun unto us, only it discovers itself by its own beams. So all the angels and saints in heaven cannot discover to our souls the love that is in the breast of God towards us, but only the Spirit of God, which *sheds it into our hearts.* Rom. v. 5. The Spirit only teaches this language, My God. It is infused only into sanctified hearts; and therefore ofttimes mean men enjoy it, when great, wise, and learned persons are strangers to it. Matt. xi. 25.

5. The Spirit when it witnesseth this to us is called the *Spirit of adoption,* and hath always accompanying it a spirit of supplication, whereby with a familiar, yet reverend boldness, we lay open our hearts to God as a dear father; all others are strangers to this heavenly intercourse. In straits they run to their friends and carnal shifts, whereas an heir of heaven runs to his father, and tells him of all.

6. Those that are God's are known to be his by special love-tokens that he bestows upon them. As 1. The special graces of his Spirit. Princes' children

are known by their costly jewels, and rich ornaments. It is not common gifts, and glorious parts that set a character upon us to be God's, but grace to use those gifts in humility and love, to the glory of the giver.

2. There is in them a suitableness and connaturalness of heart to all that is spiritual, to whatsoever hath God's stamp upon it, as his truth and his children, and that because they are his. By this likeness of disposition, we are fashioned to a communion with him; can two walk together, and not be agreed? it is a certain evidence that we are God's in Christ, if the Spirit of God hath wrought in us any impression like unto Christ, who is the image of his Father: both Christ looking upon us, and our looking upon Christ by faith as ours, hath a transforming and conforming power.

3. Spiritual comforts in distress, such as the world can neither give, nor take away, show that God looks upon the souls of his with another eye, than he beholdeth others. He sends a secret messenger that reports his peculiar love to their hearts. He knows their souls, and feeds them with his hidden manna? the inward peace they feel is not in freedom from trouble, but in freeness from God in the midst of trouble.

4. Seasonable and sanctified corrections, whereby we are kept from being led away by the error of the wicked, show God's fatherly care over us as his. Who will trouble himself in correcting another man's child? yet we oftener complain of the smart we feel, than think of the tender heart and hand that smites us, until our spirits be subdued, and then we reap the quiet fruit of righteousness. Where crosses *work together for the best* we may know *that we love God*, Rom. viii. 28, and are loved of him. Thriving in a sinful course is a black mark of one that is not God's.

5. Then we make it appear that God is our God, when we side with him, and are for him and his cause in ill times. When God seems to cry out unto us, *Who is on my side, who?* then if we can say as those in Isaiah, whereof one says, *I am the Lord's*, and another calls himself *by the name of Jacob*, and an-

other *subscribes with his hand unto the Lord,* it is a blessed sign. Thus the patriarchs and prophets, apostles and martyrs, were not ashamed of God, and God was not ashamed to own them. Provided that this boldness for God proceed not only from a conviction of the judgment, but from spiritual experience of the goodness of the cause, whereby we can justify in heart what we justify in words. Otherwise men may contend for that with others, which they have no interest in themselves. The life must witness for God as well as the tongue; it is oft easier for corrupt nato part with life rather than with lust.

This siding with God, is with a separation from whatsoever is contrary. God useth this as an argument to come out of Babylon, because we are his people; *Come out of her, my people.* Religion is nothing else but a gathering and a binding of the soul close to God: that fire which gathers together the gold, separates the dross. Nature draws out that which is wholesome in meats, and severs the contrary. The good that is to be had by God, is by cleaving to him, and him only. God loves an ingenuous and full protestation, if called to it. It shows the coldness of the times when there is not heat enough of zeal to separate from a contrary faith. God is a jealous God, and so we shall find him at last. When the day of severing comes, then they that have stood for him, shall not only be his, but his treasure, and his jewels. Mal. iii. 17.

There is none of us all but may some time or other fall into such a great extremity, that when we look about us, we shall find none to help us: at which time we shall thoroughly know, what it is to have comfort from heaven, and a God to go unto. If there be any thing in the world worth labouring for, it is the getting sound evidence to our souls that God is ours. What madness is it to spend all our labour, to possess ourselves of the cistern when the fountain is offered to us? O beloved, the whole world cannot weigh against this one comfort, that God is ours. All things laid in the other balance, would be too light.

A moth may corrupt, a thief may take away that we have here, but who can take our God away? though God doth convey some comfort to us by these things, yet when they are gone, he reserves the comfort in himself still, and can convey that, and more, in a purer and sweeter way, where he plants the grace of faith to fetch it from him.   Why then should we weaken our interest in God, for any thing this earth affords? what unworthy wretches are those, that to please a sinful man, or to feed a base lust, or to yield to a wicked custom, will, as much as in them lieth, lose their interest in God? such little consider what an excellent privilege it is to have a sure refuge to fly unto in time of trouble.   God wants not ways to maintain his, without being beholden to the devil: he hath all help hid in himself, and will then most show it, when it shall make most for his own glory.   If God be ours, it is a shame to be beholden to the devil, that ever it should be said, Satan by base courses hath made us rich.   God thinks any outward thing too mean for his children, severed from himself, therefore he gives his Son, the express *image of himself,* unto them.   For which cause David, when he had even studied to reckon up the number of God's choice blessings, concludes with advancing of *this above all, yea, rather happy are they whose God is the Lord.* If this will not satisfy the soul, what can?   Labour therefore to bring thy soul to this point with God, *Lord, if thou seest it fit, take away all from me, so thou leavest me thyself: whom have I in heaven but thee, and there is none on earth that I desire in comparison of thee?*

CHAPTER XXXII.

OF IMPROVING OUR EVIDENCES FOR COMFORT IN SEVERAL PASSAGES OF OUR
LIVES.

THAT we lose not any measure of comfort in this so sweet a privilege, we must labour for skill to improve and implead the same in the several passages and occasions of our lives, and let it appear in the retail, that whatsoever is in God is mine: if I am *in a perplexed condition,* his *wisdom* is mine: if *in great danger,* his *power* is mine; if I lie sighing *under the burthen of sin,* his *grace is mine:* if in any want, his *all-sufficiency is* mine. *My God,* saith Paul, *will supply all your wants.* If in any danger, *I am thine, Lord,* save me, I am thine, the price of thy Son's blood, let me not be lost, thou hast given me the earnest of thy Spirit, and set thy seal upon me for thy own, let me neither lose my bargain, nor thou thine. What is religion itself but a spiritual bond? whereby the soul is tied to God as its own, and then singles out of God whatsoever is needful for any occasion: and so binds God with his own covenant and promise. *Lord, thou hast made thyself to be mine, therefore now show thyself so, and be exalted in thy wisdom, goodness, and power, for my defence. To walk comfortably in my Christian course, I need much grace, supply me out of thy rich store. I need wisdom to go in and out inoffensively before others, furnish me with thy Spirit. I need patience and comfort, thou that art the God of all consolation, bestow it on me.*

In time of desertion put Christ betwixt God and thy soul, and learn to appeal, from God out of Christ, to God in Christ. Lord, look upon my Saviour, that is near unto thee as thy son, near to me as my brother, and now intercedes at thy right hand for me; though I have sinned, yet he hath suffered, and shed his precious blood to make my peace. When we are in any trouble, let us still wait on him, and lie at his feet, and never let him go till he casts a gracious look upon us.

So if we be to deal with God for the Church abroad, we may allege unto him that whatsoever provocations are therein, and deformity in regard of abuses and scandals; yet it is his Church, his people, his inheritance, his name is called upon in it, and the enemies of it are his enemies. God hath engaged himself to the friends of the Church, that *they shall prosper that love it,* Psalm cxxii. 6; and therefore we may with a holy boldness press him for a blessing upon the same.

So for our children and posterity, we may incline God to respect them, because they are under his covenant, who hath promised to be our God, and the God of *our seed,* John xvii.; *thine they were, thou gavest them me: all that I have is thine, these are those children which thou of thy rich grace hast given me. They are thine more than mine; I am but a means under thee to bring them into the world, and to be a nurse unto thy children; take care therefore of thine own children, I beseech thee, especially. when I can take no care of them myself; thou slumberest not, thou diest not, I must.*

Flesh and blood think nothing is cared for, but what it seeth cared for by itself. It hath no eyes to see a guard of providence, a guard of angels. It takes no knowledge that that is best cared for, that God cares for. Those that have God for *their God,* have enlarged hearts as they have enlarged comforts. They have an everlasting spring that supplies them in all wants, refreshes them in all troubles, and then runs most clearly and freshly, when all other streams in the world are dried and stopped up. Were we skilful in the art of faith, to improve so great an interest, what in the world could much dismay us? faith will set God against all.

It should fill our hearts with an holy indignation against ourselves, if either we rest in a condition, wherein we cannot truly say, God is our God, or, if when we can in some sincerity of heart say this, that we make no better advantage thereby, and maintain not ourselves answerable to such a condition. What a shame is it for a nobleman's son to live like a beggar? for a great rich man to live like a poor peasant? to famish at a banquet? to fall when we have so many stays to lay hold on? Whereas if we could make this clear to our souls, that God is ours, and then take up our thoughts with the great riches we have in him, laid open in Christ, and in the promises, we need trouble ourselves about nothing, but only get a large vessel of *faith,* to receive what is offered, nay enforced upon us.

When we can say, *God is our God,* it is more than

if we could say, Heaven is mine; or whatever good the creature affords is mine. Alas, what is all this, to be able to say, *God is mine*, who hath in him the sweetness of all these things, and infinitely more? If God be ours, goodness itself is ours. If he be not ours, though we had all things else, yet ere long *nothing would be ours*. What a wondrous comfort is this, that God hath put himself over to be ours? That a believing soul may say with as great confidence, and greater too, that God is his, than he can say his house is his, his treasure is his, his friends are his? Nothing is so much ours as God is ours, because by his being ours in covenant, all other things become ours: and if God be once ours, well may we trust in him. God and ours joined together, make up the full comfort of a Christian. [God] there is all to be had; but what is that to me, unless he be *my God? All-sufficiency with propriety, fully stayeth the soul.*

David was now banished from the sanctuary, from his friends, habitation, and former comforts; but was he banished from his God? No, God was his God still. When riches, and friends, and life itself cease to be ours, yet God never loseth his righteous, nor we our interest in him. This comfort that *God is ours,* reacheth into the *resurrection of our bodies,* and to *life everlasting.* God is the God of Abraham, and so of every true believer, even when his body is turned into dust. Hence it is that *the loving kindness of the Lord is better than life,* because when life departs, yet we live for ever in him. When Moses saw the people drop away so fast in the wilderness, and wither like grass, *Thou art our foundation,* saith he, *from one generation to another: thou art God from everlasting to everlasting.* When we leave the world, and are no more seen here, yet we have a dwelling place in God for ever. God is ours from everlasting in election, and to everlasting in glory, protecting us here, and glorifying us hereafter. David that claimed God to be his God is gone, but David's God is alive. And David himself, *though his flesh see corruption,* yet is alive in his God still.

That which is said of wily persons that are full of fetches and windings, and turnings in the world, that such will never break, may much more truly be said of a right godly man, that hath but one grand policy to secure him in all dangers, which is to run to his God as to his tower of offence and defence: such a one will never be at a desperate loss so long as God hath any credit, because he never faileth those that fly unto him, and that because his mercy and truth never fails. The very lame and the blind, the most shiftless creatures, when they had gotten the *strong hold of Zion*, thought then they might securely *scorn David and his host*, 2 Sam. v. 6, 7, because though they were weak in themselves, yet their hold was strong; but we see their hold failed them at length, which a Christian's will never do.

But God seems to have small care of those that are his in the world, those who believe themselves to be his jewels, *are counted the* offscouring of the world, *and most despised.*

We must know that such have a glorious life in God, but it is *hidden with Christ in God*, from the eyes of the world, and sometimes from their own; here they are hidden under infirmities, afflictions, and disgraces, but yet never so hidden, but that God sometimes lets down a beam of comfort and strength, which they would not lose to be freed from their present condition, though never so grievous. God comes more immediately to them now, than formerly he was used; nay, even when God seems to forsake them, and to be their enemy, yet they are supported with such inward strength, that they are able to make good their claim with Christ their head, and cry, *My God* still; God never so departs, but he always leaves somewhat behind him, which draws and keeps the heart to him. We are like poor Hagar, who when the *bottle of water* was spent *fell a crying*, Gen. xxi. 13, when there was a fountain close by, but her tears hindered her from seeing it; when things go ill with us in our trades and callings, and all is spent, then our spirits droop, and we are at our wits' end, as if God went

not where he was. Oh, consider if we had all and
had not God, we had nothing: if we have nothing,
and have God, we have enough, for we have him
that hath all, and more than all at his command. If
we had all other comforts that our hearts can desire,
yet if God withdraw himself, what remains but a
curse and emptiness? What makes heaven but the
presence of God? And what makes hell but the absence of God? Let God be in any condition, though
never so ill, yet it is comfortable, and usually we find
more of God in trouble, than when we are out of
trouble; the comforts of religion never come till
others fail. Cordials are kept for faintings. When a
curtain and a veil is drawn betwixt us and the creature, then our eyes are only upward to God, and he is
more clearly seen of us.

In the division of things God bequeaths himself to
those that are his, for their portion, as the best portion
he can give them. There are many goodly things in
the world, but none of these are a Christian's portion;
there is in him to supply all good, and remove all ill,
until the time come that we stand in need of no other
good. It is our chief wisdom to know him, our holiness
to love him, our happiness to enjoy him. There is in
him to be had whatsoever can truly make us happy.
We go to our treasure, and our portion in all our
wants, we live by it, and value ourselves by it. God
is such a portion, that the more we spend on him, the
more we may. *Our strength may fail,* and *our
heart may fail,* but *God is our portion for ever.*
Psalm lxxiii. 26. Every thing else teaches us by the
vanity and vexation we find in them, that our happiness is not in them, they send us to God; they may
make us worse, but better they cannot. Our nature
is above them, and ordained for a greater good; they
can go but along with us for a while, and their end
swallows up all the comfort of their beginning, as
Pharaoh's lean kine swallowed up the fat. If we have
no better portion here than these things, we are like to
have hell for our portion hereafter. What a shame will
it be hereafter when we are stript of all, that it should

be said, Lo, this is the man that took not God for his portion. If God be once ours, he goes ever along with us, and when earth will hold us no longer, heaven shall. Who that hath his senses about him, would perish for want of water, when there is a fountain by him? or for hunger, that is at a feast? God alone is a rich portion; O then let us labour for a large faith, as we have a large object; if we had a thousand times more faith, we should have a thousand times more increase of God's blessings. When the prophet came to the *widow's house*, as many vessels as she had *were filled with oil*, 1 Kings xvii. 14; we are straitened in our own faith, but not straitened in our God. It falls out oft in this world that God's people are like Israel at the Red Sea, environed with dangers on all sides: what course have we then to take but only to look up and wait for the salvation of our God? This is a breast full of consolation, let us teach our hearts to suck, and draw comfort from hence.

Is God our God; and will he suffer any thing to befall us for our hurt? Will he lay any more upon us, than he gives us strength to bear? Will he suffer any wind to blow upon us but for good? Doth he not set us before his face? Will a father or mother suffer a child to be wronged in their presence, if they can help it? Will a friend suffer his friend to be injured, if he may redress him? And will God that hath put these affections into parents and friends, neglect the care of those he hath taken so near unto himself? No surely, his eyes are open to look upon their condition; his ears are open to their prayers; a *book of remembrance*, Mal. iii. 16, is written of all their good desires, speeches, and actions; he hath bottles for all their tears, their very sighs are not *hid from him;* he hath written them upon the *palms of his hands*, and cannot but continually look upon them. Oh let us prize the favour of so good a God, who though he dwells on high yet will regard things so low, and not neglect the mean estate of any; nay, especially delights to be called the *comforter of his elect*, and the God of those that are in misery, and have none to fly unto but himself.

But we must know that God only thus graciously visits his own children, he visits with his choicest favours those only that fear his name. As for those that either secretly undermine, or openly oppose the cause and Church of God, and join with his enemies; such as savour not the things of God, but commit spiritual idolatry and adultery with God's enemies, the world and the devil; God will answer these, as once he did the Israelites, when in their necessity they would have forced acquaintance upon him, *Go to the gods whom ye have served*, Judges x. 14, to the great men whose persons you have obeyed for advantage: to your riches, to your pleasures, which you have loved more than God or goodness: you would not lose a base custom, an oath, a superfluity, a thing of nothing for me, therefore I will not own you now. Such men are more impudent than the devil himself, that will claim acquaintance with God at last, when they have carried themselves as his enemies all their days. Satan could tell Paul and Silas, they were *the servants of the living God*, Acts xvi. 17; but he would not make that plea for himself, knowing that he was a cursed creature.

Miserable then is their condition who *live in the world*, nay, in the Church, *without God*. Such are in a worse estate than Pagans and Jews; for living in the house of God, they are strangers from God, and from the covenant of grace; usurping the name of Christians, having indeed nothing to do with Christ.

Some of these like spiritual vagabonds, as Cain, excommunicate themselves from God's presence in the use of the means; or rather like devils, that will have nothing to do with God; because they are loath to be tormented before their time; they think every good sermon an arraigning of them, and therefore keep out of reach.

Others will present themselves under the means, and carry some savour away with them of what they hear, but it is only till they meet with the next temptation, unto which they yield themselves presently slaves. These showed themselves under a general profession, as they did, who called themselves Jews, and were nothing less. But alas, an empty title will bring an empty comfort at last. It was cold comfort to the *rich man* in flames, Luke xvi., that Abraham called him son. Or to Judas, that Christ called him friend. Or to the rebellious Jews, that God styles them his people. Such as our profession is, such will our comfort be. True profession of religion is another thing than most men take it to be; it is made up of the outward duty, and the inward man too; which is indeed the life and soul of all. What the heart doth not in religion, is not done.

God cares for no retainers that will only wear his livery, but serve themselves. *What hast thou to do to take his name into thy mouth, and hatest to be reformed?* Saul lived in the bosom of the Church, yet (being a cruel tyrant) when he was in a desperate plunge, his outward profession did him no good; and therefore when he was environed with his enemies, he uttered this doleful complaint, *God hath forsaken me, and the Philistines are upon me;* a pitiful case; yet so will it be with all those that rest in an outward profession, thinking it enough to compliment with God, when their hearts are not right within them. Such will at length be forced to cry, Sickness is upon me, death is upon me, hell is before me, and God hath forsaken me. I would have none of God heretofore, now God will have none of me. When David himself had offended God by *numbering the people,* then God counted him but plain David, *Go and say to David,* &c. whereas before, when he purposed to build a temple, then *Go, tell my servant David.* When the Israelites had set up an idol, then God fathers them on Moses, *Thy people which thou hast brought out of Egypt:* he would not own them as at other times, then; they are my people still whilst they keep covenant. No care, no present comfort in this near relation.

The price of the pearl is not known till all else be sold, and we see the necessary use of it. So the worth of God in Christ is never discerned, till we see our lost and undone condition without him, till conscience flies in our faces, and drags us to the brink of hell; then if ever we taste *how good the Lord is*, we will say, *Blessed is the people whose God is the Lord.* Heretofore I have heard of his loving kindness, but that is not a thousandth part of what I see and feel. The joy I now apprehend is unutterable, unconceivable.

Oh then, when we have gotten our souls possessed of God, let our study be to preserve ourselves in his love, to walk close with him, that he may delight to abide with us, and never forsake us. How basely doth the Scripture speak of whatsoever stands in our way? it makes nothing of them. What is man but vanity, and less than vanity? *All nations* but as *a drop of the bucket,* as the *dust of a balance;* things not at all considerable. Flesh looks upon them as through a multiplying glass, making them greater than they are; but faith, as God doth, sees them as nothing.

This is such a blessed condition, as may well challenge all our diligence in labouring to be assured of it; neither is it to be attained or maintained without the strength and prime of our care. I speak especially of, and in regard of the sense and comfort of it. For the sense of God's favour will not be kept without keeping him in our best affections above all things in the world, without keeping of our hearts always close and near to him, which cannot be without keeping a most narrow watch over our loose and unsettled hearts, that are ready to stray from God, and fall to the creature. It cannot be kept without exact and circumspect walking, without constant self-denial, without a continual preparation of spirit, to want and forsake any thing that God seeth fit to take from us.

But what of all this? Can we cross ourselves, or spend our labours to better purpose? one sweet beam of God's countenance will requite all this. We beat not the air, we plough not in the sand, neither sow in a barren soil, God is no barren wilderness. Nay, he never shows so much of himself, as in suffering, and parting with any thing for him, and denying ourselves of that which we think stands not with his will. Great persons require great observance. We can deny ourselves, and have mens' persons in great admiration, for the hope of some advantage; and is any more willing and more able to advance us than the great all-sufficient God? A Christian, indeed, undergoes more troubles, takes more pains (especially with his own heart) than others do. But what are these to his gains? What return so rich, as trading with God? What comforts so great as these that are fetched from the fountain? One day spent in enjoying the light of God's countenance is sweeter than a thousand without it. We see here, when David was not only shut out from all comforts, but lay under many grievances, what a fruitful use he makes of this, that God was his God. It upholdeth his dejected, it stilleth his unquiet soul: it leadeth him to *to the rock that was higher than he,* and there stayeth him. It filleth him with comfortable hopes of better times to come. It sets him above himself, and all troubles and fears whatsoever.

Therefore wait still in the use of *means* till God shine upon thee; yea, though we know our sins in Christ are pardoned, yet there is something more that a gracious heart waits for, that is, a good look from God, a further enlargement of heart, and an establishing in grace. It was not enough for David to have his sins pardoned, but to *recover the joy of salvation,* and *freedom of spirit.* Psalm li. Therefore the soul should always be in a waiting condition, even until it be filled with the fulness of God, as much as it is capable of. Neither is it quiet alone, or comfort alone, that the soul longs after, no, nor the favour of God alone, but a gracious heart to walk worthy of God. It rests not whilst any thing remains, that may breed the least strangeness betwixt God and us.

CHAPTER XXXIII.

OF EXPERIENCE AND FAITH, AND HOW TO WAIT ON GOD COMFORTABLY.
HELPS THERETO.

My God. These words further imply a special experience, that David's soul had felt of the goodness of
God, he had found God distilling the comfort of his
goodness and truth through the promises, and he
knew he should find God again the same he was, if
he put him in mind of his former gracious dealing.
His soul knew right well, how good God was, and he
could seal to those truths he had found comfort by,
therefore he thus speaks to his soul: My soul, what,
my soul, that hast found God so good, so oft, so
many ways, thou my soul to be discouraged, having
God, and my God, with whom I have taken so much
sweet counsel, and felt so much comfort from, and
found always heretofore to stick so close unto me?
Why shouldst thou now be in such a case, as if God
and thou had been strangers one to another. If we
could treasure up experiments, the former part of our
life would come in to help the latter, and the longer
we live, the richer in faith we should be. Even as in
victories, every former overthrow of an enemy helps
to obtain a succeeding victory. The use of a sanctified memory is to lose nothing that may help in time
of need. He had need be a well tried, and a known
friend, upon whom we lay all our salvation and comfort.

We ought to trust God upon other grounds, though
we had never tried him: but when he helps our faith
by former experience, this should strengthen our confidence, and shore up our spirits, and put us on to go
more cheerfully to God, as to a tried friend. If we
were well read in the story of our own lives, we might
have a divinity of our own, drawn out of the observation of God's particular dealing towards us; we
might say this and this truth, I dare venture upon, I
have found it true, I dare build all my happiness

upon it. As Paul, *I know whom I have trusted*, I have tried him, he never yet failed me, I am not now to learn how faithful he is to those that are his. Every new experience is a new knowledge of God, and should fit us for new encounters. If we have been good in former times, God remembers the *kindness of our youth*, Jer. ii. 2; we should therefore remember the kindness of God even from our youth. Evidence of what we have felt, helps our faith in that which for the present we feel not.

Though it be one thing to live by faith, and another thing to live by sight, yet the more we see, and feel, and taste of God, the more we shall be led to rely on him, for that which as yet we neither see nor feel: *Because thou hast been my helper*, saith David, *therefore in the shadow of thy wings will I rejoice.* Psalm lxiii. 7. The time was, Lord, when thou showedst thyself a gracious Father to me, and thou art unchangeable in thy nature, in thy love, and in thy gifts.

Yea, when there is no present evidence, but God shows himself as contrary to us, yet a former taste of God's goodness will enable to lay claim unto him still. God's concealing of himself is but a wise discipline for a time, until we be enabled to bear the full revealing of himself unto us for ever. In the mean time, though we have some sight and feeling in God, yet our constant living is not by it: the evidence of that we see not, is that which more constantly upholds the soul, than the evidence of any thing we see or feel.

Yea, though our experience by reason of our not minding of it in trouble, seems many times to stand us in no stead, but we fare as if God had never looked in mercy upon us: yet, even here, some virtue remains of former sense, which with the present spirit of faith, help us to look upon God as ours. As we have a present strength from food received, and digested before, vessels are something the better for that liquor they keep not, but runs through them.

But if experience should wholly fail, there is such a divine power in faith, as a very little beam of it, having no other faith than a naked promise, will uphold the soul; howsoever, we must neglect no help, for God oft suspends his comfort till we have searched all our helps. Though we see no light, yet we ought to search all crevices for light, and rejoice in the least beam of light that we may see day by. It is the nature of true faith, to search and pry into every corner, and if after all, nothing appears, then it casts itself upon God as in the first conversion, when it had nothing to look upon but the offer of free mercy. If at that time without former experience, we did trust God, why not now, when we have forgotten our experience? The chief grounds of trusting God are always the same, whether we feel or feel not; nay, though for the present we feel the contrary, faith will never leave wrestling, till it hath gotten a blessing. When faith is driven to work alone, having nothing but God, and his bare promise to rely upon, then God thinks it lies upon his credit to show himself as a God unto us. God's power in creating light out of darkness is never more exalted, than when a guilty soul is lift up by God to look for mercy, even when he seems armed with justice, to execute vengeance upon him, then the soul is brought to a near conformity unto Christ, who, 1. when he had the guilt of the sins of the whole world upon him; 2. when he was forsaken, and then after he had enjoyed the sweetest communion with his Father that ever creature could do; and not only so, but, 3. felt the weight of God's just displeasure against sin; and, 4. was abased lower than ever any creature was: yet still he held fast God as his God.

In earthly matters, if we have a title to any thing by gift, contract, inheritance, or howsoever, we will not be wrangled out of our right. And shall we not maintain our right in God, against all the tricks and cavils of Satan and our own hearts? We must labour to have something, that we may show that we are within the covenant. If we be never so little entered into the covenant, we are safe. And herein lies the special comfort of sincerity, that though our grace be little, yet it is of the right stamp, and shows us, that we are servants, and sons, though unworthy to be so. Here a little truth will go far. Hence it is that the saints in all their extremities still allege something, that shows that they are within the covenant, *we are thy children, thy people, and thy servants*, &c. God is mindful of his *covenant*, but is well pleased, that we should mind him of it too, and mind it ourselves to make use of it, as David doth here. He knew if he could bring his soul to his God, all would be quiet.

God is so ready to mercy, that he delighteth in it, and delighteth in Christ, through whom he may show mercy, notwithstanding his justice, as being fully satisfied in Christ. Mercy is his name that he will be known by. It is his glory which we behold in the face of Christ, who is nothing but grace and mercy itself. Nay, he pleads reasons for mercy, even from the sinfulness and misery of his creature, and maintains his own mercy against all the wrangling cavils of flesh and blood, that would put mercy from them; and hearken more willingly to Satan's objections, than God's arguments, till at length God subdues their spirits so far, as they become ashamed for standing out so long against him. How ready will God be to show mercy to us when we seek it, that thus presseth upon us, when we seem to refuse it? If God should take advantage of our waywardness, what would become of us? Satan's course is to discourage those that God would have encouraged, and to encourage those whom God never speaks peace unto, and he thinks to gain both ways. Our care therefore should be when we resolve upon God's ways, to labour that no discouragement fasten upon us, seeing God and his word speak all comfort to us.

And because the best of a Christian is yet to come, we should raise up our spirits to wait upon God, for that mercy which is yet to come. All inferior waitings for good things here, do but train us up in the comfortable expectation of the main.

This waiting on God requires a great strength of grace, by reason not only, 1. of the excellency of the things waited for, which are far beyond any thing we can hope for in the world. But, 2. in regard of the long day which God takes before he performeth his promise, and, 3, from thence the tediousness of delay. 4. The many troubles of life in our way. 5. The great opposition we meet with in the world; 6. and scandals ofttimes even from them that are in great esteem for religion; 7. together with the untowardness of our nature in being ready to be put off by the least discouragement. In these respects there must be more than a human spirit to hold up the soul, and carry it along to the end of that which we wait for.

But if God be our God, that love which engaged him to bind himself to us in precious promises; will furnish us likewise with grace needful, till we be possessed of them. He will give us leave to depend upon him both for happiness, and all sanctifying and quieting graces, which may support the soul, till it come to its perfect rest in God. For God so quiets the hearts of his children, as withal he makes them better and fitter for that which he provides for them; grace and peace go together; our God is the God of grace and peace, of such graces as breed peace.

1. As he is a God of love, nay, love itself to us, so a taste of his love, raising up our love, is better than wine, full of nothing but encouragement; it will fetch up a soul from the deepest discouragement; this grace quickeneth all other graces, it hath so much spirits in it as will sweeten all conditions. Love enables to wait, as Jacob for Leah, seven years, Gen. xxxix. Nothing is hard to love; it carries all the powers of the soul with it.

2. As he is a God of hope, so by this grace as an anchor fastened in heaven within the veil, he stayeth the soul; that though as a ship at anchor it may be tossed and moved, yet not removed from its station. This hope, as cork, will keep the soul, though in some heaviness, from sinking, and as a helmet bear off the blows, that they endanger not our life. Eph. vi.

3. As God is a God of hope, so by hope of patience, which is a grace whereby the soul resigneth up itself to God in humble submission to his will, because he

is our God, as David in extremity *comforted himself in the Lord his God.* Patience breeds comfort, because it brings experience with it of God's owning of us to be his. Eph. vi. The soul, shod and fenced with *this,* is prepared against all rubs and thorns in our way, so as we are kept from taking offence. All troubles we suffer, do but help *patience* to its *perfect work,* Rom. v. 3; by subduing the unbroken sturdiness of our spirits, when we feel by experience, we get but more blows, by standing out against God.

4. The Spirit of God, likewise, is a Spirit of meekness, whereby, though the soul be sensible of evil, yet it moderates such distempers, as would otherwise rob a man of himself; and together with patience keepeth the soul in possession of itself. It stays murmurings and frettings against God or man. It sets and keeps· the soul in tune. It is that which God (as he works, so he) much *delights in,* and *sets a price upon it,* as the chief ornament of the soul. The *meek of the earth seek God, and are hid in the day of his wrath,* Zeph. ii. 3; whereas high spirits that compass themselves with *pride* as with a *chain,* Psalm lxxiii. 6; thinking to set out themselves by that which is their shame, are looked upon by God afar off. Meek persons will bow when others break; they are raised when others are plucked down, and stand when others that mount upon the wings of vanity *fall,* Matt. v. 5; these prevail by yielding, and are lords of themselves, and other things else, more than other unquiet spirited men: the blessings of heaven and earth attend on these.

5. So, likewise, contentedness with our estate is needful for a waiting condition, and this we have in our God, being able to give the soul full satisfaction. For outward things God knows how to diet us; if our condition be not to our mind, he will bring our mind to our condition. If the spirit be too big for the condition, it is never quieted, therefore God will level both. These wants be well supplied that are made up with contentedness, and with riches of a higher kind. If the *Lord* be our *Shepherd,* we can *want nothing.* This lifteth the *weary hands and feeble*

knees, even under *chastisement,* wherein though the soul mourneth in the sense of God's displeasure, yet it rejoiceth in his fatherly care.

6. But patience and contentment are too low a condition for the soul to rest in, therefore the Spirit of God ariseth it up to a spiritual enlargement of joy. So much joy, so much light; and so much light, so much scattering of *darkness of spirit.* We see in nature how a little light will prevail over the thickest clouds of darkness, a little fire wastes a great deal of dross. The knowledge of God to be our God, brings such a light of joy into the soul, as driveth out dark uncomfortable conceits; this light makes lightsome. If the light of knowledge alone makes bold, much more the light of joy arising from our communion and interest in God. How can we enjoy God, and not joy in him? a soul truly cheerful rejoiceth that God whom it loveth, should think it worthy to endure any thing for him. This joy often ariseth to a spirit of glory, even in matter of outward abasement; if the trouble accompained with disgrace continue, *the Spirit of glory rests upon us,* and it will rest so long until it makes us more than conquerors, even then when we seemed conquered; for not only the cause, but the spirit riseth higher, the more the enemies labour to keep it under, as we see in Stephen. Acts vii.

With this joy goeth a spirit of courage and confidence. What can daunt that soul, which in the greatest troubles hath made the great God to be its own? such a spirit dares bid defiance to all opposite power, setting the soul above the world, having a spirit larger and higher than the world, and seeing all but God beneath it, as being in heaven already in its head. After Moses and Micah had seen God in his favour to them, how little did they regard the angry countenances of those mighty princes, that were in their times the terrors of the world; the courage of a Christian is not only against sensible danger, and of flesh and blood, but against *principalities and powers of darkness* against the whole *kindom of Satan,* the god of the world, whom he knows *shortly* shall be *trodden*

under his feet. Rom. xvi. 20.   Satan and his may
for a time exercise us, but they cannot hurt us.   True
believers are so many kings and queens, so many
conquerors over that which others are slaves to ; they
can overcome themselves in revenge, they can despise
those things that the world admires, and see an excellency in that which the world sets light by, they
can set upon spiritual duties, which the world cannot
tell how to go about, and endure that which others
tremble to think of, and that upon wise reasons, and
a sound foundation, they can put off themselves, and
be content to be nothing, so their God may appear
the greater, and dare untertake and undergo any
thing for the glory of their God.   This courage of
Christians among the heathen was counted obstinacy, but they knew not the power of the Spirit of
Christ in his, which is ever strongest, when they are
weakest in themselves, they knew not the privy ar-
mour of proof that Christians had about their hearts,
and thereupon counted their courage to be obstinacy.

Some think the martyrs were too prodigal of their
blood, and that they might have been better advised ;
but such are unacquainted with the force of the love
of God kindled in the heart of his child, which makes
him set such a high price upon Christ and his truth,
that he counts not *his life dear unto him.* Acts. xx.
24; he knows he is *not his own,* but he hath given up
himself to Christ, and therefore all that is his, yea, if he
had more lives to give for Christ, he should have them.
He knows he shall be no loser by it.   He knows it
is not a loss of his life, but an exchange for a better.

We see the creatures that are under us will be
courageous in the eye of their masters, that are of
a superior nature above them, and shall not a Christian be courageous in the presence of his great Lord
and Master, who is present with him, about him, and
in him? undoubtedly he that hath seen God once in
the face of Christ, dares look the grimmest creature
in the face, yea, death itself under any shape.   The
fear of all things flies before such a soul.   Only a
Christian is not ashamed of his confidence.   Why

should not a Christian be as bold for his God, as others are for the base gods they make to themselves?

7. Besides a spirit of courage (for establishing the soul) is required a spirit of constancy, whereby the soul is steeled and preserved immoveable in all conditions, whether present or to come, and is not changed in changes. And why? but because the spirit knows that God on whom it rests is unchangeable. We ourselves are as quicksilver, unsettled and moveable, till the Spirit of constancy fix us. We see David sets out God in glorious terms, borrowed from all that is strong in the *creature*, to show that he had great reason to be constant, and cleaving to him. *He is my rock, my buckler, the horn of my salvation, my strong tower*, &c. God is a rock so deep, that no floods can undermine; so high, that no waves can reach, though they rise never so high, and rage never so much. When we stand upon this rock that is higher than we, we may overlook all waves, swelling, and foaming, and breaking themselves, but not hurting us. And thereupon may triumphantly conclude with the Apostle, that *neither height, nor depth, shall ever separate us from the love of God.* Rom. viii. 39. Whatsoever is in the creature he found in his God, and more abundant; the soul cannot with an eye of faith look upon God in Christ, but it will be in its degree as God is quiet and constant, the spirit aimeth at such a condition as it beholdeth in God towards itself.

This constancy is upheld by endeavouring to keep a constant sight of God, for want of which it oft fares with us, like men, that having a city or tower in their eye, passing through uneven grounds, hills, and dales, sometimes get the sight thereof, sometimes lose it, and sometimes recover it again, though the tower be still where it was, and they nearer to it than they were at first. So it is oft with our uneven spirits; when once we have a sight of God, upon any present encouragement, we let fall our spirits, and lose the sight of him, until by an eye of faith we recover it again, and see him still to be where he was at first. The cherishing of passions take away the sight of God, as clouds take away the sight of the sun: though the sun be still where it was, and shineth as much as ever it did. We use to say, when the body of the moon is betwixt the sun and us, that the sun is eclipsed, when indeed not the sun but the earth is darkened, the sun loseth not one of its glorious beams. God is oft near us, as he was unto Jacob, and we are *not aware of it.* God was near the holy man Asaph, when he thought him afar off. *I am continually with thee,* saith he, *thou holdest me by my right hand.* Psalm lxxiii. 27. Mary in her weeping passion could not see Christ before her, he seemed a stranger unto her. So long as we can keep our eye upon God, we are above the reach of sin or any spiritual danger.

CHAPTER XXXIV.

OF CONFIRMING THIS TRUST IN GOD—SEEK IT OF GOD HIMSELF—SINS HINDER NOT: NOR SATAN—CONCLUSION, AND SOLILOQUY.

§ I. But to turn to the drawing out of our trust by waiting. Our estate in this world is still to wait, and happy it is that we have so great things to wait for; but our comfort is, that we have not only a *furniture of graces,* 2 Pet. i. 5; one strengthening another as stones in an arch, but likewise God vouchsafeth some drops of the sweetness of the things we wait for, both to increase our desire of those good things, as likewise to enable us more comfortably to wait for them. And though we should die waiting, only cleaving to the promise with little or no taste of the good promised; yet this might comfort us, that there is a life to come, that is a life of sight and sense, and not only of taste but of *fulness,* and that for *evermore.* Psalm xvi. 11. Our condition here is to live by faith and not by sight; only to make our living by faith more lively, it pleaseth God when he sees fit, to increase our earnest of that we look for. Even here God waits to *be gracious* to those *that wait for him.* Isa. xxx. 18. And in heaven Christ waits for us, we are part of his *fulness,* Eph. i. 23; it is part of his joy that *we shall be where he is,*

John xvii. 24: he will not therefore be long without us. The blessed angels and saints in heaven wait for us. Therefore let us be content as strangers to wait a while till we come home, and then *we shall be for ever with the Lord;* there is our eternal rest, where we shall enjoy both our God and ourselves in perfect happiness, being as without need, so without desire of the least change. When the time of our departure thither comes, then we may say as David, *Enter now my soul into thy rest.* This is the *rest which remaineth for God's people,* that is worth the waiting for, when we *shall rest from all labour of sin and sorrow,* and *lay our heads in the bosom of Christ for ever.*

It stands us therefore upon to get this great charter more and more confirmed to us, that God is our God, for it is of everlasting use unto us. It first begins at our entering into covenant with God, and continues not only unto death, but entereth into heaven with us. As it is our heaven upon earth to enjoy God as ours, so it is the very heaven of heaven, that there we shall for ever behold him, and have communion with him.

The degrees of manifesting this propriety in God are divers, rising one upon another, as *the light clears up by little and little till it comes to a perfect day.* 1. As the ground of all the rest, we apprehend God to be a God of some peculiar persons, as favourites above others. 2. From hence is stirred up in the soul a restless desire, that God would discover himself so to it, as he doth to those that are his, that he would *visit our souls* with the salvation of *his chosen.* 3. Hence follows a putting of the soul upon God, an adventuring itself on his mercy. 4. Upon this, God, when he seeth fit, discovers by his Spirit that he is ours. 5. Whence followeth a dependence on him as ours, for all things that may carry us on in the way to heaven. 6. Courage and boldness in setting ourselves against whatsoever may oppose us in the way, as the three young men in Daniel, *Our God can deliver us if he will. Our God is in heaven,* &c. 7. After which springs a sweet spiritual security, whereby the soul is freed from slavish fears, and glorieth in God as ours in all conditions. And this is termed by the Apostle, not only *assurance* but the *riches of assurance.* Yet this is not so clear and full as it shall be in heaven, because some clouds may after arise out of the remainder of corruption, which may something overcast this assurance, until the light of God's countenance in heaven for ever scatters all.

There being so great happiness in this nearness betwixt God and us, no wonder if Satan labour to hinder the same, by interposing the guilt and hein-ousness of our sins, which he knows of themselves will work a separation: but these, upon our first serious thought of returning, will be removed. As they could not hinder our meeting with God, so they may cause a strangeness for a time, but not a part-ing, a hiding of God's countenance, but not a banish-ing of us from it. Peter had denied Christ, and the rest of the Apostles had left him all alone; yet our Saviour, after his resurrection, forgets all former un-kindnesses; he did not so much as object it to them, but sends Mary, who herself had been a great sinner, as an apostle to the apostles, and that presently, to tell them that he was risen; his care would have no delay. He knew they were in great heaviness for their unkindness. Though he was now entered into the *first degree* of his glory, yet we see his glory made him not forget his poor disciples. Above all, he was most careful of Peter, as deeper in sin than the rest, and therefore deeper in sorrow. *Go tell Peter* he needs *most* comfort. But what is the mes-sage? that *I ascend* not *to my Father* alone, but *to your Father;* not to *my God* only, but to *your God.*

And shall not we be bold to say so after Christ hath taught to us, and put this claim into our mouths? If once we let this hold go, then Satan hath us where he would, every little cross then dejects us. Satan may darken the joy of our salvation, but not take away the God of our salvation. David, after his cry-ing sin of murder, prays, *Restore unto me the joy of thy salvation,* Psalm li; this he had lost: but yet in the same psalm he prays, *Deliver me from blood, O God thou God of my salvation :* therefore, whatsoever *sense, reason, temptation, the law,* or *guilt upon conscience* shall say, nay, however God himself, by his strange carriage to us may seem to be, yet let us cast ourselves upon him, and not suffer this plea to be wrung from us, but shut our eyes to all, and look upon God *All-gracious* and *All-sufficient,* who is the *Father,* the begetter of *comfort,* 2 Cor. i. 3; *the God,* the creator *of consolation,* not only of things that may comfort, but of the comfort itself conveyed through these unto us.   *Who is a God like unto our God, that passeth by the sins of the remnant of his people?*   This should not be thought on without admiration; and indeed there nothing so much deserves our wonderment as such mercy, of such a God, to such as we.

Since God hath *avouched us to be his peculiar people,* let us avouch him, and since he hath passed his word for us, let us pass our words for him that we will be his, and stand for him, and to our power advance his cause.   Thus David out of an enlarged spirit saith, *Thou art my God, and I will praise thee; thou art my God, and I will exalt thee.* Whatsoever we engage for God, we are sure to be gainers by.   The true Christian is the wisest merchant, and makes the best adventure.   He may stay long, but is sure of a safe and a rich return.   A godly man is most wise for himself.   We enter on religion, upon these terms, to part with ourselves, and all, when God shall call for it.

§ II. God much rejoiceth in sinners converted, as monuments of his mercy, and because the remembrance of their former sins whets them on to be more earnest in his service, especially after they have felt the sense of God's love; they even burn with a holy desire of honouring him, whom before they dishonoured, and stand not upon doing or suffering any thing for him, but cheerfully embrace all occasions of expressing obedience.   God hath more work from them than from others; why then should any be discouraged?

Neither is it sins after our conversion, that nullify this claim of God to be ours. For this is the grand difference betwixt the two covenants, that now God will be merciful to our sins, *if our hearts by faith be sprinkled with the blood of Christ.* Though one sin was enough to bring condemnation, yet the free gift of grace in Christ is of many offences unto justification. And we have a sure ground for this, for the righteousness of Christ is God's righteousness, and God will thus glorify it, that it shall stand good to those that by faith apply it against their daily sins, even till at once we cease both to live and sin. For this very end was the Son of God willingly *made sin,* that we might be freed from the same. And if all our sins laid upon Christ could not take away God's love from him, shall they take away God's love from us, when by Christ's blood our souls are purged from them?

O mercy of all mercies, that when we were once his, and gave away ourselves for nothing, and so became neither his nor our own, that then he would vouchsafe to become ours, and make us his by such a way, as all the angels in heaven stand wondering at; even his Son not only taking our nature and miserable condition, but our sin upon him, that that being done away, we might through Christ have boldness with God as ours, who is now in heaven appearing there for us, until he bring us home to himself, and presents us to his Father for *his* for ever.

Think not then only that we are God's and he ours, but from what love and by what glorious means this was brought to pass; what can possibly disable this claim, when God for this end hath founded a covenant of peace so strongly in Christ, that sin itself cannot disannul it? Christ was therefore manifest, *that he might destroy* this greatest *work of the devil.* 1 John iii. 5, 8. Forgiveness of sins now is one chief part of our portion in God. It is good therefore not to pore and plod so much upon sin and vileness by it, as to forget that mercy that rejoiceth over judgment. If we once be God's, though we *drink this deadly poison*, it *shall not hurt us.* Mark xvi. 18. God will make a medicine, an antidote of it; and for all other evils, the fruit of them is by God's sanctifying the same, the *taking away sin* out of our natures; so that lesser evils are sent to take away the greater. If God could not over-rule evils to his own ends, he would never suffer them.

§ III. I have stood the longer upon this, because it is the one thing needful, the one thing we should desire, that this one God in whom, and from whom is all good, should be ours. All promises of all good in the new covenant, spring first from this, that God *will be ours and we shall be his.* Jer. xxxii. What can we have more; and what is in the world less that will content us long, or stand us in any stead, especially at that time when all must be taken from us? Let us put up all our desires for all things we stand in need of, in this right we have to God in Christ, who hath brought God and us together; he can deny us nothing, that hath not denied us himself. If he be moved from hence to do us good, that we are his; let us be moved to fetch all good from him, on the same right that he is ours.

The persuasion of this will free us from all pusillanimity, lowliness, and narrowness of spirit, when we shall think that nothing can hurt us, but it must break through God first. If God give quietness, who shall *make trouble?* Job xxxiv. 29. If God be with us, who can be against us? This is that which puts comfort into all other comforts, that maketh any burthen light; this is always ready for all purposes; our God is a present and a seasonable help. All evils are at his command to be gone, and all comforts at his command to come. It is but, go comfort, go peace, to such a man's heart, cheer him, raise him: go salvation, rescue such and such a soul in distress. So said and so done presently. Nay, with reverence be it spoken, so far doth God pass over himself unto us, that he is content himself to be commanded by us.

Concerning the work of my hands command you me;
lay the care and charge of that upon me. He is content to be out-wrestled and over-powered by a spirit
of faith as in Jacob, and *the woman of Canaan;* to
be as it were at our service. He would not have
us want any thing wherein he is able to help us.
And what is there wherein God cannot help us?
If Christians knew the power they have in heaven
and earth, what were able to stand against them?
What wonder is it if faith overcome the world, if it
overcomes him that made the world? that faith should
be almighty that hath the Almighty himself ready
to use all his power for the good of them to whom he
hath given the power of himself unto? Having therefore such a *living fountain* to draw from, such a
centre to rest in, having all in one, and that one
ours, why should we knock at any other door? we
may go boldly to God now, as made *ours, being
bone of our bone, and flesh of our flesh.* We may
go more comfortably to God, than to any angel or
saint. God in the second person hath vouchsafed
to take our nature upon him, but not that of angels.
Our God, and our man, our God-man is ascended
unto the high court of heaven to this and our God,
clothed with our nature. Is there any more able and
willing to plead our cause, or to whom we may trust
business with, than he, who is in *heaven for all
things for us, appertaining to God?* Heb. v. 1.

It should therefore be the chief care of a Christian,
upon knowledge of what he stands in need of, to
know where to supply all. It should raise up a holy
shame and indignation in us, that there should be so
much in God, who is so near unto us in Christ, and
we make so little use of him. What good can any
thing do us if we use it not? God is ours to use, and
yet men will rather use shifts and unhallowed policies, than be beholding to God, who thinks himself
never more honoured by us than when we make use
of him. If we believe any thing will do us good, we
naturally make out for the obtaining of it. If we believe any thing will hurt us, we study to decline it.

19

And certain it is, if we believed that so much good were in God, we would then apply ourselves to him, and him to ourselves; whatsoever virtue is in any thing, it is conveyed by application and touching of it; that, whereby we touch God, is our faith, which never toucheth him, but it draws virtue from him; upon the first touch of faith, spiritual life is begun. It is a bastard in nature, to believe any thing can work upon another without spiritual or bodily touch. And it is a monster in religion, to believe that any saving good will issue from God, if we turn from him, and shut him out, and our hearts be unwilling. Where unbelief is, it binds up his power. Where faith is, there it is between the soul and God, as betwixt the iron and the loadstone, a present closing and drawing of one to the other. This is the beginning of *eternal life*, so to *know God the Father and his Son Christ*, John xvii. 4; as thereby to embrace him with the arms of faith and love, as ours, by the best title he can make us, who is truth itself.

Since then our happiness lies (out of ourselves) in God, we should go out of ourselves for it, and first get into Christ, and so unto God in him; and then labour, by the Spirit of the Father and the Son, to maintain acquaintance with both, that so God may be ours, not only in covenant but in communion, hearkening what he will say to us, and opening our spirits, disclosing our wants, consulting and advising in all our distresses with him. By keeping this acquaintance with God, *peace and all good is conveyed to us.* Job xxii. 21.

Thereafter as we maintain this communion further with him, we out of love study to please him, by exact walking according to his commands; then we shall feel increase of peace as our care increaseth, then he will *come and sup with us,* and be free in his refreshing of us. Then he will show himself more and more to us, and manifest still a further degree of presence in joy and strength, until communion in grace ends in communion in glory.

But we must remember, as David doth here, to

desire and delight in God himself more than in any thing that is God's; it was a sign of Paul's pure love to the Corinthians, when he said, *I seek not yours, but you.* We should seek for no blessing of God so much as for himself.

What is there in the world of equal goodness to draw us away from our God? If to preserve the dearest thing we have in the world, we break with God, God will take away the comfort we look to have by it, and it will prove but a dead contentment, if not a torment to us. Whereas, if we care to preserve communion with God, we shall be sure to find in him whatsoever we deny for him, *honour, riches, pleasures, friends, all:* so much the sweeter, by how much we have the more immediately from the spring head. We shall never find God to be our God more, than when for making of him to be so, we suffer any thing for his sake. We enjoy never more of him than then.

At the first we may seek to him, as rich to supply our wants, as a physician to cure our souls and bodies, but here we must not rest till we come to rejoice in him as our friend, and from thence rise to an admiration of him for his own excellencies, that being so high in himself, out of his goodness would stoop low to us. And we should delight in the meditation of him, not only as good to us, but as good in himself; because goodness of bounty springs from goodness of disposition; *he doth good because he is good.*

A natural man delights more in God's gifts than in his grace. If he desires grace, it is to grace himself, not as grace, making him like unto God, and issuing from the first grace, the free favour of God; by which means men come to have the gifts of God without God himself. But alas, what are all other goods without the chief good? they are but as flowers, which are long in planting, in cherishing and growing, but short in enjoying the sweetness of them. David here joys in God himself; he cares for nothing in the world, but what he may have with his favour; and whatever else he desires, he desires only that he

may have the better ground from thence to praise his
God.

§ IV. The sum of all is this, *the state of God's dear
children in this world is to be cast into variety of
conditions,* wherein, they consisting of nature, flesh,
and spirit, every principle hath its own and proper
working. They are sensible as *flesh and blood;* they
are sensible to discouragements as sinful flesh and
blood; but they recover themselves, as having a higher
principle (God's Spirit) above flesh and blood in them.

In this conflicting state, every principle labouring
to maintain itself, at length by help of the Spirit, back-
ing and strengthening his own work, grace gets the
better, keeping nature within bounds, and suppress-
ing corruption. And this the soul, so far as it is spiritual, doth by gathering itself to itself, and by reasoning the case so far, till it concludes, and joins upon this
issue, that the only way to attain sound peace is, when
all other means fail, *to trust in God.* And thereupon
he lays a charge upon his soul to do, so it being a
course grounded upon the highest reason, even the
unchangeable goodness of God; who, out of the
riches of his mercy, having chosen a people in this
world, which should be to the glory of his mercy, will
give them matter of setting forth his praise, in showing some token of good upon them, as being those on
whom he hath fixed his love, and to whom he will
appear not only a Saviour, but salvation itself. *Nothing but salvation;* as the sun is nothing but light,
so whatsoever proceeds from him to them tends to
further salvation. All his ways towards them lead
to that; which ways of his, though for a time they are
secret, and not easily found out, yet at length God will
be wonderful in them, to the admiration of his enemies themselves, who shall be forced to say, God hath
done great things for them; and all from this ground,
that God is *our God in covenant:* which words are a
stern that rule and guide the whole text.

For why should we not be disquieted when we are
disquieted? Why should we not be cast down when
we are cast down? Why should we trust in God as a

Saviour? but that he is *our God,* making himself so to us in his choicest favours: doing that for us which none else can do, and which he doth to none else that are not his in a gracious manner. This blessed interest and intercourse betwixt God's Spirit and our spirits, is the hinge upon which all turns: without this no comfort is comfortable; with this, no trouble can be very troublesome.

Without this assurance there is little comfort in soliloquies; unless, when we speak to ourselves, we can speak to God as ours. For in desperate cases, our soul can say nothing to itself, to still itself, unless it be suggested by God. Discouragements will appear greater to the soul than any comfort, unless God comes in as ours.

See therefore David's art; he demands of himself why he was so cast down? The cause was apparent, because there were troubles without, and terrors within, and none to comfort. Well, grant this, saith the Spirit of God in him (as the worst must be granted;) yet saith the Spirit, *Trust in God—So I have.*

Why then, wait in trusting; *light is sown for the righteous:* it comes not up on the sudden, we must not think to sow and reap both at once. If trouble be lengthened, lengthen thy patience.

What good will come of this?

God will wait to do thee that good; for which *thou shalt praise him;* he will deal so graciously with thee, as he will deserve thy praise; he will *show thee his salvation.* And new favours will stir thee up to sing new songs; every new recovery of ourselves or friends, is, as it were, a new life, and ministers new matter of praise. And upon offering this *sacrifice of praise,* the heart is further enlarged to pray for fresh blessings. We are never fitter to pray, than after praise.

But in the mean time I hang down my head, whilst mine enemies carry themselves highly, and my friends stand aloof.

God in his own time (which is best for thee) will be the *salvation of thy countenance:* he will compass thee about with songs of deliverance, and make it appear at last that he hath care of thee.

But why then doth God appear as a stranger to me?

That thou shouldst follow after him with the stronger faith and prayer; he withdraws himself, that thou shouldst be the more earnest in seeking after him. God speaks the sweetest comfort to the heart in the wilderness. Happily thou art not yet low enough, nor purged enough. Thy affections are not thoroughly crucified to the world, and therefore it will not yet appear that it is God's good will to deliver thee. Wert thou a fit subject of mercy, God would bestow it on thee.

But what ground hast thou to build thyself so strongly upon God?

He hath offered, and made himself to be *my God*, and so hath showed himself in former times; and I have made him *my God*, by yielding him his sovereignty in my heart. Besides the present evidence of his blessed Spirit, clearing the same, and many peculiar tokens of his love, which I daily do enjoy; though sometimes the beams of his favour are eclipsed. Those that are God's, besides their interest and right in him, have oft a sense of the same even in this life, as a foretaste of that which is to come. To the seal of grace stamped upon their hearts, God superadds a fresh seal of joy and comfort, by the presence and witness of his Spirit. And shows likewise some outward token for good upon them, whereby he makes it appear that *he hath set apart him that is godly for himself, as his own.* Psalm iv. 3.

Thus we see that discussing of objections in the consistory of the soul, settles the soul at last. Faith at length silencing all risings to the contrary. All motion tends to rest, and ends in it. God is the centre and resting place of the soul, and here David takes up his rest, and so let us. Then whatsoever times come, we are sure of a hiding place and sanctuary.

Although the fig-tree shall not blossom, neither shall fruit be in the vines, the labour of the olive shall fail, and the fields shall yield no meat, &c., yet I will rejoice in the Lord, I will joy in the God of my salvation. Hab. iii. 17.

He that dwelleth in the secret place of the most High, shall lodge under the shadow of the Almighty. I will say of the Lord, He is my refuge, and my fortress; My God, in him will I trust. Psalm xci. 1, 2.

My strength and my heart faileth, but God is the strength of my heart, and my portion for ever. Psalm lxxiii. 26.

THE END.

BIBLIOLIFE

Old Books Deserve a New Life
www.bibliolife.com

Did you know that you can get most of our titles in our trademark **EasyScript**[TM] print format? **EasyScript**[TM] provides readers with a larger than average typeface, for a reading experience that's easier on the eyes.

Did you know that we have an ever-growing collection of books in many languages?

Order online:
www.bibliolife.com/store

Or to exclusively browse our **EasyScript**[TM] collection:
www.bibliogrande.com

At BiblioLife, we aim to make knowledge more accessible by making thousands of titles available to you – quickly and affordably.

Contact us:
BiblioLife
PO Box 21206
Charleston, SC 29413

40588532R00171

Made in the USA
Lexington, KY
11 April 2015